RISE OF THE
BLACK QUARTERBACK

WHAT IT MEANS FOR AMERICA

JASON REID

ANDSCAPE
LOS ANGELES · NEW YORK

First Edition, August 2022
10 9 8 7 6 5 4 3 2 1
FAC-004510-22168
Printed in the United States of America

This book is set in Chalet Comprine and Acta
Designed by Amy C. King

Library of Congress Cataloging-in-Publication Control Number: 2022935339
ISBN 978-1-368-07662-3
Reinforced binding

Visit www.AndscapeBooks.com

FOR JOSH AND MAYA

CONTENTS

[1]

THE YEAR OF THE BLACK QUARTERBACK

AS DINNER WAS WINDING down and three NFL colleagues prepared to depart a popular Northern Virginia steakhouse, the most prominent among them offered one final observation. And when Doug Williams talks, well, people listen.

It was July 2019, and Williams, the first Black man to both quarterback a team to a Super Bowl championship and win the game's Most Valuable Player Award, still cut an imposing figure nearly 30 years after he last took a snap from center. Even seated, at a muscular 6 foot 4 with a booming voice, Williams commanded the room, let alone the dinner table.

This had been the last chance for the small group to fellowship over a good meal before embarking on another journey. Sharing

1

seafood and laughs over several hours, the men would all, in different capacities, soon begin the grind of the NFL season. They discussed the upcoming season, of course, but Williams also often steered the conversation to the most important topics affecting Black men in the NFL, which were meaningful to him as much because of his role as a high-ranking executive for Washington's NFL franchise, the same franchise he led to Super Bowl glory as a young man, as his standing as an African American icon. Not surprisingly, Williams that night was especially interested in the state of play at the most important position in professional sports: quarterback.

Quarterbacks are the most celebrated players in football and among the most scrutinized and highest-paid in professional sports. The QB, as the position is commonly known, has an outsized role in determining a team's success. Quarterbacks are at the center of the action on offense, barking out directions through play calls, handling the ball on almost every snap and passing it often in the pass-heavy NFL. From the lowest levels of youth football through high school, college, and the NFL, star quarterbacks are the face of the game. A "franchise QB" is a passer considered to be so talented that team owners build their clubs around them in pursuit of long-term success. Major decisions both on and off the field–roster construction, offensive philosophy, marketing strategies, etc.–are made to capitalize on a franchise QB's strengths.

As NFL team owners sought to expand the league's popularity through the decades, with an emphasis on filling their franchises' coffers by securing bigger television contracts, they approved rule changes intended to increase scoring, which excites fans. Quarterbacks benefitted most from the changes. Game officials afforded them more protection than other players while restrictions were placed on the defense in its efforts to cover a QB's targets. The adjustments produced the owners' desired effect: The passing game took off, scoring increased, the NFL became king among the major professional sports leagues, and quarterbacks ascended to a position of prominence in popular culture, once the exclusive domain of male movie stars. In a white, patriarchal society, the QB has come to personify the ideal form of masculinity. In professional football, a sport full of alpha males, the QB is king. He's a matinee idol, the smartest guy in the room and the coolest to boot. He's everything the "average guy" wishes he could be but can't.

Despite all this focus on the position, for decades, NFL quarterbacks were not always the most gifted athletes on the team. There had been one requirement, never plainly stated, that the game's owners and coaches had insisted on, an attribute that had nothing to do with talent: whiteness.

That fact of history, a history both distant and recent, was the context, the undercurrent, and the 300-pound gorilla lurking in the room among the white linen and fine china.

Although the other two men present at the gathering were also "football lifers"–Williams was flanked on one side by a top league public relations official and on the other by a longtime NFL writer–Williams was, by far, the most qualified to evaluate the game's best passers. And he did, commenting in general on future Hall of Famers Tom Brady, Aaron Rodgers, and Drew Brees, among others. Then, shortly before the party dispersed into the night, Williams reignited the QB portion of the conversation. He had been holding his most salient consideration until the end–the fast-rising newcomers who were pushing the old guard: a cadre of elite Black signal-callers.

"You look at these young guys, you look at their talent, what they've done so far and where they are right now . . . it's gonna be something different this year," Williams said. "You're gonna see these young guys really do some things. They're gonna show where they are. We haven't seen it before. It'll be new."

And with that, he was done. It was more of a declaration than an observation. His comments inspired further discussion at the table–as well as a few eye rolls. Williams being bullish on the potential of Black QBs was nothing new. He rooted for them as if they were part of his extended family. And given what he endured to help light their path, it wasn't surprising that he embraced the cheerleader role. But his optimism sometimes outpaced the results of those he promoted.

Not this year. The unfolding months would prove Williams's assessment of the state of Black NFL QBs was supported by fact. As the 2019 NFL season drew near, the league had never had more talented African American passers playing at one time in the game's 100-year history. All still were young; none had yet peaked. The previous season, Patrick Mahomes of the Kansas City Chiefs had won the Associated Press Most Valuable Player Award. Perennial Pro Bowler Russell Wilson, then the only other Black QB to have started in a Super Bowl victory, was still going strong. Deshaun Watson of the Houston Texans and Dak Prescott of the Dallas Cowboys also were voted to Pro Bowl teams. Lamar Jackson of the Baltimore Ravens was coming off a promising rookie season. Heisman winner Kyler Murray, the No. 1 overall pick in the 2019 NFL draft, would be the Arizona Cardinals' starter. Williams, though, wasn't merely saying that those young men would continue to play well in the upcoming season. He expressed confidently, some would have said foolishly, that the NFL, then on the eve of its 100th season, was at the threshold of a new era on the field: the era of the Black quarterback.

And as it turned out, he couldn't have been more prescient.

—

During the 2019 season, Mahomes led the Kansas City Chiefs to their first Super Bowl title in 50 years. In doing so, he was voted the Super Bowl MVP, making him, at then only 24, the youngest player ever to have a Super Bowl title, a Super Bowl MVP award, and a league MVP award. With each step Mahomes took toward the title that season, Black quarterback pioneers swelled with pride. More than 30 years had passed since Williams took a sledgehammer to the racist myth that Black passers lacked the smarts and leadership ability to win championships. By the time Wilson helped the Seattle Seahawks crush the Denver Broncos in the 2014 Super Bowl, his race wasn't the biggest story of the day. Likewise, when Cam Newton led the Carolina Panthers to the 2016 Super Bowl, he didn't face a volley of questions about whether he measured up. At that point, both former Houston great Steve McNair and Newton had brought home league MVP trophies. For more than a decade, Warren Moon, the only Black quarterback to be enshrined in the Pro Football Hall of Fame, had his bust among the game's all-time greats in Canton, Ohio. Randall Cunningham, the onetime Philadelphia Eagles star, was known as the Ultimate Weapon. Mahomes wasn't the first highly accomplished Black quarterback.

Here's the thing, though: Cunningham and Moon played during an era in which Joe Montana, Dan Marino, and John Elway took turns standing atop the mountain. From the time Newton and Wilson entered the league, the long-running debate was whether Manning and Rodgers were better than Brady. But in the Year of the Black Quarterback, it became clear that Mahomes could become the first African American passer to be the consensus No. 1 player in the league in any era, let alone for a long stretch. The potential for Mahomes to maintain that rank pleased pioneer James "Shack" Harris.

Harris was the first Black quarterback to start a season opener (doing so in 1969 for the Buffalo Bills of the American Football League, which in 1970 merged with the NFL) as well as the first to start and win an NFL playoff game. A longtime NFL player-personnel executive as well, Harris studied Mahomes's game closely during the Chiefs' Super Bowl run. "I couldn't have been more impressed," Harris recalled. "What you have to have to be great, to be special, is to play quarterback with instinct. It's not something you teach. You've just got to have that. He does. He throws the ball from a lot of different angles with accuracy. He has great pocket awareness. When he makes mistakes, he plays through it."

Mahomes delivered a steely Super Bowl performance as the Chiefs overcame a late deficit and rallied for a 31–20 win over the NFC Champion San Francisco 49ers. That result only reinforced the pioneers' belief in Mahomes. The Chiefs became the first team in a single NFL postseason to overcome three double-digit deficits in victories. On the final night of the 2019 season, Mahomes ascended to a position of enormous power within the NFL. As a result of his youth and historic success, Mahomes quickly came to occupy a space few superstar athletes have attained. As the Chiefs enjoyed a confetti shower and Mahomes held the Vince Lombardi Trophy above his head at Miami's Hard Rock Stadium, Williams recalled his words from that night more than six months earlier, wondering aloud about what the future would bring for the NFL's best player–a Black quarterback.

"Everyone is looking at him now, looking to try to get to where he is now because he's at the front [of the line]," Williams said of Mahomes. "But when you're out there and everyone is following you, what do you do? What do you do with the position you have? That's what everybody is watching for next."

—

While Mahomes broke free from the pack of Black quarterbacks, the pack was nonetheless outstanding. During the playoffs after the 2019 season, four of the eight teams in the NFC and AFC division series, the playoff quarterfinals, were led by Black quarterbacks. For the NFL, that was a first. Mahomes, Watson, and Jackson were voted into the three QB spots on the AFC Pro Bowl roster. Guess how many times Black passers had previously occupied every roster spot for either the AFC or NFC Pro Bowl teams? Here's a hint: It's the same number that had won the Super Bowl before Williams accomplished the feat.

Each season, the AP picks two All-Pro teams. The first- and second-team members are considered to be the top two players at their positions in the entire NFL. That season, with Jackson and Wilson selected, Black QBs occupied both spots on the team for the first time. The AP has been picking All-Pro teams since 1940.

Houston's Watson, selected 12th, two picks after Mahomes in the 2017 draft, proved to be a wizard whether working from the pocket or on the move. Watson completed nearly 70 percent of his passes, displaying all the best attributes of the greatest pocket passers: to be able to stay cool in the face of the pass rush, survey the field, and link up with receivers far more often than not. Watson's signature play occurred in the playoffs that season against the Buffalo Bills.

Late in the game, Watson, as he often does, somehow eluded a fierce pass rush, spinning out of a sack and extending the play just long enough to complete a pass that led to the game-winning field goal. Watson rallied Houston to a victory in overtime after it trailed by 16 points on its home field. You know what you call someone who gets the job done like that? A great quarterback.

Murray, whose elusiveness as a runner was nearly as impressive as his accuracy within the pocket, was selected the AP Offensive Rookie of the Year. The Seahawks' Wilson, a future Hall of Famer and, at 31, the dean of the group, continued to deliver. Wilson had 31 passing touchdowns and only five interceptions. For the seventh time in Wilson's eight seasons to that point, he led the Seahawks to at least 10 victories in a season.

In his fourth impressive season as the leader of the Cowboys, "America's Team," Dak Prescott passed for 4,902 yards, finishing only one yard short of the franchise single-season record established by Tony Romo in 2012.

Throughout the 2019 season, Black quarterbacks excelled in every major statistical metric, pushing bars higher in the process. Black QBs occupied five of the top seven spots in Total QBR (quarterback rating), a measurement of a quarterback's all-around performance. Jackson led the league with a mark of 83.0 on a scale to 100. Jackson was followed by Mahomes (77.7), Prescott (71.9, fourth), Wilson (71.5, sixth), and Watson (70.5, seventh). During the season, five NFL quarterbacks finished games with a perfect passer rating (calculated differently than the 100-point maximum QBR) of 158.3. Black signal-callers accounted for four of them. What's more, Jackson, Mahomes, Prescott, Watson, and Wilson combined for a higher collective yards per attempt (8), touchdowns-to-interceptions ratio (3.8), completion percentage (66%), and passer rating (104) than the career rates of Hall of Famer Peyton Manning and even all-time great Brady.

Now, ponder these numbers: 24, 23, 24, 22, 26, and 31. Those were the ages, respectively, of Mahomes, Jackson, Watson, Murray, Prescott, and Wilson at the end of the 2019 season. Talk about a group poised to lead the NFL into its next 100 years.

No question that 2019 was every bit the banner year for Black quarterbacks that Williams had predicted before it kicked off. It was an easy call, Williams said. It had been in the making for 100 seasons.

"It's all about finally getting the opportunities," Williams said. "For a long, long time in the NFL, we, Black quarterbacks, didn't get the opportunities to show what we could do. We didn't get the opportunities to show who we could be. But once we started getting them, you saw what we could do. So [the 2019 season] was really just a matter of time. You saw what developed. It took too long, but the time finally came."

[2]

THE FIRST

ONLY A FEW FEET and one imposing would-be tackler separated eight-year-old Fritz Pollard III from an imaginary goal line and fanciful athletic glory in the backyard of his family's home at Hyde Park, Chicago. Although his previous attempts to outdo his beloved grandfather and namesake had ended badly, Pollard III resolved, on that fall day in 1963, to finally succeed.

The boy oozed confidence as he cradled the ball and displayed the nifty moves the old man had taught him, darting in one direction and zigzagging in another. In his mind's eye, he could see it so clearly–leaving Fritz Pollard Sr. grasping at his shadow. At long last, the child would get the better of his larger-than-life elder at the game Grandpapa knew so well. Pollard III even envisioned his touchdown celebration, featuring a long stretch of joyful, impromptu dancing. After being schooled by one of the best to ever lace up a pair of football cleats, the student was poised to become the teacher.

But youth, alas, would not be served.

Breaking into daylight, Pollard III dropped his guard–providing just the opening his grandfather needed. Suddenly, caught from behind and stripped of the football, Pollard III wound up on his back, wondering, "What just happened?"

"I wasn't paying attention . . . and he hit me so hard. He would really knock me around back there," Pollard III said, punctuating the sentence with a hearty laugh. "Here I am, this little kid, figuring my grandfather was just playing around with me. Then all of a sudden–boom.

"I really didn't expect that. But I learned my lesson: Stay focused until the task is completed. He was teaching me the right way to play football, the way he learned, and about getting the job done in life. And my grandfather, let me tell you, he was great at both."

———

Fritz Pollard III idolized his grandfather. A major presence in his grandson's life until he passed away in 1986 at the age of 92, when Pollard III was 31, the elder Pollard stirred a love of football first in his son, Fritz Pollard Jr., and then in his son's son. In fact, many of Pollard III's earliest memories involve his grandfather and the game. When Pollard III was an infant, his grandad put a football in his crib. By the time Pollard III was a toddler, Fritz Sr., in the backyard of junior's house, was well into teaching him the finer points of how to elude defenders and make open-field tackles.

Back then, Pollard III had no idea his hero was also a pioneering football legend who achieved many firsts for Blacks in both college and the professional ranks. But in a couple of years, Pollard III got an inkling that he was a descendant of football royalty. His first hint came in the summer of 1964. Pollard III spent the entire time with his doting grandfather in New York City. Between afternoons spent watching baseball at Yankee Stadium, and trips to Central Park and tours of the Empire State Building and other Big Apple landmarks, Fritz Sr. showed off his grandson to longtime friends from his college days at Brown University, the prestigious Ivy League school located in Providence, Rhode Island.

Invariably, the adults Pollard III met waxed nostalgic about his grandfather's athletic exploits and accomplishments. That's when Pollard III also first learned about his grandfather's adventures in business–Fritz Sr. founded a number of businesses and was a successful casting agent and film producer–but the sports stories the Brown alums shared with Pollard III most piqued his curiosity. Every anecdote about his grandfather's college football career made him eager to hear another. To merely call Pollard a standout athlete at Brown is akin to simply describing Donald J. Trump as a one-term president. The information is accurate–but there's a whole lot more to the story.

Long after Fritz Sr. last cracked a book during an all-night cram session, he remained a big man on campus. As a teenager, Pollard III frequently accompanied his grandfather on trips to Brown. Each time, Pollard III witnessed the star treatment Fritz Sr. received there.

Often, he stood at his grandfather's side as Brown administrators, faculty members, and students moved into formation like airplanes awaiting takeoff clearance in hopes of getting a few seconds of face time with a Brown living legend. Pollard III draws a straight line from those moments to his love for Brown, which he also attended. He swelled with pride while witnessing the celebrity his grandfather had earned by excelling at the game they played together for countless hours in the backyard. And the young man was only beginning to understand the entire compelling story. Pollard III still wasn't aware that his grandfather played a major– and largely uncredited–role in launching professional sports' most successful and powerful league: the NFL.

—

As Pollard III matured, he recalled many conversations among adult relatives about his grandfather that didn't make sense to him when he sat at the kids' table. During family cookouts, holidays, or whenever the extended Pollard clan gathered, discussions about how the NFL mistreated his grandad were sure to occur. The more bits and pieces Pollard III remembered, the more he wanted to complete the puzzle. He peppered his father with questions about his grandfather's involvement in the early years of the NFL. Fritz Jr. had all the answers.

Pollard III's dad explained that Fritz Sr. was among the league's founding members. As the NFL struggled to gain legitimacy in the early 1920s, Fritz Sr. was one of its biggest draws. He was the NFL's first Black player, first Black All-Pro, first Black quarterback (even if he rarely threw a forward pass, which was barely utilized during that era in the NFL), and first Black head coach. He was the leader of the NFL's first championship team. When the NFL banned Black players for a 12-year stretch beginning in 1934, Fritz Sr. reminded NFL owners what they were missing: He coached an all-Black team, his presence at the club's helm making it the most visible one of its kind in the nation. Fritz Jr. told his son that the head of their family accomplished all of that and so much more as a pro player.

Pollard III reveled in his father's recounting of the stories Fritz Sr. had handed down about the then-upstart league that became an enduring part of American culture. A star athlete himself, Pollard Jr. also briefly attended Brown before transferring to the University of North Dakota. A great running back on the North Dakota football team, Pollard Jr. competed on the university's boxing squad as well. As a member of the United States Olympic team, Fritz Jr. won the bronze medal in the 110-meter hurdles at the 1936 Summer Olympics in Berlin—joining Jesse Owens in dealing a blow to Hitler's white-supremacist mythology right to the Führer's face. He went on to earn a law degree and had a long career in the State Department as a Foreign Service Officer.

Pollard III was fiercely proud of his father, who taught him how to be a strong man. Pollard III's hero worship of his grandfather, though, created a unique bond between them. And as Pollard III devoured all the information he could uncover about his grandfather's efforts in helping to lay the NFL's foundation, his frustration grew proportionally. More people should know about his grandfather's role in the growth of the NFL, Pollard III told his father, and Fritz Sr. should receive the recognition he had unfairly lacked for far too long. Based on what he achieved in the NFL, and the fact that his accomplishments were forged in the face of soul-crushing racism, he had surely earned it.

Pollard III would soon discover that the honor his grandfather so richly deserved for a long list of completely obvious reasons would not be easily attained. His initial impulse became an obsession, which would morph into a crusade. He worked the phones, leveraged contacts, and toiled steadily for years on end, but what should have been a simple correction of a clear injustice remained elusive.

That Pollard's football career happened at all was almost an accident. In a country ridden with virulently racist Jim Crow laws and strictly enforced segregation, Pollard only slipped into a prominent role because so few people were paying attention to the shoestring attempt to create a major professional football league that had been sputtering along for 30 years around the dawn of the twentieth century. In that time, paying someone to play football was considered poor sportsmanship. The first compensated players were handed cash under the table. The games were little more than muddy and bloody sandlot scrimmages before a few hundred screaming onlookers. But once Pollard and his fellow immortal, Native American Jim Thorpe, began to thrill spectators with the potent and now-familiar combination of power, speed, dexterity, and violence—spiced with heart-stopping end-to-end sprints that left defenders grabbing at air—crowds began to grow, and so did the dream that professional football could become something other than an obscure regional pastime.

—

Frederick Douglass Pollard was born in Rogers Park, now a suburb of Chicago, on January 27, 1894, to John William Pollard, a barber, and Catherine Amanda Hughes, a seamstress. While Catherine was pregnant with Fritz, the Pollards attended an event at which Frederick Douglass, the great champion of equal rights, spoke.[1] Moved by Douglass's rousing speech, the Pollards quickly agreed on the name for their unborn child.

The seventh of the Pollards' eight children, Frederick soon became a fixture on the fields and sandlots of the up-and-coming community of about 3,500 in the 1890s. Many of its settlers had arrived from Germany, and Frederick Pollard would rarely be referred to by his given name once he began mingling on the neighborhood playgrounds. He was being called "Fritz" by the time he entered grade school.[2]

John William owned a barbershop and had been a champion boxer during the Civil War. To say the Pollards were an athletic family would be an understatement. Fritz's older brother, Luther J., played football at Lakeview High School and Northwestern University in the 1890s. Another brother, Leslie, was a standout player at Dartmouth. Later, he became coach and athletic director at Lincoln University. It was a third brother, Hughes, who kick-started Pollard's own football career at Lane Tech High in Chicago. As Pollard recalled late in life, "[Hughes] was the big shot on the team and he told the coach if his kid brother couldn't play, he wouldn't play, either. I weighed all of eighty-nine pounds. But as the years went by, I became the star of the team."[3]

Pollard believed in his own talent and, beginning in 1912, bounced from college to college trying to find the best showcase for it. From Northwestern to Dartmouth to Harvard to Bates College in Maine, his nomadic journey ended in the fall of 1915, when he entered Brown as a 21-year-old freshman. In the era of the so-called "tramp athlete," nothing about Pollard's travels in search of the optimal football fit was in the least bit shocking.

At the turn of the century, it was fairly common for tramp athletes to wander from campus to campus, offering their football talents to the highest bidder for cash. Most of these athletes only vaguely posed as students and often played for many years, sometimes at a number of different colleges. When Pollard, newly graduated from high school, set out for Evanston to attend football practice at Northwestern in September 1912, his primary goal "was the thought of playing four more years of football."[4]

Although he reported for freshman practice at Northwestern, Pollard had one minor problem: He never bothered to actually enroll in school. The dean of admissions met with Pollard after classes started and asked why he was at Northwestern. "I'm here to play football," Pollard replied. Unfortunately for Pollard, at Northwestern in 1912, solely playing football was not an acceptable reason for being on campus. Pollard was sent on his way.[5]

From Northwestern, Pollard headed to Brown. For years, a longtime customer of Pollard's mother, who was a seamstress, had lavished praise on the school, focusing on the good connections one could make there to help in career building after graduation.

Pollard, cocksure and persuasive throughout his life, wrangled a meeting with Brown's president, who granted him "special student" status. Seeing something in Pollard (perhaps mostly his potential to bolster the university's football team), the president waived the standard process for applying to the university. To gain formal admittance, though, Pollard needed to complete language courses required for incoming freshmen. Buoyed by the meeting, Pollard enrolled in Columbia College in New York City in the summer of 1913 in an effort to meet the language requirement, taking courses in French and Spanish. Brown accepted the French work, but Pollard didn't receive a passing grade on the required Spanish exam.[6]

—

Hoping admission was just around the corner the following semester, Pollard remained in Providence, found a job as a busboy, and rented a room. It appeared Pollard's once-promising football career might be permanently derailed after he fell in love with his landlord's daughter. Ada Laing became pregnant, and the couple eloped in June 1914. (Fritz Jr. arrived in 1915, and his three sisters would follow.) Out of school and needing to support a wife with a baby on the way, Pollard opened an ironing shop on Brown's campus. For one dollar a month, the Pollard Varsity Pressing Club would press an unlimited number of clothes and repair them if needed. When students left campus for the summer, Pollard moved his business south to glitzy Narragansett Pier, Rhode Island, located near the Atlantic Ocean.[7]

At 20, Pollard was a family man and business owner–both full-time jobs. Still, the allure of potentially becoming a college football star was too strong for him to ignore. He temporarily left his family in Providence and gave Dartmouth a try.

Pollard joined the team and began practicing. But he soon was forced to pack his bags yet again: Once Dartmouth learned Pollard had recently been a "special student" at Brown, his brief time at the school concluded. Next, Pollard was on to Boston to check out Harvard.

Two days after departing from Dartmouth, Pollard became a Harvard man. One could only imagine the varying accounts Pollard offered to school officials as he moved throughout what would become the Ivy League in search of a landing spot to primarily play football.

Pollard suited up for the season opener against Bates College from Maine but sat on the bench for the Crimson's 44–0 blowout victory. The inactivity made Pollard question whether he should remain at Harvard. He quickly found his answer.[8]

During the game, one of the Bates College coaches recognized Pollard from when he was a standout prep football player in Chicago. Before leaving the field, the coach approached Pollard and asked, "Why sit when you can play?" The next day, Pollard was on a train headed to Lewiston, Maine, where he quickly learned that, football aside, Maine was too damn cold for him. Dejected, Pollard took to the road again, heading back to Boston.[9]

Seeking only to play football, Pollard had attended three colleges in a matter of weeks. Even for a tramp athlete, Pollard was entering a league of his own. Clearly, Pollard's approach wasn't working. He needed a new one.

In Boston, a group of his brother Leslie's friends reached out to Pollard and staged what's currently known as an intervention. They told the floundering young man that he needed to get back to high school, earn the missing foreign language credits, and return to Brown. Heeding their advice, Pollard enrolled in a Springfield, Massachusetts, high school. In May 1915, Pollard received his long-awaited acceptance letter from Brown.[10]

—

That year would be a momentous one for Black America. Boxer Jack Johnson lost his world heavyweight title; D. W. Griffith debuted the thoroughly racist movie *The Birth of a Nation*; and the esteemed Booker T. Washington, one of the most influential Black leaders of his time, died.[11]

Pollard's performance as a college football player would also be historically significant for Black folk.

Shortly after his admittance to Brown as a full student, Pollard reestablished his laundry business. Pollard Varsity Pressing Club flourished. The business would help give its owner a reputation for sharp dressing on campus.

In fact, more than one customer was said to have seen his suit jacket gliding across a dance floor on the back of Fritz Pollard.[12]

"My grandfather was the best-dressed man on campus," Pollard III said. "He had many satisfied customers—and a great wardrobe."

But more important, his entrepreneurial spirit attracted the attention of one of the richest men in America. John D. Rockefeller Jr., an 1897 Brown graduate, had been the university's junior class president and managed the football team. On many levels, Rockefeller's years at Brown were among the most fulfilling of his life. In those days, the Rockefellers possessed the nation's greatest fortune. Not surprisingly, Brown reaped a windfall in donations from the Rockefeller family as a result of the experience John Jr. enjoyed at the school.

According to Pollard family lore, as news of Fritz's growing business spread across campus, Rockefeller, a devotee of both Brown football and bootstrap entrepreneurship, put the word out that he was eager to meet the successful young entrepreneur and freshman running back. After being introduced, Rockefeller and Pollard apparently hit it off. Rockefeller was so impressed, the story goes, that he not only promised to pay Pollard's tuition, room, and board, but offered to pay for a second dorm room so he could expand his laundry service. It was a relationship that would stretch beyond college. After Pollard finished playing and coaching in the NFL, Rockefeller invested in him again, providing a $29,000 business loan.

━━

In the fall of 1915, Pollard reported for football practice for his fifth college team. To say the least, the 5-foot-9, 150-pound halfback was not greeted with open arms by coach Eddie Robinson and the players. When Pollard arrived at Marston Field House, he was told the last practice suit had already been distributed. Even after athletic director Frederick W. Marvel intervened to make sure the freshman had a uniform, it was the oldest one in the locker room. Pollard's issued cleats were at least two sizes too large. Nobody would room with Pollard. When he hit the showers, his new teammates cleared out. During practices, Robinson exiled Pollard to one side of the field to focus on punting. The day of Brown's first game, the day Pollard had been dreaming of since graduating high school three years earlier, he arrived at the field house to pick up his uniform. That's when he learned he had not been assigned one. Pollard found a quiet spot in the corner of the field house, sat down, and cried.[13]

Fortunately for Pollard and the future of football, Clair "Mike" Purdy, Brown's 6-foot, 190-pound captain, saw past Pollard's skin tone to his immense talent and cleared the way for him both on and off the field. As Pollard would later recall, "Mike would say to me in the huddle, 'Just stay a step-and-a-half behind me Fritz. I'll get you where you want to go.' I never played with a man in college or in the pros who could clear out an end for the runner and then manage to get down field and put a block on the defensive back."[14]

Pollard found Purdy just as instrumental in blocking the inevitable racially motivated objections to his playing and living with his all-white teammates. Just as his own brother had, Purdy "used to say that if I couldn't play, he wouldn't play.

"He fought off all the objections."

Of course, the fact that the Rockefeller family gave large buckets of money to Brown helped, too. With the family's backing, "I could overcome a lot of nonsense," Pollard recalled. "It made things go easier."

But even the Rockefellers couldn't protect him at the bottom of a pileup on the field. In those days, what went on beneath the bodies heaped on the gridiron made World Wrestling Entertainment villains look like meek gentlemen. When white opponents—or teammates, for that matter—wanted to keep a Black man in his place, whatever sporting restraint they had turned to brutal aggression. Pinned to the ground, Pollard was the particular target of kicks with sharpened cleats, punches, and, thanks to the lack of a face guard in those days, even eye gouges. For self-preservation, Pollard quickly became adept at rolling on his back, whenever he could, and raising his legs. No one wanted to get cut by Pollard's spikes, so would-be assailants backed off.

Eventually, though, with the help of Purdy, Pollard got his opportunity and seized it. He dazzled on the practice field, displaying elite speed and quickness. What most impressed Brown's coaches was that it was hard to hit Pollard squarely. His bobbing running style—imagine a stationary boxer ducking and moving side to side almost rhythmically in an effort to avoid blows—made Pollard the most elusive halfback the coaching staff had ever seen. Robinson determined the freshman was simply too good to constrain. Pollard had to play.

—

"Playing football for Brown was rough. They'd call me 'nigger' from the stands. . . . 'Kill the nigger! Don't let him do that!' was all I heard. That was the first year. Then things started working out."[15]

Well, at least on Brown's campus.

When Brown played on the road, though, Pollard was the target of the most dehumanizing invective imaginable. The threats were most troubling. Threats that opponents would take cheap shots at him. Threats that he would be physically attacked by fans. And, worst of all, threats on his life.

The Yale crowd was especially awful. Once, in an effort to avoid confrontation with fans during a game there, Pollard snuck into the Yale Bowl field through a secluded entrance, Pollard III said.

"All of those schools were horrible to him—not just Yale. That stuff happened all over [what in 1954 became] the Ivy League," his grandson said. "They shouted the N-word nonstop and threw things at him. His freshman season, this went on everywhere he played. There were always threats. The fans were awful. He just came to accept that's what he would always have to deal with if he wanted to play. And he refused to let any of it stop him."

Pollard had a sensational freshman season, emerging among the top newcomers in the college game. And led by Pollard—who had big runs of 32 and 23 yards—Brown defeated Yale that season for the first time since 1910. Following Yale's defeat, an opposing tackle named Sheldon paid the freshman halfback perhaps the most backhanded compliment possible, saying, "You're a nigger—but you're the best goddam football player I ever saw."[16]

Largely due to the fresh respect Pollard and the Bears had earned, Brown was selected to play Washington State in the Rose Bowl on January 1, 1916.

The oldest currently operating bowl game, the Rose Bowl is fittingly nicknamed "the Granddaddy of Them All." But way back in 1916, the Rose Bowl was in its infancy and experiencing growing pains. The Tournament of Roses Parade began in 1890 in Pasadena as a way to raise the national profile of Southern California. In 1902, the Tournament of Roses Association decided to add a football game to the festivities. The idea was to match the best collegiate team in the East with the best team in the West. The first game was called the Tournament East-West Football Game, and the first invitees were the University of Michigan and Stanford. Michigan routed Stanford, 49–0. Game officials granted Stanford's request to end the game with eight minutes remaining. The play was so humiliating to the West Coast team that the Tournament of Roses Association abandoned the idea of having future football games in tandem with the parade. Other contests became part of the event, including chariot races and ostrich races.[17]

By 1916, apparently, enough time had passed to erase the stink of the 1902 game, and the Rose Bowl decided to try football again with the Brown–Washington State matchup. In this grand reintroduction, Pollard represented a fly in the ointment.

"Nothing was said at first," Pollard said. "But then the bowl game officials and everybody else said they didn't want the nigger to play, meaning me, of course."[18]

On the weeklong train trip from Providence, Rhode Island, to

Pasadena, California, Pollard would only occasionally be served in the dining car. "Black waiters just wouldn't even come over to him," Pollard III said. "He would go in there and it was like he was invisible. They either were told not to serve him or just didn't think he belonged in there, but his teammates mostly had to bring him food. Here he is one of the best players on the team as a freshman, his performance was a big part of the reason Brown was even going to the Rose Bowl, and that's the treatment he got on the train out to California."

Things also didn't go swimmingly for Pollard after Brown arrived at its destination.

The front-desk clerk at the Hotel Raymond in Pasadena refused to check him in. Brown's coaching staff rebelled, and after tense negotiations, Pollard was permitted to occupy a small room by himself. "That whole thing was a big mess," Pollard III said. "What my grandfather always remembered was how the whole team was willing to stand up for him. And they were already out in California. The Rose Bowl needed Brown to play."

In the game, Pollard faced the same taunts from the crowd he'd grown used to, but of more concern was the weather. Sunny California had greeted his historic appearance with torrential rains that turned the field into a big bowl of mud soup. Expecting the famous California sunshine, the team had left its foul weather gear, including cleats designed to track through mud, back in Providence. Sluicing through the mud, minus his ability to cut on a dime, Pollard only managed to gain 47 yards, the lowest total of his career, without scoring. Brown lost the game, 14–0.

One columnist reported sympathetically, "Considering the price of real estate in Pasadena, it is estimated the Brown athletes had at least $125,000 worth of mud clinging to them when they left the field."[19]

—

Though Brown finished on a disappointing note, Pollard's freshman season was a resounding success. But it only set the stage for his historic second season at Brown. Armed with the knowledge he could compete with the sport's best after his fabulous freshman season, especially considering the burden he carried daily, Pollard sprinted to stardom as a sophomore. There's an adage in college sports: The best thing about freshman is they become sophomores. In Pollard's case, that sentiment was only amplified.

Beginning in spring 1916, Pollard would set a world record in low hurdles on Brown's track team, qualify for the Olympic team (the 1916 Summer Olympics were canceled because of World War I), then go on to lead Brown to an 8–1 record with 12 touchdowns. His dominance on the field was unprecedented. Against Yale, he gained 144 yards rushing, another 74 on kickoff returns, and 76 on punt returns. It was the same incredible story against Harvard: 148 yards rushing, 44 on punt returns, and 51 as a pass receiver in Brown's first-ever victory over Harvard.[20]

Generally, statistics from that era are notoriously unreliable. But Brown officials have painstakingly reviewed Pollard's games to be as precise as possible about his accomplishments.

Pollard definitely impressed Walter Camp.

Known as "the Father of American Football," Camp is credited with several innovations that helped the game evolve, including setting a line of scrimmage and a system of downs. Camp is also known for picking the earliest All-American teams, beginning in 1889. Camp chose Pollard for the 1916 team, making Pollard only the second Black All-American—and the first to be selected for a backfield position.

Of Pollard, Camp said, he's "the most elusive back of the year or of any year."[21]

Pollard's selection to the All-American team as the first Black backfield player made him an instant national celebrity. In the first half of the twentieth century, when the struggle for equality was second only to that of survival in the Black community, Blacks held up their sports heroes to challenge the racist dogma that whites were inherently superior. Pollard became a coveted public speaker. Civil rights organizations honored him. The Black press lionized him. He was pulled in many directions. Pollard was heady with fame.

As he recalled, "I began receiving invitations from all over the country to make speeches." During the Christmas recess and well into the second semester, Pollard remembered speaking "in Chicago, Philadelphia, Pittsburgh, Washington, D.C., Baltimore, and many other places, especially New York where the NAACP held a very large reception for me as did other places."[22]

With his family at home, Pollard reveled in his newfound status. In less than two years, he went from being an unknown athlete in search of a major university at which to showcase his considerable skills to the toast of Black America. He was having the time of his life. Is there any formerly obscure twentysomething who wouldn't bask in the glory of being feted often by elites? Pollard's time on the rubber-chicken circuit, however, resulted in predictable conse-quences. He was having too much fun: Pollard dropped the ball on his studies. Undoubtedly, Pollard saw the cliff ahead, said Dr. Stephen Towns, Pollard's other grandson. But the ride to the edge was so exhilarating, Pollard declined to pump the brakes.

"Being an All-American was great for him, but becoming a big star like that . . . let's just say he was having a great time and got a little bit wild. He just stopped going to school," Towns said. "Education is very important in our family. Education was very important in the home he grew up in. But he wound up not graduating from Brown."

As the 1917 spring semester began, Pollard, who in the process of acquiring fame lost direction, was everywhere except in class at Brown. By his own account, his celebrity would benefit him in business and socially for the rest of his long life–but it cost him a college degree.

By 1918, unable to scale the academic hole he dug for himself, Pollard dropped out of school and joined the military. The United States was well into World War I (on August 6, 1917, the US formally entered the global conflict), and Pollard wound up being assigned as a physical director in the war department's new Student Army Training Corps program, which was designed to train commissioned and noncommissioned officers on college campuses. He received orders to report to the SATC detachment at Lincoln University near Oxford, Pennsylvania, located about 40 miles southwest of Philadelphia. Given the fact that his brother Leslie had been a football coach at Lincoln, there is reason to suspect that Pollard used his influence both within the army and in the Black community to secure the appointment.[23]

Pollard's military training duties included serving as the college's head football coach. Following the war, Pollard retained his position as athletic director at Lincoln, which paid $50 a month, but soon realized that he needed to supplement that income to support his family, which by that point included his wife and three children.[24]

At this point, Pollard really wasn't thinking about professional football. But professional football was thinking about him. In 1919, the Akron Ohio Indians club, which the following year would become one of the founding teams in the American Professional Football Association, approached Pollard about joining the team.

Despite being a few years removed from the height of his nationwide fame, Pollard still had a high profile within the football world and name recognition with college football fans, the group professional teams needed to win over. In short, he had what the sputtering effort to create a truly national professional football league desperately needed.

[3]

THE BAN

IN ITS EARLY YEARS, the nascent professional football league wasn't highly structured, to put it kindly. Akin to the American Wild West of the late nineteenth century, when much of the territories west of the Mississippi River were lawless, among the various professional leagues no agreements prevented teams from raiding opponents' rosters, which changed weekly as players moved from city to city chasing the biggest paycheck.

That's the way things had been since the professional game took root in small- and medium-sized cities in Western Pennsylvania and the Ohio Valley, starting on August 31, 1895, when the first game was played at Latrobe, Pennsylvania.[25]

No Blacks played in the first professional football game, or for the seven years following. It wasn't until 1902 that Blacks emerged on rosters. Charles W. Follis of Cloverdale, Virginia, was the first. Follis played for the Shelby Athletic Association in Ohio. Cloverdale was born on February 3, 1879, and moved to Wooster, Ohio, and played at Wooster High there. The *Wooster Republican* newspaper, in one write-up of Wooster High's victory over Alliance High, praised Follis's performance. "The ball was kicked off and Follis brought it back half way across the field, plugging through the Alliance boys as if they were paper." Follis joined the Shelby Athletic Association after he was wooed away from the Wooster Athletic Association amateur team. In their first game with Follis, Shelby defeated Freemont, 58–0. One of Follis's teammates was Branch Rickey, a student at Ohio Wesleyan and later the president and general manager of the Brooklyn Dodgers. Rickey's firsthand observation of Follis's unruffled handling of prejudice, on the field and off, influenced his decision to introduce Jackie Robinson to Major League Baseball in 1947.[26]

The proto-professional football world that Pollard entered in 1919 was in many ways indistinguishable from the one in which Follis thrived near the turn of the century. Follis, and three other Black professional players during the period before the NFL, put cracks in the wall. Pollard was the first one to burst through it in a big way. Pollard's smashing second season in professional football would also mark a new era in the game.

In 1920, George Halas, manager, coach, and player of the Staley Starchmakers, wrote a letter to Ralph Hay, manager of the Canton Bulldogs, suggesting that some of the better football teams get together and form a league. On September 17, 1920, managers of eleven professional clubs met in the showroom of Hay's Automobile Agency in Canton, Ohio, to discuss Halas's suggestion. The APFA was formed at this meeting. Jim Thorpe—winner of two gold medals at the 1912 Summer Olympics in Stockholm, Sweden—was elected president, and eleven franchises (with rosters averaging about 20 players) were awarded at a cost of $100 each: Canton Bulldogs, Cleveland Indians, Dayton Triangles, Akron Professionals, Massillon Tigers, Rochester All-Stars, Rock Island Independents, Muncie Tigers, Decatur Staleys, Hammond Pros, and Chicago Cardinals.

(Only two of the original eleven franchises are still active in the National Football League: the Chicago Bears, formerly known as the Decatur Staleys, and the Arizona Cardinals, formerly called the Chicago Cardinals.) On June 24, 1922, the APFA was renamed the National Football League.[27]

Without question, Pollard was the Pros' most important player as they raced toward the first league title. Of course, Pollard had help. One of his best teammates in those early years was the person whom he persuaded to join the 1921 Pros: his friend Paul Robeson.

———

When Pollard briefly relocated his laundry operation to Narragansett Pier, he met the then-16-year-old Robeson, who was working as a waiter in the Rhode Island seaside town.

Pollard and Robeson became fast friends and remained close for the rest of their lives. Robeson went on to become an All-American football player at Rutgers University. And Robeson's accomplishments off the field dwarfed anything he did on it. Among the most influential Blacks of the twentieth century, Robeson would become a scholar, a lawyer, an acclaimed concert performer, an accomplished stage and film actor, and a political activist who championed the cause of civil rights.

William Drew Robeson, Paul's father, was born a slave in Martin Country, North Carolina, on July 27, 1845. He escaped at age 15, joined the Union Army, and after the Civil War attended Lincoln University in Pennsylvania. There he met and married Maria Louisa Bustill. The couple moved to Princeton, New Jersey, in 1879, and their fifth child, Paul Leroy, was born on April 9, 1898. Their child became one of the most heralded citizens in the history of Black America. The young Robeson attended the segregated Jamison Elementary School and performed well, considering the premature death of his mother in 1904. At racially mixed Somerville High in Somerville,

New Jersey, Robeson played fullback on the football team. His thoughts of college centered on Lincoln because of his father, but he changed his mind when he scored the highest marks ever attained on the New Jersey High School Examination. He entered Rutgers in the fall of 1915.[28]

A gifted athlete who would ultimately grow to 6 foot 3 and weigh about 220 pounds at the peak of his playing career, Robeson made the Rutgers varsity as a freshman, playing tackle and end. As a sophomore, Robeson faced Pollard in a Rutgers-Brown game on October 28, 1916. Pollard scored twice—once on a 48-yard run—and Brown won, 21–3. That season, however, Robeson was involved in a shameful incident. On October 14, 1916, he was left off the team in a game against Washington and Lee (Virginia), which refused to play against Blacks. Rutgers could have canceled the game in protest or insisted that all its varsity members take the field with no exceptions. Instead, it left Robeson in New Jersey.[29]

But when West Virginia made the same demand, Rutgers coach G. Foster Sanford, who had regretted giving in to Washington and Lee, refused. [30]

By 1917, Robeson was clearly one of the best players in the nation.

The *New York Times* of October 14, 1917, said of Robeson, "the giant colored end from New Brunswick stood head and shoulders above his teammates in all around playing. . . . He was a tower of strength on the Scarlet defense. . . . He towered above every man on the field, and when he stretched his arms up in the air, he pulled down forward passes that an ordinary player would have to use a stepladder to reach." Later, the November 28, 1917, *New York Herald* was equally lavish in praise: "Paul Robeson, the big Negro end of the Rutgers eleven, is a football genius." Camp called him the finest end that ever played the game—college or professional—and named him to his first-team All-American roster in 1918.[31]

Robeson entered his senior year as one of the most prominent athletes on the East Coast, if not the whole country. With another game against Washington and Lee on the Scarlet Knights' schedule, the team's white players, coaches, and university administrators would have sent a powerful message by either demanding that Robeson be permitted to play or canceling the game. Once again, however, Rutgers chose the easiest path: Robeson was benched. As Robeson went on to crusade for civil rights in the nascent stage of the movement during the first half of the twentieth century, it's easy to imagine that his humiliation at the hands of college football coaches lingered in his mind.

After graduating Phi Beta Kappa, he planned to eventually attend law school. But first he accepted his pal Fritz Pollard's offer to come join him in the new professional football league. Correctly, Robeson surmised he'd be able to make enough money in the new league to help pay for his tuition at Columbia Law School. And this time, Robeson would have the reassurance of knowing his fate wouldn't be in the hands of a white coach, willing to abandon him at the first difficulty, but with Pollard, who would share the reins of the Pros as their co-coach for the 1921 season.

—

With Pollard and Robeson, the 1920–21 Pros were a formidable bunch. Of their first 23 games in the APFA/NFL, the Pros had 16 victories, only three losses and four ties. Pollard continued his rushing heroics, and Robeson made an immediate impact playing both tackle and end, repeatedly breaking through defenses to bust up plays before they could begin. Although the new league's club owners by no means openly recruited Black players after Pollard and Robeson excelled, they nonetheless reluctantly gave Black players opportunities to participate. More joined the league to begin the 1922 season.

That season, Pollard helped organize, played for, and coached the new Milwaukee Badgers squad. In Milwaukee, Pollard was again joined by Robeson and another Black All-American from the University of Iowa, Fred "Duke" Slater, a 6-foot-4 tackle who divided the season between the Milwaukee and Rock Island teams. Then there was Jay "Ink" Williams, whom Pollard had opened doors for years earlier at Brown.

Williams, from Monmouth, Illinois, arrived on campus the year after Pollard showed what Black football players could do. A freshman on Brown's great 1916 Rose Bowl team, Williams, who played end, roomed with Pollard, and they became lifelong friends. By 1922, Williams was in his second season with Hammond as their left end. He was joined on the team by John Shelbourne, a Dartmouth graduate. So in 1922, the NFL had at least five Black players. Although these few Black players were given opportunities to play, they did not come without repercussions. Later in life, Williams recalled that their relationships with white players were "very poor in some instances." Most white players would only begrudgingly acknowledge the existence of a Black teammate. During practices and games, it wasn't uncommon for a white player to completely ignore a Black player lined up alongside him. Off the field the struggle against legal segregation was constant. While sitting in a hotel in Green Bay, Wisconsin, Williams and Pollard were "paged out of the dining room," then taken to the office and told, "We don't allow colored people to eat in our hotel." In Canton, Ohio, seated with teammates, Williams was allowed to go on eating–the management simply put a screen around the table."[32]

Daily, the league's Black players had to swallow their pride to navigate the racism all around them. And embarrassment was the least of their worries. Their physical safety was at stake.

One afternoon after the Akron Pros defeated a team in the hills of Western Pennsylvania, the windows of the team bus were shot out. Fortunately, no one was aboard the bus at the time.[33]

A few more Black players trickled into the league in 1923. Pollard was still going strong as a player-coach. Robeson, though, had moved on. Having completed his goal of earning enough money to pay his law school tuition, Robeson was done with the inherent physical risks of football. He also had burgeoning theatrical and singing careers to nurture. Robeson's excellence in so many endeavors reduced his impressive athletic career to a footnote in his life's story. But the end of Robeson's time in professional football would not mark the end of his professional partnership with Pollard.

Pollard, who reinvented himself multiple times when his playing days were finished, became a theatrical agent. When Robeson made the movie *The Emperor Jones*, Pollard, as the film's uncredited casting agent, supplied most of the Black talent for it.

—

By 1925, the hiring of new Black players had stopped cold. Pollard, now in his 30s, was no longer quite the dominant figure he had been during the league's first few seasons. And while the NFL had steadily garnered more interest among sports fans, it still lagged far behind baseball, college football, and boxing in terms of widespread appeal. The NFL's major problem, owners surmised, was the absence of a white star. Pollard was still a draw, if only for the fact he piqued the curiosity of white fans. But for the most part back then, white stars appealed to white fans and put their fannies in the seats. The environment was ripe for a white hero, especially one who played in the most glamorous position, which at the time was halfback, to help broaden the NFL's appeal on a national level.

Almost as if on cue, along came Harold "Red" Grange from the University of Illinois. Nicknamed "the Galloping Ghost," Grange was the embodiment of the owners' hopes. The speedy, shifty halfback was a three-time All-American at Illinois, led the school to the theoretical 1923 national championship, and, most important, was white. In 1924, Grange attained legend status after his signature six-touchdown performance in a 39–14 victory over the University of Michigan. In the first quarter, Grange scored on runs of 95, 67, 56, and 44 yards. After halftime, he scored a fifth rushing touchdown and capped the stunning display with a touchdown pass. On November 21, 1925, Grange led Illinois to a 14–9 victory over Ohio State in front of 85,295 at Columbus, Ohio. Minutes after the game, he stunned reporters by declaring that he was dropping out of college—and signing with the Chicago Bears.[34]

It was by far the most important NFL signing to that point and ranks among the most consequential in the history of professional sports in North America.

Grange, born on June 13, 1903, in Forksville, Pennsylvania, first became a star football player at Wheaton High in Illinois before entering the University of Illinois. Grange emerged as the nation's idol in the early 1920s, his eye-opening football exploits for the Fighting Illini chronicled weekly in newspapers, on radio, and in newsreels. Millions of Americans followed Grange, whose presence in the league accelerated the legitimization of the NFL. Grange's role in the ascendancy of pro football as a major sport cannot be overstated. Though Pollard had thrilled fans and excited new interest in professional football, given his built-in handicap, there was a ceiling to what he could accomplish. He was Black.

Grange's arrival, a shooting star of talent wrapped in a pale complexion, marked the moment the NFL began its long climb to becoming a professional sports league second to none.

■

The day after Illinois defeated Ohio State, Grange joined the Bears in Chicago. He sat on the bench and watched his new team beat the Green Bay Packers, 21–0, at Cubs Park (in 1926 the name would be changed to Wrigley Field). Four days later, on Thanksgiving Day, Grange made his NFL debut in the Bears' scoreless tie against the Chicago Cardinals in front of a standing-room crowd of 36,000–the largest in pro football history at the time–packed into Cubs Park to watch Grange work.[35]

George Halas, the Bears' owner, had big plans to capitalize on Grange's immense popularity. In an effort to drum up more interest in the Bears and the NFL as a whole, Halas, following the completion of the 1925 season, led the club on a 19-game, 67-day "barnstorming tour" during the winter of 1925–26 with Grange getting top billing throughout the road show. This was long before the advent of commercial television, which enabled people across the United States to watch college and professional sporting events regardless of where schools and clubs were located. Taking to the road, performing in areas where the NFL hoped to expand its footprint and, hopefully, its fan base, provided the best showcase for the league.

The success of the Grange-inspired coast-to-coast tour exceeded Halas's wildest dreams. Quickly, the Bears became the hottest sports story of the day. Whenever the Bears showed up in a new town, large crowds turned out, primarily to watch Grange dazzle with the football in his hands. The tour resulted in newspaper headlines, major radio coverage, and many newsreels.

While in college, Grange realized his earning potential and hired Champaign, Illinois, theater owner and promoter C. C. "Cash and Carry" Pyle as his agent and manager. Given Pyle's flair for hyperbole in furtherance of hyping, well, any business project he was part of, it's likely his accounts of the tour's financial success were at least somewhat inflated. That established, there's no debating the tour stirred unprecedented national interest in the Bears and, in turn, the NFL. The immediate economic impact to the league was immeasurable.

Halas and Pyle apparently agreed to a 50-50 split of revenue.

Halas was expected to assume all costs of the tour, providing Grange played in all the games. The Bears' final tally after expenses is unknown, but the franchise reportedly produced its first significant profit as a result of the groundbreaking collaboration between a professional sports franchise and its biggest star. Reportedly, the cut for Grange and Pyle after the tour's first stage was $100,000, which they split equally.

After a week of rest, Grange and the Bears hit the road again. They wound their way through the South with three games in Florida and one in New Orleans before heading to the West Coast to play in Los Angeles, San Diego, San Francisco, Portland, and Seattle. At the completion of the tour, Grange and Pyle supposedly split another $100,000.[36]

From the NFL season, the tour and Pyle-brokered endorsements combined, Grange is believed to have raked in north of $125,000 (the equivalent of $1.8 million today)—an eye-opening sum in any occupation during the mid-1920s and a staggering amount relative to what pro football players were earning. Typically, salaries in that era were less than $100 per game. At Pollard's zenith as a player in Akron, he had a better chance of being elected president of the United States than earning anything close to what Grange made in his rookie season. Pollard's salary while playing for Akron is one of those intriguing questions that may never be answered accurately.

Pollard claimed in a number of interviews that he was paid $1,500 per game for important contests with Akron, which put him ahead of the $1,000 per game he said Jim Thorpe earned. The Professional Football Researchers Association estimates that the average pro salary for that era was $75 to $150 per game, with star players receiving a little more. The highest documented per-game salary for 1920 is $300 that the Chicago Cardinals paid star quarterback Paddy Driscoll. George Halas, who paid the salaries of the Decatur Staleys in 1920, maintained that his players averaged $125 per game and that

Guy Chamberlin received the largest amount for the entire season: $1,650. It appears that Pollard exaggerated his per-game salary. Given his superior play for Akron, his contributions as coach, and his enormous appeal as a gate attraction, however, there is little doubt that Pollard was one of the highest-paid players in the APFA in 1920.[37]

Grange, after only one year in the league, had earned more money and would have more future opportunities to profit in the NFL than any player before him, especially the Black players. Pollard noticed.

"He understood what was happening," Pollard III said. "In the beginning, my grandfather was really one of only two stars in the league, him and Jim Thorpe, but the NFL had no interest in promoting someone who looked like my grandfather.

"So once the league had a white star, there were suddenly all these different ways to make more money. With money comes more power, which the owners didn't want my grandfather to have."

—

In a bold move, Grange tested his power.

Because of Grange's barnstorming success, Pyle informed the Bears, Grange would not play for Chicago in 1926 unless Halas and his partner, Ed "Dutch" Sternaman, gave Grange one-third of the team. They refused, so Pyle decided he and Grange should start their own NFL franchise and place it in the media center of the world, New York City, to capitalize fully on the star's popularity. At the league's annual postseason meeting, Pyle proposed putting his team in Yankee Stadium, but New York Giants owner Tim Mara refused to allow it, claiming territorial infringement. When the league backed Mara, Pyle announced he was forming his own circuit–the American Football League–with his own team. To add insult to injury, he even appropriated the name of the Giants' rival for the sporting attention of New Yorkers. His new team would be called the New York Yankees.[38]

Beset with problems from the start, even despite Grange's larger-than-life presence, the American Football League lasted only one season. After sitting out the 1928 season because of a knee injury, Grange in 1929 returned to the NFL–a league that no longer included Pollard.

Pollard played his last game for Akron on October 10, 1926, against the archrival Canton Bulldogs. It was perhaps a fitting conclusion to Pollard's NFL career in that he faced his old rival, Jim Thorpe, one last time.

Thorpe, being a Native American and of mixed ancestry, undoubtedly faced a level of racism in a league that was overwhelmingly white. But the indignities Thorpe faced never approached the level of what Pollard contended with daily. Nominally the first NFL president, Thorpe commanded respect for his athletic prowess and, most significantly, the fact that he wasn't Black. The different paths Pollard and Thorpe traveled to induction in the Pro Football Hall of Fame tell the story. Despite Thorpe and Pollard being equal draws at the dawn of the league, Thorpe became a Hall of Famer 42 years before Pollard.

In the final Pollard-Thorpe showdown, Akron and Canton played to a scoreless tie. After the game, Frank Nied, Akron's treasurer, gave Pollard, who was 32, his unconditional release as player and coach. An Akron news release stated that management took the action because Pollard "failed to play up to the form expected of him." Pollard was quoted as saying that he had intended to retire after the season and wanted to end his professional career in an Akron uniform. He added that he "never counted on being fired."[39]

Being cast aside unceremoniously, after the league benefitted so greatly from his efforts in those early years, wounded Pollard deeply. He knew it was time to walk away, his mind still capable but his body no longer cooperating consistently after so many years playing a brutal game. But this? This was a cruel betrayal.

"He helped the league get going, he brought in fans, and all of them [NFL owners] knew it," Pollard III said. "Then, after he does all of that, after he's really one of their only two stars and also a successful coach, he just gets thrown aside."

—

The combination of Grange's ascent and Pollard's forced retirement in 1926 proved to be a harbinger of a major change in the NFL's unwritten policy about Black players. Suddenly, many club owners, who had previously been willing to scatter a handful of African American players on team rosters, now focused on filling their rosters with white players exclusively. After Grange left the Bears for the 1926 season in his futile attempt to get the American Football League off the ground, the NFL struggled and teams folded. Fewer job opportunities resulted in Black players being shown the door first.

While 22 teams began the 1926 season, only 12 competed for the championship the following season. In 1926, the league featured five Black players. The following season, there was only one: Duke Slater of the Chicago Cardinals. Over the next six seasons, only three other Black players played in the NFL.[40]

In addition to the contraction of the NFL and collapse of the American Football League, there were other factors that contributed to Black players being squeezed out.

By the mid-1920s, players were making about $1,500 to $1,800 per season—today's equivalent of roughly $22,000 to $27,000. White players didn't want to share that much money with Black teammates.

Resentment fueled racial tension within the NFL. On November 5, 1926, New York Giants players refused to take the field in a game against Canton at the Polo Grounds. Giants management maintained that the large crowd might object to the presence of Canton's only Black player, Sol Butler, on the field. After a 10-minute delay, Butler withdrew "voluntarily," advising his teammates to play and not disappoint the crowd.[41]

Primarily because of the racist views of white fans and white players, Black players were increasingly required to clear an even higher bar than they had previously merely to receive consideration from NFL teams.

Beginning with Pollard, Black players had to fit a certain mold: high performers who'd been a sensation at white universities. NFL executives didn't scour the Black press for information on players at Historically Black Colleges and Universities. They viewed Black coaches as being inferior to their white counterparts at major colleges and universities. They considered it a waste of time to evaluate Black players, who played a supposedly substandard brand of college football. The seeds of the NFL's deplorable record on inclusive hiring in coaching and its executive ranks were sown during this period.

As the 1920s drew to a close, even top Black players weren't receiving a second look from the league. The pool of standout Black players at white schools was small to begin with. Once team owners decided to ignore that group, it was a certainty the NFL would become an all-white league.

Pollard saw the writing on the wall. In 1928, before the ban began, Pollard organized a Black professional team in Chicago: the Chicago Black Hawks. For three seasons, the Black Hawks played on the road during the fall and winter months. Most of their opponents were white semipro teams in California. Semipro teams did not participate full-time in sports, and players on those clubs were compensated at much lower rates than players in major professional leagues. With the depression worsening, however, the Black Hawks were forced to disband in California during the 1931–32 season because of poor attendance. Many of the players, nearly broke, were stranded on the West Coast.[42]

———

In 1931, America was in the midst of the Great Depression. By 1933, unemployment reached 20 percent. It was within this atmosphere of economic despair that the last two Black players in the NFL–Joe Lillard and Ray Kemp–were sent packing.[43]

The NFL wouldn't hire another Black player for 13 years. It strains credulity to believe this was a matter of happenstance. Of course, that's what some of the most prominent white figures in the game's history would contend for the remainder of their lives, failing to concede their culpability. Decades after the ban was finally lifted, Pittsburgh Steelers owner Art Rooney said, "I can say there never was any racial bias." In 1970, George Halas of the Chicago Bears declared that there had been no unwritten exclusionary agreement "in no way, shape or form." And Tex Schramm, of the Los Angeles Rams and later the Dallas Cowboys, said he had no recollection of a gentleman's agreement. "You just didn't do it [sign Blacks]. It wasn't the thing that was done."[44]

Although Grange's debut season stirred buzz that helped the NFL attract more white fans, the dwindling number of Black players was alienating Black sports fans, especially after Pollard was ushered out. Without major Black stars with whom they could identify, Black sports fans mostly committed their resources to other sports—especially baseball. With the color barrier firmly in place in Major League Baseball, Blacks turned their attention to a professional baseball league organized by entrepreneurs, the Negro National League. Teams sprang up in Chicago, Cincinnati, Dayton, Detroit, Indianapolis, Kansas City, and St. Louis, all siphoning off fan support that could have been going to the NFL.

—

The NFL was done with Fritz Pollard—but he wasn't finished with it. Not even close. Just as at the start of the league, Pollard remained a key figure during the most disgraceful era in NFL history.

No written documentation about the 13-year ban on Black players has ever been revealed publicly. No correspondence among team owners; no hiring directives for club officials. The creation of the color barrier appears to have been implemented stealthily. And, judging by the historical record, quite effectively.

The forced exodus of Blacks from the NFL meant that Black football players in college, at both schools with overwhelmingly white enrollment and Historically Black Colleges and Universities, could not continue their playing careers in a league that had emerged as the best ever in professional football. The situation created a void that Pollard—who throughout his life identified areas for growth where others only saw a blank space—viewed as an opportunity.

Pollard didn't waste energy sulking about his unceremonious departure from the league whose growth was, literally, in large part due to his blood, sweat, and tears. He accepted that another chapter of his life was finished and it was time to begin the next. Sure, Pollard would have preferred to walk away on his own terms, retiring instead of being given the boot. But he believed the entrepreneurial spirit that had served him so well at Brown would continue to light his path. Off the field, he first saw an opening in financial planning.

During this period, the small but growing group of affluent Blacks in the United States had increasing amounts of discretionary income that they could invest. But there were no Black-owned investment firms dedicated to serving the Black community. Pollard founded the first: F.D. Pollard and Co. Although potential clients were partly drawn to Pollard because of his recent history as a high-profile player in the upstart NFL, he was still widely known—and most important, trusted—because of his trailblazing accomplishments at Brown. But the enduring name recognition that helped launch the investment business would soon inspire him to go in another direction—back into the game he just couldn't quit.

—

Locked out of the NFL, Black football players followed their counter-parts in baseball and formed semipro teams. They played each other and, occasionally, integrated semipro teams and semipro teams with all-white rosters.

From this raw material, Pollard sought to create a competitive Black professional team. If NFL owners would consent to playing Black teams, Pollard thought, they might be prompted to sign Black players again.[45]

Decades later, Pollard explained his thinking in detail to his grandson. "It was pretty simple: He wanted to show them what they were missing," Pollard III said. "He really believed that, from a business standpoint, the NFL would have to reconsider its position once owners saw so many talented Black players on one team at the same time.

"He wasn't naive at all about how the owners felt about Black players. He was thinking about it based on what would be best for the league to improve its talent and make money. He was hoping green would help them change their thinking about Black."

Late in the summer of 1935, Pollard initiated his plan by accepting an offer to coach a professional, all-Black Harlem football team organized and managed by Herschel "Rip" Day, an athletic promoter and Lincoln University alumnus. The team was named the Brown Bombers in honor of rising heavyweight boxing contender Joe Louis. Day was determined to make the Brown Bombers the finest Black pro team in the nation, on par with Bob Douglas's famed New York Renaissance Big Five basketball team.[46]

As he had earlier attempted in Chicago with the Black Hawks, Pollard tried to showcase the best available Black football talent in an effort to demonstrate once again that Blacks could compete on the field with whites without serious incident. He was deter-mined to schedule exhibition games with the local NFL teams–the Brooklyn Dodgers and the New York Giants–to underscore his point. During the season, Lewis Dial of the *New York Age* printed a rumor, most likely started by Pollard, that the Giants had challenged the

Bombers to a game in late November. Dial quoted Pollard as saying that if the November date was not acceptable, "a post season game will be arranged." In fact, neither of New York's NFL teams had expressed any interest in playing the Brown Bombers or any other Black team.[47]

As Pollard continued to try to lure the NFL into playing the Bombers, he and Day went about assembling a top-notch professional team, built around former standout Chicago Cardinal halfback Lillard, one of the last two players in the NFL before the ban. In the meantime, they played a motley collection of white semipro teams from the Northeast at Dyckman Oval, near Harlem. Although the city's Black newspapers gave the Bombers ample coverage and duly praised Pollard and his players, the club struggled financially. Average attendance at Dyckman Oval was about 1,500 per game, barely enough to cover players' salaries.[48]

Giants owner Tim Mara ignored Pollard's attempts to engage him publicly and drum up interest in a Giants–Brown Bombers matchup. Pollard would come to believe that the color line remained in effect so long largely because of the recalcitrance of Mara and George Halas of the Bears.

With hope of a high-profile matchup with an NFL team dwindling, Pollard tried to stir interest in the team and help boost poor attendance by instituting trick plays and unorthodox formations, including one called the "aeroplane shift" that the *Amsterdam News* claimed baffled opponents.[49]

On the field, at least, the Bombers thrived, providing a showcase for Black players who were walled off from the NFL. But off it, financial troubles only increased. Pollard's tenure as coach would end after three seasons when, before the 1938 season kicked off, he learned that the Bombers would not be allowed to use Dyckman Oval for their home games. With no suitable stadium close to Harlem available, the Bombers became exclusively a road team. Pollard didn't sign up for that.

Pollard fell short in his ultimate aim of chipping away at the color barrier. NFL owners, he discovered, were entrenched on maintaining the ban no matter how many great Black football players could have potentially helped them win and grow the league.

But in Pollard's time with the Bombers, he again emerged as one of the most important figures in the evolution of the NFL. In addition to his body of work as a trailblazing player and head coach in the league, Pollard also was on the right side of history in attempting to show owners that their color line was a horrible mistake. Pollard's monumental contribution to pro football can best be characterized in four words: He was a leader.

If a person of Pollard's stature in the game wasn't worthy of induction into the Pro Football Hall of Fame, the organization shouldn't exist.

—

In the early 1990s, visitors to the office of former NFL commissioner Paul Tagliabue departed with a gift: a book about the life of Fritz Pollard.

Tagliabue thoroughly enjoyed *Fritz Pollard: Pioneer in Racial Advancement*, written by John M. Carroll. First published in 1991, the book topped Tagliabue's recreational reading list. Among friends, colleagues, and associates, Tagliabue trumpeted Carroll's illuminating profile of a key figure in the NFL whose accomplishments had been reduced to merely a footnote in history. Tagliabue, who first served as the NFL's general counsel and then, beginning in 1989, ran the league for almost 17 years, found Pollard's story to be among the most compelling he had read about the pro game's earliest pioneers.

"I used to have a case of those books in my office," Tagliabue said. "From that book, I started talking about him [with NFL employees].

I asked the question, 'Why shouldn't he be in the [Pro Football] Hall of Fame?'"

Good question. By that point, Pollard III had already been asking it for years.

One could argue, and Pollard III did, that considering Pollard's importance while the NFL was striving to gain a foothold, he should have been inducted in the inaugural 1963 Pro Football Hall of Fame class, which included peers Harold Edward "Red" Grange, George "Papa Bear" Halas, Green Bay Packer cofounder Earl Louis "Curly" Lambeau, and Jim Thorpe. In that era, however, NFL owners and other league power brokers still hadn't come to terms with their racist history.

For the remainder of his life, Pollard was denied the bronze bust he deserved. As far back as 1976, Pollard III kicked around the idea of formally making a case for his grandfather to be inducted into the Pro Football Hall of Fame.

In 1990, armed with the historical information he had collected, Pollard III began working the phones. He attempted to make contact with officials in the league office in New York City and staff at the Pro Football Hall of Fame in Canton, Ohio. Almost immediately, he realized things could take a while.

"I could never seem to get in touch with the right person," Pollard III recalls. "I would call someone over in one area, hoping to have a conversation, and leave a message. They would call me back and say they weren't the right person to talk to.

"They'd give me a number of another person. But when I'd call that person, I'd get the same answer: I had the wrong person for what I needed. I don't know how long it went like that. It seemed like forever. I knew it would take a lot of time."

And that's one thing Pollard III never had enough of while providing for the two greatest joys in life: his son, Marcus, and his daughter, Meredith Kaye Pollard Russell.

During the week, Pollard III stayed on the go in his position as a civilian employee with the Maryland-National Capital Park Police. Then, on weekends, Marcus and Meredith Kaye, who were both active in sports, always had a game somewhere. The fact that Pollard III was a single parent made his perpetual time crunch all the worse. As a little girl, Meredith Kaye remembers how hard her father worked at three jobs: being a parent, earning a living, and attempting to get the right people interested in Fritz Pollard's story.

"Whenever he was home, he was either dead tired, passed out asleep, or he was on the phone in his office making calls about his grandfather," said Pollard Russell, an early-education teacher.

"He was trying to gain traction. He was trying to get people to listen to him. It went very slowly. He would have worked on it full-time if he could, it was that important to him, but he had two children to take care of. He made so many calls."

—

By the mid-1990s, Tagliabue was making calls on behalf of Pollard, too.

Tagliabue reached out to longtime *Washington Post* sportswriter Leonard Shapiro, whom he had known for years. In addition to his source-reporter relationship with Shapiro that developed over the journalist's long, distinguished career at the *Post*, Tagliabue wrote the foreword to Shapiro's 1991 book, *Big Man on Campus: John Thompson and the Georgetown Hoyas*. Tagliabue had been a standout forward for the Hoyas in the early 1960s.

For 29 years, Shapiro was a member of the Pro Football Hall of Fame selection committee. Tagliabue had a lot to say about why Pollard was worthy of significant consideration for induction. On Tagliabue's strong recommendation, Shapiro read Carroll's biography of Pollard. Then Shapiro entered the fight.

"Lenny got interested in the cause," Tagliabue said. "He made it a priority."

No arm-twisting was required, Shapiro insists.

"When the commissioner of the NFL says to you, 'Hey, Len, you ought to take a look at this guy. I think he's really worthy,' you do it," Shapiro said. "It wasn't an order. He just suggested it. And it was a good suggestion."

For Shapiro, Carroll's book was a great starting point–but a *Post* reporter always wants to know more. Shapiro initiated his own fact-finding project, reading as much as he could find about Pollard. In becoming further educated on the man's NFL career, Shapiro realized Tagliabue had nailed it.

"Was I a Fritz Pollard scholar? Well, obviously, no. But after he [Tagliabue] put me on to the guy, based on what Pollard accomplished, it was clear to me that he should be in the Hall of Fame," Shapiro said.

Shapiro connected with other committee members, putting Pollard on their radar. He also tracked down Fritz Jr. and introduced him to Tagliabue. Fritz Jr. told Tagliabue that his son was leading the family's efforts regarding the Pro Football Hall of Fame. That's when things finally got going in earnest. Still, the process moved at a glacial pace.

"There wasn't as much emphasis on the senior part as there was [on candidates from the modern era]," Shapiro said. "With the structure of the Hall of Fame committee back then, it was really easy for guys to slip through the cracks."

Despite being in plain sight, Pollard for decades had been invisible to the committee. The group's lack of diversity in the past could have been part of the problem. Although it's always dangerous to make sweeping generalizations about race, it's not a stretch to suggest that an overwhelmingly white Pro Football Hall of Fame electorate may not have readily understood the social significance of voting to induct Pollard largely for being the NFL's first Black pioneer.

By 2003, the NFL's ongoing internal struggle with racism—which dated from its opening kickoff more than 80 years earlier—sparked renewed interest in Pollard's story among Black league employees. Many came together that year to form an affinity group dedicated to advancing inclusive hiring within the NFL. Today, the Fritz Pollard Alliance assists the league in enforcing compliance of hiring guidelines and counsels the commissioner on all matters of workplace diversity. Through the eponymous organization's earliest efforts to expand opportunities for people of color from the front office to the field, Pollard was back in pro football's spotlight for the first time since the Roaring Twenties.

There's no doubt about it—Shapiro and the alliance's leadership were helpful in advancing the ball on Pollard's candidacy. But in Tagliabue, Pollard III had the coach he needed to eventually win the game.

"The former commissioner was very instrumental in helping me," Pollard III said. "Once he got involved, I started to feel like we were finally moving in the right direction. But just because he was helping me didn't mean the selection committee would let my grandfather in. The selection committee does things its own way, which I found out."

—

The list of Pro Football Hall of Fame voters was intimidatingly long.

There were so many names, so many phone numbers, just so many people who needed to be contacted and cajoled. That's always the first thing that comes to mind whenever Pollard III reflects on the yearlong campaign he spearheaded, beginning in the summer of 2004, on behalf of his family to finally right a wrong.

First, Pollard III had to persuade Hall of Fame voters to research his grandfather's career, which required most to break new ground. Few had heard of Pollard. Even those who had some inkling of Pollard knew little about his reign as a big draw in the league's early years.

Pollard III was persistent. He left phone messages. If calls were not returned, he followed up with more. If committee members seemed ambivalent about Pollard, Pollard III would keep them on the phone until they promised to at least take a quick look at his grandfather's NFL career.

Fortunately for Pollard III, he had help.

Meredith Kaye, 16 at the time, became her father's de facto secretary. She structured his office so he could most efficiently begin his night gig. All of the day's messages, including brief call summaries, were neatly arranged on his desk. She even wrote out a daily to-do list for him.

Repeatedly, committee members informed Pollard III they couldn't find any information on his grandfather. It was as if he never played in the NFL, they said.

Of course, members were looking in all the wrong places: the archives of major metropolitan newspapers. Calmly, time after time, Pollard directed committee members to the Black press. The *Chicago Defender*, the *New York Amsterdam News*, the *Baltimore Afro-American*, and many others–Pollard III assured them all that's where they'd find what they needed.

"They didn't understand that only the Black press covered Black players at that time," Pollard III said. "Then after they went back and looked, they'd call me back and say, 'Did you know your grandfather did this and that and this? Did you realize he did all of these things?' I certainly did. That's exactly what I was trying to tell them."

—

With Tagliabue, Shapiro, and Black league officials all rowing in the same direction as Pollard's committed grandson, Pollard was finally nominated for the Hall of Fame class that would be enshrined in 2005–one of two senior candidates that year. He had been rejected on the regular ballot from 1963–69 and again in 1971 before he began regularly appearing on the senior ballot in 1977. Pollard's outspokenness through the years about whom he wanted held accountable for the racist color line may have contributed to the lack of interest in his candidacy. But on August 7, 2005, in front of a sun-splashed crowd, the Pollard family was focused on the present: Fritz was inducted posthumously into the Pro Football Hall of Fame, part of a four-member class that included quarterbacks Steve Young and Dan Marino and fellow senior player Benny Friedman. Despite being the first Black quarterback, Pollard was enshrined as a halfback, the position he was best known for playing. From Chicago and Washington, D.C., Pollard's family made the trek to Canton, Ohio, to celebrate a moment more than 40 years overdue–and which, without Pollard III's labor of love, may never have happened.

His work done, Pollard III was filled with a sense of satisfaction. His grandfather was finally where he belonged. But Pollard III also reflected on the damaging impact of the NFL's color line on his grandfather and so many other Black football players–and the long struggle they faced even after it was lifted.

"It wasn't like everything was suddenly great for Black players once the NFL let them back in," he said. "The NFL still had a long way to go to make things right. And in many ways, it's still trying to get there."

[4]

REINTEGRATION

CLEVELAND BROWNS ROOKIE OFFENSIVE lineman John Wooten had just dropped his luggage when he heard a knock on the hotel room door in December 1959. Mike Brown, a young Browns club official and the son of Paul Brown–Cleveland's legendary cofounder and head coach, whom the NFL team was named after–needed to speak privately with defensive back Bernie Parrish, Wooten's roommate.

After conferring briefly with Mike Brown in the hallway, Parrish reentered the room and quickly gathered his things. Before exiting again, he turned to Wooten and sheepishly said, "Woot, I had nothing to do with this."

A mix-up at check-in had resulted in Wooten, who is Black, and Parrish, who was white, being paired up before Cleveland's road game versus the Philadelphia Eagles. In the NFL during that era, Blacks and whites were prohibited from rooming together–a remnant of the league's 12-year color barrier that had finally fallen 13 years earlier. The experience left Wooten demoralized.

"It was a long time ago, but I remember all the details of it so well because it was just so blatant," Wooten said. "I played at an integrated high school [in New Mexico] and then at the University of Colorado in college. And even though there weren't many Blacks on the team [at Colorado], we always roomed by position, so that kind of situation never came up. So there I was, I'm in my first year in the NFL, and I had no idea what was going on.

"But Bernie knew. Bernie played at the University of Florida, in the Jim Crow South, so he understood that's just the way things were. Even after they started to let us [Black players] back into the league, that was the type of thinking that still existed. And what was even worse was that the prejudice we played under carried over to so many other parts of the game. It's why they didn't let us play certain positions. It's why back then and for a long, long time, you would just never see any Black quarterbacks."

Even after reintegration resumed slowly in 1946–the process wasn't completed until 1962, when Washington franchise owner George Preston Marshall, an avowed segregationist, finally capitulated to having Black players on his team's roster amid a threat from the federal government, pressure from civil rights organizations, and withering criticism of his actions from the Black press and the *Washington Post*–the NFL's Black players remained on unequal footing with their white counterparts for most of the league's history. And until relatively recently, Black QBs were the league's most marginalized group. Team owners tolerated Black talent at some positions to help them steadily increase the value of their franchises, but still refused to acknowledge the ability and intellect of Black quarterbacks–a recurring theme throughout the league's first 100 years, from Fritz Pollard to Colin Kaepernick.

Perhaps no one is more qualified than Wooten to evaluate the rise of the Black quarterback in the NFL. In his previous roles as a pioneering player, scout, agent, and high-ranking club executive, Wooten occupied a front-row seat in history–and helped shape it.

Born in 1936, Wooten was 10 when Black players began trickling back into the NFL. Although the league became the first in major professional sports to lower its color barrier during the period following World War II, it did so reluctantly, ultimately surrendering to political pressure in pursuit of commercial success. As a standout player in high school and college, Wooten, unlike many before him denied the same opportunity merely because of their Black skin, knew he would have an opportunity to pursue his dream of playing the game he loved at the highest level professionally. What surprised Wooten was that he'd have to travel such a rough road to achieve work-life fulfillment.

"Even by the time I got to the league, even thirteen years later, there were a lot of things that were still really difficult, things that made you angry," Wooten said. "But we had to get back in to get started on this road that we're still on. That's what finally happened in '46."

As so often is the case, history had a little assist from greed.

—

Only 27 days after winning their first NFL championship in 1945, the new Los Angeles Rams became the first major pro sports team to take up residence on the West Coast. Since he had purchased the team in 1941, owner Dan Reeves had dreamed of plugging into the lucrative and fast-growing Pacific market. Concluding that airplane travel was finally feasible, he shocked the team's Cleveland patrons by going west. The Rams and the newly formed Los Angeles Dons of the AAFC, yet another short-lived upstart football league, hoped to use the 103,000-capacity Coliseum, which was publicly owned, for their home games.[50]

That's when the Black press pushed back.

At a Coliseum Commission meeting held in late January 1946, several Black writers, including Halley Harding of the *Los Angeles Tribune* and Herman Hill, the West Coast correspondent of the

Pittsburgh Courier, objected to the use of the Coliseum by any organization that practiced racial discrimination. Harding delivered a dramatic speech for integration. He traced the early beginnings of pro football, pointing out that Fritz Pollard, Paul Robeson, Sol Butler, Duke Slater, and other Black athletes had played prominent roles in the league's success, only to be completely barred since 1933. Harding reminded the commissioners of the sacrifices and ambitions of World War II veterans.[51]

Harding hit the mark.

After representatives of the Dons and Rams quickly signaled their intention to sign Black players, the Coliseum Commission agreed to the lease. With that, the NFL's long color barrier had been breached. As with most things, however, there was more to the story.

By 1945, the NFL was keeping a close eye on what was happening in Major League Baseball—by far the nation's most popular team sport. On October 23 of that year, the Brooklyn Dodgers signed Jackie Robinson, the former four-sport star at UCLA and shortstop for the Kansas City Monarchs of the Negro Leagues, to a minor league contract. The first Black man to sign with a MLB team, Robinson received a monthly salary of $600 and a $3,500 signing bonus. Branch Rickey, one of Brooklyn's owners as well as its team president and general manager, orchestrated the highly controversial move with the intention of having Robinson integrate professional baseball for the first time since the 1880s. Realizing Robinson would face enormous pressure, Rickey assigned him to the Montreal Royals, the Dodgers' International League affiliate in Canada. Robinson's transition would be easier, Rickey believed, if Robinson played for a minor league team outside of the United States. The thought being that Robinson would face fewer hostile crowds north of the border, enabling him to get acclimated and prepare for his monumental task ahead in relative peace. Rickey played it well.

Robinson excelled with the Royals, batting .349 with 40 stolen bases. Robinson's success at the top rung of the minors set the stage for his historic debut with the Dodgers on April 15, 1947. The attention, most of it positive, that Robinson was getting no doubt impressed the NFL owners.

For 12 years, they had remained in lockstep to keep out Black players. But with Robinson, they felt a changing wind. Almost certainly, a majority of the owners had given the Rams their tacit support in the reintegration deal the team had signed with the Coliseum Commission. Soon all their competitors would follow. All except for George Preston Marshall, who held the line for another 16 years in the nation's capital.

—

The NFL's ban on Black players officially ended on March 21, 1946. On that day, the Rams acquired former UCLA star running back Kenny Washington, Jackie Robinson's teammate on both the Bruins football and baseball teams. The Rams purchased Washington's contract from the semipro Hollywood Bears.

Washington had been among the most notable victims of the NFL's color line. He was arguably college football's best player in 1939. By the time Washington, who joined the Los Angeles Police Department after college, signed with the Rams, his body was battered from years in the Pacific Coast League. The PCL was considered a high level of semipro football–but it was still the minors.

The racist roommate policy that Cleveland offensive lineman John Wooten would encounter 13 years later provided the opening for Woody Strode to become the NFL's second Black player post-ban. Washington's teammate on the Hollywood Bears, Strode, an Olympic decathlete, also starred with Washington and Jackie Robinson in UCLA's loaded backfield. In mid-May 1946, the Rams purchased Strode's contract from the Hollywood Bears. Like Washington, Strode's best on-field days were behind him. But as Strode, who went on to become a successful actor, explained in his autobiography, *Gold Dust: The Warm and Candid Memories of a Pioneering Black Athlete and Actor*, the Rams didn't sign him to help them win football games.

"When Kenny signed, they had to get him a roommate. He could have gotten along with the white boys on the team, Bob Waterfield and Jim Hardy and all of those boys from UCLA and USC. But the thinking then was that he had to have a running mate, another Black person to live with on the road. They asked him to select somebody. Kenny told them he wanted me. They spoke of my marriage to a Hawaiian. They tried to use my marriage to keep me off the team. But Kenny had power at that point and he said, 'I want my buddy.'"[52]

Although the Dons of the AAFC violated their pledge to sign a Black player during their inaugural season in Los Angeles (they brought in Black players a season later), another team in their league made two groundbreaking signings in 1946: the Cleveland Browns.

On August 2, co-owner and head coach Paul Brown invited former Ohio State All-American tackle Bill Willis to training camp at Bowling Green State University in Bowling Green, Ohio. Brown had coached Willis at Ohio State. After college Willis had become the head football coach at Kentucky State College. After one year of coaching, Willis realized he still wanted to play. Two weeks later, another Black player, Marion Motley, arrived at Browns training camp. Motley, too, had played under Paul Brown at the Great Lakes Naval Training Center in Great Lakes, Illinois, where he starred as the team's fullback. Following his discharge, Motley returned home to Canton, nearly 27 with a family to support. He took a mill job until Brown invited him to try out. Once at the Browns' training camp, Motley outran everyone on the team in the timed sprints and left little doubt that he, too, had the ability to play professionally.[53]

Washington, Strode, Willis, and Motley highlighted a promising future for Black football players. But their troubles, and those of the players who followed in their cleat marks, especially any who dreamed of playing under center, were far from over.

John Wooten played 10 years in the NFL (his first nine with the Cleveland Browns) and was a two-time Pro Bowler. After a brief stint as a sports agent, Wooten returned to the league and climbed the corporate ladder in scouting with the Dallas Cowboys, eventually occupying a top position in their player-personnel department. Later, with the Philadelphia Eagles, Wooten held the title of vice president of player personnel. Following his retirement from the NFL, Wooten had a long run as the chairman of the Fritz Pollard Alliance, the independent advocacy group that arose from the struggle to recognize Pollard in the Hall of Fame. Of the myriad experiences Wooten had during 60 years working in the NFL, none impacted him more than what he witnessed in his first few seasons as a player.

The unsettling hotel situation in Wooten's rookie season inspired him, at least partly, to become a civil rights activist. From then on, he was a vocal proponent of social justice. Browns co-owner and head coach Paul Brown was actually ahead of the curve on reintegration in the NFL, having played a leading role in starting it by signing Willis and Motley in 1946. But having players room together on the road based on their race was a standard NFL practice that Paul Brown adhered to as well, likely without giving it much thought. After superstar running back Jim Brown, widely regarded as the greatest player in NFL history, and several other Browns veterans asked Paul Brown to reconsider the team's policy, the powerful head coach permitted veterans to choose their roommates. Brown further revised the policy to have rookies assigned roommates alphabetically. "Like with a lot of things the Browns did, other teams followed," Wooten said. "That eliminated that situation from ever happening again."

For Wooten, the arrival of the expansion Dallas Cowboys in 1960 provided another lesson about racism at professional football's premier league.

Many Dallas-area hotels prohibited Black guests. During trips to play the Cowboys, Black players on most clubs stayed with local Black families. On game day, Black players would meet their white coaches and teammates at the team hotel and ride the team bus with them to the stadium. Just another dehumanizing experience in a long list of many the NFL inflicted on its second-class citizens. Cleveland did things differently: The Browns always stayed together on the road. A hotel near Dallas Love Field Airport provided rooms for the entire team.

"I would have had a hard time staying in someone's house I didn't know, getting up the next morning to go down to the team hotel to have a pregame meal and then playing. I would have really had trouble with that," Wooten said. "I had a lot of friends on other teams who did it. They weren't happy about it. They didn't want to do it. But I would have really struggled with that. There were things that happened on other teams that just didn't happen on the Browns."

In the NFL of the 1950s and 1960s, many locker rooms were divided along racial lines. And Black players mostly bottled their rage in the face of daily indignities, though not always.

"We were hearing stuff from all over the league about all these racist guys on other teams, about fights in locker rooms, but we never had fights in the locker rooms or anywhere else," Wooten said. "You have to understand that so many of the white players were from the South. There were so many guys from Mississippi, Alabama, Georgia—and there were problems. We had Southern guys on our team as well. But we didn't have those types of issues on our team. It just didn't happen. And I have to give Paul Brown a lot of credit for that.

"On the first day of training camp every year, Paul Brown would gather everyone together and give this speech. He'd stand up in front of the room and say, 'We don't have any Black Browns, we don't have any white Browns. Everyone in this room is part of the Cleveland Browns. And if anyone has a problem with that, let us know right now and we'll get you on your way.' There was never any name calling. You never heard the N-word in that locker room or anywhere else. What he did went a long way to showing us what the Browns were about."

Nowadays, an NFL head coach who publicly embraced positions on race contrary to Brown's, in the context of team building, wouldn't remain a head coach for long. Brown was ahead of his time in so many ways, including in understanding that open racial strife within the locker room would likely be an impediment to success on the field. On the other hand, Brown also maintained the insulting practice of prohibiting Black and white players from rooming together on the road. Despite his forward thinking in some respects on race, he was still very much a product of racist times.

[5]

THE THINKING POSITIONS

IT'S IMPOSSIBLE TO OVERSTATE Paul Brown's influence on pro football.

Before the Browns joined the NFL in 1950, Brown led the franchise to all four AAFC titles. He also guided the club to NFL championships in 1950, 1954, and 1955. An innovative tactician, Brown was the first coach to hire a full-time staff of assistants and use game film to scout opponents. He's also credited, among other things, with inventing the modern face mask. Whenever Paul Brown tried something new, other coaches were sure to take notice–and follow. Brown's trust in Wooten indirectly challenged the longstanding, ignorant notion that Black players lacked the intellect to play certain positions.

After reintegration, owners and coaches were vehemently opposed to Black players playing the so-called "thinking positions," such as interior offensive line, middle linebacker, and, of course, quarterback. The players in those jobs make the initial play calls and pre-snap adjustments based on opponents' offensive and defensive alignments. Not surprisingly, they're usually the smartest guys in the locker room. On offense, quarterbacks are the conductors. But Paul Brown took the baton from the Browns' passers. He thought he could run the show better.

Brown, during an era in which advanced electronic communications were not in use in professional sports, devised a method to connect Browns signal-callers with the person calling the plays on the sidelines, employing "messenger guards" to convey his orders. Throughout games, Brown directed the Browns' offense through his starting guards. The offensive linemen had to understand Paul Brown's thinking well enough to articulate the coach's plans to teammates in the huddle. Wooten was Cleveland's first Black "messenger guard." And he was great at the gig. On every play in Paul Brown's playbook, Wooten knew where everyone was supposed to line up and wind up, and, most important, he understood Paul Brown's thinking about each X and O. By succeeding in a role instrumental to the Browns' success, Wooten emerged as a trailblazer in the struggle to end positional segregation.

"With the quarterback, the middle linebacker, and the center and guard, the up-the-middle positions that provided a team's foundation, the reason they didn't want us there all goes back to the prejudice we played under," Wooten said. "It really was as simple as they just didn't think we were smart enough. Coaches didn't think we could be at center and guard, which is pretty much the same position for what we're talking about, because those guys had to make the [pass-protection] calls and determine who would stay in and who would pull [on running plays]. Middle linebackers . . . they're the leaders of the defense. They're quarterbacks on the defense.

"Coaches didn't think we could get the plays called in time and have the whole defense follow us. But the thinking was even worse with quarterbacks. Your quarterback is really the guy everyone was supposed to follow on the field. But you have these coaches who not only thought we couldn't play there because we supposedly weren't smart enough, which was just racist and ridiculous, but the leadership part of it was even a bigger problem for them. They just couldn't see us being the leaders of teams all over the league. You look back at that time, you just didn't see any of us at quarterback. Even the few guys who did break through a little, they didn't really get opportunities. And they didn't last long."

—

No quarterback ever had a cooler name: Willie Thrower.

When one hears it, visions of picturesque deep balls, efficient two-minute drills, and fourth-quarter comebacks immediately come to mind. Much more important than his great name, though, is what Thrower accomplished during his brief time in the NFL. In only two career games, Thrower, who died at 71 in 2002, cleared one of the biggest hurdles in professional sports. From the bottom, Thrower was the Black quarterback who started the group's trek to the top of the league.

"He broke the ice," said Warren Moon, the only Black quarterback inducted into the Pro Football Hall of Fame. "He was the first one to give little African American boys the belief that maybe, just maybe, they could one day play quarterback, too. That's what he did for me."

In 1953, Thrower became the first Black man to play quarterback in the NFL's modern era—an era defined by the elevation of the role of quarterback to the pinnacle of the sport.

The duties of the modern quarterback are much different than his predecessors at the position, which dates to the late 1880s. That's when American colleges in what's now known as the Ivy League—whose members are Brown University, Columbia University, Cornell

University, Dartmouth College, Harvard University, the University of Pennsylvania, Princeton University, and Yale University–began modifying rugby rules to form a new game. Walter Camp, a standout multisport athlete and rugby player at Yale, would come to be hailed as the "Father of American Football" for streamlining the hodge-podge of rules that amounted to little more than organized chaos, creating the outlines of the game that has grown into a national obsession and elevated superstar NFL quarterbacks to the status of pop-culture royalty. But it didn't start out that way.

In Camp's vision of the position, the quarterback's primary role was to receive the snap from the center and immediately toss or hand it to halfbacks and fullbacks. For much of the early part of the twentieth century, quarterbacks mostly blocked for running backs. In fact, until 1906, the forward pass was prohibited by rule in football. By the 1940s, however, the rise of the quarterback began in earnest because of significant rule changes–including scrapping penalties for multiple incomplete passes and even modifying the shape of the football to make it more passer-friendly–to liberalize the passing game. By the 1960s, the QB was the undisputed star of the game. But of all the top-notch Black players who entered the NFL in the 1950s and 1960s, none had played the highest-profile position. Thrower finally broke through on October 18, 1953.

During a 35–28 loss to the San Francisco 49ers, Thrower, then a Bears rookie, replaced starting quarterback and future Pro Football Hall of Famer George Blanda. Thrower completed three of eight passes, for 27 yards. Of course, Thrower's performance that day is almost irrelevant. The fact that Thrower got in the game was the story. It's what should be remembered most about his short-lived NFL career.

Harry Edwards, the renowned sociologist who since the 1960s has been at the forefront of the discussion about race, sports, and politics, has studied Thrower's career. He laments the fact that his significant achievement is mostly overlooked or forgotten. "In every social change situation, there is always somebody who is the first, someone who bears the pressure and scrutiny of the change moment," Edwards said. "The first is always a legacy that is more than just worthy of being memorialized. The saga of challenge and change is not only incomplete without encompassing recognition of the first; it is to a substantial degree untrue."

Thrower was a standout halfback at New Kensington High in western Pennsylvania. His talent was so pronounced that he had been invited to play in a 1948 high school all-star game in Texas as captain on the East team. But when the game's organizers discovered he was Black, Thrower was told he could not take the field.[54]

"Every college in the country wanted me—schools like Miami, Georgia, Kentucky—but as soon as they saw I was Black, that was the end of it," Thrower said. "So I went north to Michigan State."[55]

Recognizing Thrower had phenomenal arm strength, Michigan State's coaching staff quickly converted him to a quarterback. Thrower backed up starter Tom Yewcic on Michigan State's 1952 national championship team.[56]

Once reintegration resumed, NFL teams wouldn't draft African Americans to play quarterback. No matter how Black players performed at the position in college, they were almost always immediately converted to other positions in the NFL. A few players here and there, however, slipped through. Thrower, who went undrafted, was one. He made the Bears' roster and signed a one-year contract to play quarterback.

"I got in the San Francisco 49er game as a quarterback after [Bears owners and head coach] George Halas got dissatisfied with George Blanda. I took them from our 45-yard line all the way down to about the 15. All of a sudden, Halas sends Blanda back in. The fans really jumped on him: 'Leave Willie in! Leave Willie in!' But that was it; the end of the game for me."[57]

—

What motivated Halas to pull Thrower with the Bears driving? Well, whatever it was has been lost to history. It wouldn't be surprising, though, if Halas was concerned about support building among Bears fans for Thrower to play more. Permitting Thrower to play a little with Blanda struggling was one thing. But sticking with Thrower for an extended stretch, and opening himself up to the potential for Thrower to succeed–less than 10 years after reintegration resumed– was likely a bridge too far for Halas.

During one more game in the 1953 season, Thrower played briefly. The Bears released him before the start of the next season. Halas's decision to abruptly cut the cord on his Thrower experiment lends credence to the notion that the situation was fraught politically for the owner-coach. Halas had likely viewed the athletically gifted Thrower as a project and decided to put Thrower on the roster to see how things would play out. It wouldn't be surprising if Halas privately got blowback from fellow owners for even having a second-string Black quarterback on the Bears' roster. And Halas had proven before he was vulnerable to the prejudices of his peers. More than a decade earlier, Halas had expressed interest in possibly signing UCLA All-American Kenny Washington but abandoned the idea after he failed to get the backing of other owners.

As further proof that the NFL overall thought Halas got it wrong on even signing Thrower, no other team acquired the young passer after the Bears dumped him. With the NFL in his rearview mirror, Thrower had a good run in Canada, playing four more seasons until a separated shoulder ended his football career. After football, Thrower became a social worker in New York. He eventually returned to New Kensington and operated two taverns. Few of his patrons have any idea of his important contribution to NFL history.

"On one given Sunday, every QB in the NFL should wear a small 'WT' patch on his helmet," said Edwards.

One who hasn't forgotten is Doug Williams.

"When you talk about pioneers, I came into the league in 1978. Willie Thrower set the pioneer bar in 1953. He was a quarter century ahead of me," Williams said. "You look at me, I was given more opportunities than Willie Thrower was given. But he still managed to help me and a lot of other guys. He deserves that pioneer crown. And for a quarterback, you really can't get a better name."

On the football field, George Taliaferro wasn't actually ubiquitous, though one could hardly blame opponents for thinking he was everywhere. During his seven-year career in the All-America Football Conference, which merged with the National Football League, Taliaferro played seven positions: quarterback, running back, wide receiver, punter, kick returner, punt returner, and defensive back.

Just like Willie Thrower, Taliaferro also played quarterback during the 1953 season. Only weeks after Thrower's historic moment, Taliaferro became the second African American to complete a pass in the NFL. The versatile former Indiana University star and three-time NFL Pro Bowler, who died at 92 in 2018, is best known for having been the first Black player selected in the NFL draft. Under owner-coach George Halas, the Chicago Bears chose Taliaferro in the 13th round of the 1949 draft. Taliaferro, however, never played for Chicago, instead choosing to sign with the Los Angeles Dons of the AAFC before the NFL draft.

Born in Tennessee, Taliaferro was an infant when his parents moved to Gary, Indiana, where his father was employed at a steel mill. Like many Black kids during that time, Taliaferro grew up admiring Joe Louis and wanted to be a boxer. He even caddied for Louis when the fighter would drive from Chicago to play golf in Gary. "He said he liked me because I'd always find his balls," Taliaferro said. But Taliaferro's mother forbade him to box. "My dad insisted that I do something to burn off energy," he said. "Football was that something."[58]

During sandlot games, Taliaferro could have easily dipped, sidestepped, and run around his friends, but he chose a different approach. "I was running over people," he said. He maintained that on-the-field toughness as a star at all-Black Roosevelt High School in Gary. In his senior year, the coach of an all-white school in Chicago reached out to the Roosevelt coach and requested a scrimmage game as a tune-up for the Illinois state championship. Playing in his first game against a top-level all-white team, Taliaferro was dominant. "That coach from Chicago told the coach at Indiana [University] about me," Taliaferro said. "That's how I wound up in Bloomington [Indiana, where the university is located]."[59]

Taliaferro didn't realize Blacks weren't permitted to live on campus. He was unprepared for the racism he encountered there. Playing for the Hoosiers wasn't worth losing his dignity. The freshman was ready to pack up and head back to Gary. A conversation with his father, as would be the case often in Taliaferro's life, prompted him to reevaluate his position.

"I called my father and told him I didn't want to be in a place where I couldn't live on campus, where I couldn't swim in the pool, and where I couldn't sit in the bottom section of the movie theater," Taliaferro said. "My father told me there were other reasons I was there, and then he hung up the phone on me. I was never so hurt because I thought the one person who could understand being discriminated against was him."[60]

His father totally understood.

That tough love stemmed from two things his parents, neither of whom went past sixth grade, told him every day as he grew up. "They'd say, 'We love you,'" he recalled. "And, 'You must be educated.'"[61]

—

Taliaferro toughed it out–and became a college football star.

As a freshman, Taliaferro led Indiana to its only undefeated season in school history (9–0–1), its only outright Big Ten title (the Hoosiers shared the 1967 title with the Minnesota Golden Gophers and the Purdue Boilermakers), and its highest ranking in a season-ending poll (fourth, by the Associated Press). He also earned the first of three All-American team selections.

Drafted into the army after his freshman year and shipped to an army base in Virginia, Taliaferro was one of 66 men on the bus from Indiana to Virginia. When he arrived, the other 65 were taken to the barracks; Taliaferro was taken to the office of the commanding officer.

"He said, 'I'm happy to have you as a member of our company, and I'm looking forward to having you bring us a championship team in football,'" Taliaferro recalled. "I got hot, right there, and I told him I didn't plan to play."[62]

The commanding officer then leaned forward in his seat, put his elbows on his desk, and laid out two options for Taliaferro: Play football during his one-year commitment or go to officer's candidate school with an enlistment of three years. "I said, 'I'll see you at the football practice,'" Taliaferro said. "I had been hit on the head [playing football], but I hadn't had my brain knocked out."[63]

Some critics would undoubtedly contend that Taliaferro entered into a Faustian bargain with the commanding officer, casting aside his conviction about not playing football in the army for a shorter enlistment period. To take such a stance, however, one would have to be ignorant to the fact that Black men in the army in the 1950s–or anywhere in the United States at that time, for that matter–lacked the standing to be openly defiant against white men. Based on his interaction with white men to that point, Taliaferro also likely feared that if he rejected the commanding officer's proposal, a longer enlistment period would have been merely a portion of his punishment. Running afoul of the commanding officer could have made Taliaferro's time in the army a living hell. As countless numbers of Black men have done throughout the course of American history, Taliaferro swallowed his pride and did what he needed to do to survive. He played it smart.

Taliaferro held up his end: He captained an army team that won the Mid-Atlantic title and returned to school after completing his one-year military commitment. He wound up leading Indiana once in passing, twice in rushing, and three times in punting.

Despite his success in college, Taliaferro figured he wouldn't be selected in the NFL draft—and based on the league's history of never having drafted a Black player, no holes were visible in his reasoning—so he might as well get going on his professional football career with the Dons and the upstart AAFC. When the Bears unexpectedly made history by picking him, Taliaferro considered reneging on his Dons deal. The Dons couldn't compete in status. The Bears were one of the most prominent teams in the established league. Taliaferro was drawn to the brighter lights. But on recalling his deceased father's words about what it means to be a man, Taliaferro's internal struggle ended.

"He was the man in our home. He never told me to do anything. He always asked. And I always did what my father asked—except this one time. He asked me to turn over the soil in the empty lot next to our house so he could plant his garden. He wanted me to have it done by the time he got home from work. I said, 'Sure.' But I went out and started swimming and forgot all about it. My father got home 15 minutes after I did. He said to me, 'A man is no more, no less than his word.' At one in the morning, my mother was out there with a lantern while I dug. She said, 'Son, you need to eat and you need to go to bed. You can do this tomorrow.' I said, 'Mom, he'll never have the opportunity to say that to me again.' When I was drafted by the Bears, my father was dead. I said to my mother, 'All I have to do is tear up this contract I signed with the Los Angeles Dons and give them back their $4,000 signing bonus, and I can sign with the Bears.' Do you know what she said? 'What did your father tell you?'"[64]

The decision was clear: Taliaferro stuck with the Dons. Following his rookie season, the AAFC and the NFL merged. The Dons were not one of the AAFC teams that joined the NFL intact. Taliaferro wound up with the New York Yankees. He would go on to play for three more NFL teams.

Taliaferro was an immediate success. Beginning in the 1951 NFL season, Taliaferro was selected to three consecutive Pro Bowls as a halfback. He was both productive as a ball carrier and a receiver out of the backfield. But he could pass, too. Playing for Baltimore in 1953, Taliaferro started two games at quarterback.

"The team's three quarterbacks had gotten hurt the previous Sunday. On Tuesday, I was walking to the practice field . . . when head coach Keith Molesworth put his hand on my shoulder and said, 'George, have you ever played quarterback?' I said, 'Ain't nothing but another position, coach.' There was no free agency. The Colts had to go with what they had, and they had me. I started with four days of practice and damn near beat the Rams. I threw an interception that was returned for a touchdown [in Baltimore's 21–13 loss]. That was the difference between winning and losing."[65]

Taliaferro attempted only two more passes in his career. The next season, Baltimore fired head coach Keith Molesworth and replaced him with Weeb Ewbank, who wasn't interested in playing Taliaferro at quarterback. After two seasons with Baltimore, Ewbank sent Taliaferro packing.

After three games with the Philadelphia Eagles in 1955, Taliaferro walked away from professional football. Taliaferro even passed on a chance to finally play for the Chicago Bears, the franchise that in 1949 made him the first Black player selected in the NFL draft.

"I never said a word to the Bears until 1955, when I finished my career with the Philadelphia Eagles and George Halas called to ask me to play for Chicago," Taliaferro said. "I told him, 'Thank you, Mr. Halas, but no thank you. I am no longer the football player that I set the standard for me to be. I am going on with the rest of my life.' And that was it."[66]

Some players may have tried to hang on longer, but Taliaferro had already been in the league a long time, especially for back in those days. He took a beating playing halfback for seven seasons. He knew his best was behind him, and no doubt the Eagles knew it, too. None of that diminishes his legacy. In his seven pro seasons, Taliaferro had 2,266 rushing yards, 1,300 receiving yards, and 1,633 passing yards, and accounted for 38 total touchdowns (15 rushing, 12 receiving, 10 passing, and one on a punt return). Many of his passing yards came as a halfback. Additionally, he was productive in the return game, averaging 21.4 yards on kickoff returns and 8.9 on punt returns. As a punter, he averaged 37.5 yards.

His playing days over, Taliaferro earned a master's degree from Howard University in Washington, D.C., taught in Maryland, and became the dean of students and an unpaid assistant football coach at Morgan State in Baltimore, Maryland. In 1972, Taliaferro returned to Bloomington, Indiana, to become a special assistant to the school president at Indiana University.

Because Taliaferro played many positions and was only utilized as a stopgap passer and Thrower's NFL career was over in a blink, both men have been largely lost to history. Their names are not mentioned often in the discussion about the evolution of Black quarterbacks. But at the start of a long slog, Thrower and Taliaferro broke new ground. They confronted an immovable object and nudged it forward.

—

It wasn't a coincidence that both Willie Thrower and George Taliaferro came to the NFL from the Big Ten Conference. For much of the previous century, Blacks weren't permitted to play at many traditional football strongholds in the Jim Crow South. It wasn't until 1967 that the first Black football player appeared in a game for the powerful Southeastern Conference, which is headquartered in Birmingham, Alabama, when Nate Northington of the University of Kentucky took the field against the University of Mississippi. Under legendary head coach Paul "Bear" Bryant, the University of Alabama was one of the nation's most dominant programs in the 1960s and '70s. John Mitchell was the first Black player to appear in a game for Alabama–in 1971. Even after the SEC finally began to integrate in the late 1960s and early 1970s, its members didn't heavily recruit Black high school quarterbacks. In 1972, Condredge Holloway of the University of Tennessee became the conference's first Black starting signal-caller. Over the ensuing decades in the SEC, the position stayed almost lily-white.

For Black high school quarterbacks who aspired to continue playing in college, Historically Black Colleges and Universities provided most of the options. Those who dreamed of competing at major college football programs at predominantly white institutions, however, were mostly limited to pursuing scholarship opportunities at schools in the West and on campuses in middle America. The Big Ten was one of the most welcoming big-time conferences. Beginning in the late 1940s with Thrower, Big Ten coaches displayed a willingness uncommon in their day to recruit Black quarterbacks and–most important–give them a legitimate chance to compete for playing time at their desired position. During the recruiting process, coaches from many schools across the nation would lure Black high school quarterbacks with promises of being given a fair shot to battle for playing time, only to switch them to wide receiver or defensive back after they arrived on campus. By the late 1950s, Big

Ten coaches had proved they would stick to their word. Realizing they could benefit from a mostly untapped talent pool, Big Ten coaches eagerly signed passers who were ineligible to play at schools in the South because of their skin color alone.

In 1956, the University of Wisconsin's Sidney Williams Jr. became the conference's first Black starting passer. At the University of Minnesota, Sandy Stephens led the school to consecutive Rose Bowl appearances after the 1960 and 1961 seasons—and the 1960 national championship. Then Jimmy Raye II accomplished everything he set out to do at Michigan State, including quarterbacking the school to a share of the 1966 national title. Having watched Stephens and Raye thrive at Minnesota and Michigan State, respectively, a high school quarterback making big plays in Jackson, Michigan, figured he could make it in the Big Ten, too. One day, Tony Dungy would emerge as the most important figure in the ongoing struggle of Black NFL assistant coaches to be recognized for their ability. But it was during his stellar run quarterbacking the University of Minnesota football team that Dungy served notice he did not intend to allow his leadership to be ignored.

As quarterbacks, Williams, Stephens, Raye, and Dungy proved themselves in one of the best conferences in college football. The NFL didn't care: None ever played quarterback in the league. After selecting Stephens in the second round of the 1961 draft, the Cleveland Browns made it known they would not let him play at quarterback. Though Browns co-owner and head coach Paul Brown had helped to end the 12-year color barrier by signing two of the first four Black players to reintegrate major professional football and helped chip away at positional segregation by leaning on a Black player to convey offensive play calls in the huddle, the notion of potentially partnering with a Black passer in the early 1960s was apparently too radical for Brown.

Denied the chance to fulfill his dream in the NFL, Stephens

played in the Canadian Football League. For years, Stephens, who died in 2000 at 59, continued to hope he would get another chance at the NFL. But from the 1950s through the 1970s, there just wasn't much of a path to the NFL for Black quarterbacks unless they were willing to change positions.

"If you evaluated a Black quarterback, the first thing they [senior team officials] would ask you is, 'Did you talk to him about changing positions?'" said John Wooten, a pioneering NFL player and player-personnel executive. "No matter how good the report was, that was the first thing that came to mind because they weren't going to draft him to play quarterback. Were there talented guys who could have done it and had good careers in the NFL? Absolutely. But if they wanted to play in the NFL, they wouldn't be playing quarterback. That was kind of an unwritten rule. And it was [in place] a long time."

As were many other despicable unwritten rules governing Black bodies in various workplaces throughout the nation's history. The NFL's determination to keep the quarterback position lily-white was economically disenfranchising for generations of Black passers, whose professional careers were either adversely affected because they had to change positions or outright ruined because they were incapable of lining up elsewhere and succeeding. And that should not only anger Black people, but anyone who believes in the so-called American dream and the right of every citizen to pursue it.

—

Jimmy Raye II knew he had no business lining up at defensive back during Los Angeles Rams training camp in the summer of 1968. The Rams were well into practice that day on the campus at Cal State Fullerton, and Raye couldn't shake the feeling that everything was wrong. And who could blame him?

Raye had been one of the nation's most successful college

quarterbacks. He helped lead Michigan State to championships. Yet there he was, trying to learn the free safety position as an NFL rookie. He was basically a square peg being shoved into a round hole because of racism.

"I had never played defense before, so it definitely wasn't my area of expertise, and I was trying to make a living playing defense at the highest level of the game," Raye said. "Playing defense wasn't my athletic calling, and I'm competing with people who were proficient at it. So it was a double whammy in that I'm in the NFL and not being given a chance to play quarterback, something that I've shown I can do very well, and I'm competing with guys to do something they're already good and great at.

"It was a physical and mental adjustment, something I had never experienced before, but I was out of options if I wanted to have an NFL career. My other option was to go to Canada. That's not something I wanted to do. I wanted to play in the NFL. On the one hand, I was a good enough athlete, I had some ability, so they figured they would draft me and convert me. But I was a quarterback. I had always been a quarterback. And at that time in the NFL, Black quarterbacks were persona non grata. We just didn't think of ourselves as professional quarterbacks. I kind of understood that based on what happened to Sandy [Stephens]."

Still, despite knowing that Stephens—who starred at the University of Minnesota a few years before Raye enrolled at Michigan State—was unfairly prohibited from competing at quarterback for the Cleveland Browns, Raye, deep down inside, thought he might overcome the institutional racism that crushed the hopes of Stephens and so many others through the years.

"My mindset at the time, the reason I wanted to just get into the NFL, was that I thought I would somehow beat the odds," Raye said. "I thought that if I could just get in, even if I had to start out at another position, that something would happen and I would get a shot at quarterback, which was all I wanted. None of us expected to be handed anything. We just wanted a fair shot to compete. In college, I started on championship teams and set school records and all of that. I thought that maybe there was an outside chance I would get a chance eventually."

That's the mindset of elite athletes: They're capable of overcoming seemingly insurmountable obstacles that would derail those less physically gifted and emotionally resilient. Partly, it's about the unwavering belief in their skills, but there's much more to it than that. Elite athletes expect to impose their will on opponents. And by nature of the unique leadership position they occupy, quarterbacks exude this powerful combination of skill and confidence in their every action. Even being Black during an era in which the NFL had no interest in handing the ball to Black quarterbacks, Raye still maintained a flicker of hope because of his innate belief in himself and what he had already proven he could do on the football field.

Being Black was Raye's first disadvantage, but not his only one. Listed at 6 feet tall, he didn't measure up on the height chart.

At that time, professionals at the position were supposed to measure about 6 foot 3. The thought being that quarterbacks had to be tall enough to see over the offensive line to locate receivers. (More than 40 years later, the success of Russell Wilson of the Seattle Seahawks, who supposedly lacked the key measurement to shine at QB, finally inspired NFL officials to reevaluate their anachronistic thinking.) Essentially, Raye entered the batter's box with three strikes.

"There was some unwritten law about the size you had to be back then to play in the pocket," Raye said. "I played more like a Russell Wilson . . . and we now see that you can win with that type of quarterback. You can definitely win."

As the days progressed during Rams training camp, Raye realized he wasn't progressing much at free safety. Not surprisingly, his heart wasn't in it.

"It was hurtful," he said. "I was trying, in part because I wanted to stick and see if maybe something would happen and I would get a chance at quarterback. But coming from the segregated South with the Jim Crow laws, I knew the reality of the fact that things weren't the way they were supposed to be and opportunities weren't equal. I had an internal battle with what I knew what the situation was in my head, but in my heart I was hoping something would change."

Each day after practice, Raye returned to his dorm room expecting to hear a knock on the door from someone informing him he had been cut. The Rams kept him around on the taxi squad (now known as the practice squad), a supplemental roster of players who practice with the team but are ineligible to play in games. It's designed for clubs to retain developing players who are not ready for a spot on the active roster.

Raye never appeared in the regular season for the Rams. After two games for the Philadelphia Eagles in 1969, his NFL career ended. But his time in pro football was far from over. Raye began his coaching career with his alma mater. He left Michigan State and returned to the NFL in 1977 as an assistant with the San Francisco 49ers, embarking on a 36-year coaching career in the league. Raye served as an offensive coordinator—typically the senior assistant position on an offensive staff—for seven teams. After he retired from coaching, Raye was hired as a senior adviser to Troy Vincent, the NFL's senior vice president of football operations. Objectively, Raye had a long, impressive run as an NFL coach.

There are still moments, albeit few and far between, when Raye wonders what might have been if he had come of age during an era in which being born Black wouldn't have effectively disqualified him from playing quarterback in the NFL.

"Sometimes, in a moment of solitude, I'll look at the photo of me in my Ram uniform with my No. 12 jersey on, and I think about it," Raye said. "I could have played. I could have played quarterback in the NFL. I know that."

Would Raye have made it as a quarterback in today's NFL? Obviously, the question is impossible to answer. Despite the tectonic change that has occurred over the last 50 years in how team owners, executives, and coaches view Black men who aspire to play under center in the league, and the relatively recent willingness of those who control the marionette strings to also end the discriminatory practice of heightism, there's no way of knowing for sure whether Raye would have cleared the bar. Many QBs who were stars in college never get off the bench at the game's highest level, or even get close to occupying a seat on it. What's clear, though, is that Raye, and so many like him, was denied an opportunity to make his case because the playing field wasn't level, and that will forever be a black eye on a league that has benefitted immeasurably from its Black talent.

Each week during the NFL season, millions of television viewers watch analyst Tony Dungy on NBC's *Football Night in America*. Longtime NFL fans remember him as one of the league's best head coaches. And among many African Americans, Dungy is revered for both being the first Black coach to win a Super Bowl as well as a vocal advocate of inclusive hiring throughout the NFL workplace. What isn't as widely known about Dungy, however, is that he was once a successful college quarterback who, like so many before him, was denied an opportunity to prove he could play the position in the NFL. Unlike the Black quarterbacks who currently dominate the game, Dungy and others who proved themselves in college during the 1960s and 1970s were too far ahead of their time for a league that was still stuck in its racist past.

"My kids and other young people are kind of amazed at this group that includes Mahomes, Jackson, Watson, and Russell Wilson, and I tell them all the time that I played against guys, or I saw guys play in that era, who were like these guys now," Dungy said. "But back then, the NFL wasn't looking to do things that way and turn those guys loose. People weren't thinking outside the box. There was a mold of how you had to play the position. An even though there were exceptions . . . it was just a different era."

In Dungy's era, he was one of the top quarterbacks in the Big Ten Conference.

As a junior at the University of Minnesota in 1975, Dungy led the Big Ten in passing yards, passing efficiency rating, and total offense. He was selected the Golden Gophers' most valuable player. During his senior year, Dungy again had a strong season, ranking among the conference's statistical leaders in many categories. For the second consecutive season, Dungy hauled off Minnesota's MVP hardware. Throughout his college career, Dungy displayed talent, smarts, and leadership–as a senior, he was Minnesota's captain and also won an award signifying joint athletic and academic excellence–the attributes NFL owners and head coaches most want in quarterbacks. At his core, Dungy believed he possessed what it took to make it as an NFL quarterback. He was ready to deliver. All he needed was a chance.

Unfortunately for Dungy, the year was 1977. The NFL's persistent racist mindset at that point in time was perfectly articulated in one *Saturday Night Live* skit from that year, a presumably tongue-in-cheek dialogue between SNL's Garrett Morris and 1975's Associated Press NFL MVP, Fran Tarkenton.[67]

Morris had previously used his parody of a highbrow talk-show segment, *Black Perspective*, to take some vicious swipes at racist stereotypes, not by criticizing them but by satirically embracing them. It was edgy stuff. Amazingly, he got people with household names to play along. In one episode, he got civil rights activist and then–NAACP chairman Julian Bond to say with a straight face that light-skinned Blacks were smarter than those with darker skin.

But it was arguably an even bigger coup to get Tarkenton, a white superstar quarterback, to say out loud the racist tropes that were unfortunately accurate characterizations of the thinking in the 1970s NFL.

Morris kicked off the skit by getting Tarkenton to mouth the Pollyannaish PR version of the league's position on race: "The only color that exists is the color of a player's jersey."

"Right on," Morris responded. "But still, man, even in 1977, you know, some stereotypes still exist, wouldn't you agree?"

At first, Tarkenton denied it.

But Morris pressed him: What about the myths that a Black man didn't have the smarts or the leadership abilities to make it as a pro quarterback?

That's where the skit took a surprising turn.

Those myths are "absolutely true," Tarkenton said. "It's not a myth, it's a fact. Every Black I know has trouble with area codes, let alone numbers of plays!"

It went on from there, with Tarkenton spouting even worse racist bromides, including a joke about Black quarterbacks being more interested in "a bucket of fried chicken in the parking lot" than winning the game on the field.

The skit ends as Tarkenton sums things up: "And Garrett, let's face it—try to be objective. If you were on the offensive line, would you turn your back on a Black guy standing behind you? Especially during a night game?"

The folks at home split a gut, but for Dungy, it wasn't even slightly funny. In the 1977 NFL draft, 335 players were selected. Dungy was not among them.

At 6 feet, Dungy ran into the same wall that also contributed to crushing the dreams of Sandy Stephens, who preceded Dungy in starring at quarterback for the Golden Gophers, and Jimmy Raye II, who quarterbacked Michigan State to titles. But there are exceptions to rules. The NFL made one for Fran Tarkenton, who also was listed at 6 feet. The Minnesota Vikings drafted Tarkenton in the third round of the 1961 NFL draft. In 1975, Tarkenton was selected as the Associated Press NFL Most Valuable Player. Tarkenton was inducted to the Pro Football Hall of Fame in 1986. Of course, Tarkenton is white. But it gave Dungy hope.

"I felt like some things were changing. I held out hope throughout my junior year and my senior year of college that I would get an opportunity," Dungy said. "After my senior year, I was talking to scouts and getting workouts, so you feel like maybe it will happen. I thought it would. But I didn't get drafted. It was a shock to me. I had to make a decision. And I wanted to play in the NFL."

—

Wilbur Dungy taught his children to pursue their dreams—and instilled the confidence in them to do just that. As a young man, Wilbur first displayed the same determination that powered his kids to achieve. One is one of the nation's leading doctors specializing in perinatology—an obstetrical subspecialty focusing on the care of the fetus and complicated, high-risk pregnancies. The other children are a dentist, a nurse, and a Pro Football Hall of Fame football coach. Wilbur, unable to serve as a pilot in the segregated military at the outset of World War II, was undeterred. Traveling from his birthplace of Jackson County, Michigan, the elder Dungy made his way to a small town in Alabama to link up with a newly formed squadron that would become America's first Black military pilots. The group is better known as the famed Tuskegee Airmen.

After the war, Wilbur retuned to Jackson and attended Jackson Junior College, earning his associate's degree in 1948. He then went on to receive his bachelor's and master's degrees from the University of Michigan, and his doctorate in zoology from Michigan State

University. Whenever young Anthony Kevin Dungy would complain about unfair treatment, Dr. Wilbur Dungy would encourage his son to push through and find a different path to achieve his goals. As a standout high school athlete in Jackson and at the University of Minnesota, Dungy had always managed to make things work as a quarterback. The backward thinking of NFL decision-makers presented an insurmountable challenge to Dungy continuing his career at the position he loved.

Heading to the Canadian Football League was an option Dungy briefly considered. The Montreal Alouettes held his rights. The team was led by general manager Bill Polian–whom Dungy would partner with decades later to lead the Indianapolis Colts to a Super Bowl championship–and head coach Marv Levy, who would go on to lead the Buffalo Bills to four consecutive Super Bowl appearances (all losses). "I remember talking to those guys and negotiating and feeling like, 'Hey, I could go to Canada and play quarterback,'" Dungy said. "But I wanted to play in the NFL. So I switched positions."

Dungy signed with the Pittsburgh Steelers as an undrafted free agent and moved to safety. During his two seasons with the Steelers, Dungy developed a well-deserved reputation for being one of the smartest players in the game. He led Pittsburgh with six interceptions in 1978, helping the team win the Super Bowl. Traded to the San Francisco 49ers, Dungy played his third and final NFL season with that franchise. Football players often joke that the word NFL, in fact, is not an acronym for National Football League but actually one with a more ominous meaning, "Not for Long." With younger, less-expensive players battling with him for roster spots each season, Dungy, as a player, had outlived his usefulness to those who controlled the marionette strings.

In 1980, Dungy began his coaching career back at the University of Minnesota. After one season, he left his alma mater to return to the NFL as an assistant with the Steelers in 1981. Dungy, who would become one of the NFL's top defensive coordinators, landed his first head coaching position with the Tampa Bay Buccaneers. Four times during Dungy's six seasons at the Buccaneers' helm, they qualified for the playoffs. With the Indianapolis Colts, Dungy won five division titles and the Super Bowl after the 2006 season. He was inducted into the Pro Football Hall of Fame in 2016. Two years later, Mike Tomlin of the Pittsburgh Steelers, a Dungy protégé, became the second African American head coach to win a Super Bowl. Dungy is coming from a place of experience in his belief the NFL can only benefit from improving its poor record on inclusive hiring, which is why he has pushed owners to consider more qualified people of color when seeking executives and coaches to run their franchises.

Although Dungy wasn't given a chance to make his mark as an NFL quarterback, he has had an enduring impact on the league. No one need shed a tear for how the NFL has treated Dungy overall. It has been very good to him and his family. When Dungy reflects on how many gifted African American passers were denied getting their fair shots over the years, however, he can't help but be disappointed.

"Many people don't realize how great some of those guys were," Dungy said. "And that to me is the shame of it, that had they come along in a different era we'd be celebrating them now. That's the sad part."

—

A hush fell over the room at Dallas Cowboys headquarters as scout John Wooten delivered his detailed report before the 1978 NFL draft. Some of the most accomplished men in the history of professional football flanked Wooten in the seats arrayed around a large conference table, including Cowboys president and general manager Tex Schramm, head coach Tom Landry, and Gil Brandt, the team's vice president of player personnel. The highly accomplished trio formed the brain trust of an organization that won more regular season games and appeared in more Super

Bowls than any other league franchise during the 1970s. In matters of professional football, Schramm, Landry, and Brandt were innovative thinkers whose winning efforts on behalf of the Cowboys would result in all three being inducted into the Pro Football Hall of Fame.

On that afternoon in 1978, however, none of them could see into the future as clearly as Wooten.

Schramm, Landry, and Brandt were left speechless by the report Wooten filed on a college quarterback at the University of Washington: Warren Moon. Wooten raved about Moon's arm strength, his elusiveness both inside and outside of the pocket, his ability to connect with receivers whether throwing from a stationary position or on the run, his intellect, and his leadership ability. Based on what the Cowboys valued most in quarterbacks, Moon, Wooten declared without the slightest hint of apprehension, was the complete package. And by doing so, Wooten knew what was coming next.

"Well," someone in the room finally said to shatter the silence, "did you discuss with him about playing another position?"

As late as 1978, most NFL clubs were still not comfortable with the idea of having Black quarterbacks on their rosters, let alone expending valuable draft picks, the main method of roster construction, on them. The same old racist tropes were still in circulation, though the fabricated criticisms of Black QBs weren't discussed as openly as previously in NFL history. The whispers still had a familiar ring: Black quarterbacks supposedly lacked work ethics, lacked the intelligence to comprehend NFL playbooks, lacked the confidence to lead white men, and lacked the toughness to play through pain. Wrong, wrong, wrong, wrong. No one understood this better than Wooten.

As a pioneering NFL player in the late 1950s and 1960s, Wooten experienced racism in the league firsthand. While climbing the ranks as a scout with the Cowboys after he took off his pads for the last time, Wooten learned more about how race factored into the construction of draft boards. The NFL had a certain way of doing things—and drafting Black quarterbacks to actually *play* quarterback was not part of it. But Moon, Wooten recalled, was simply too good at quarterback for Wooten to even picture him playing another position. Turning to the men who had launched his second career in the NFL, Wooten spoke truth to power.

"I said, 'No, I didn't [speak with Moon about playing another position]. I didn't have to because I wasn't going to write him up at another position,'" Wooten said. "I wrote him up as he is. He's a quarterback. He can play quarterback in this league."

Wooten then doubled down, telling the club's senior leaders that not only was Moon a gifted quarterback, he was one of the top 50 players, regardless of position, in the draft. The Cowboys were loaded at the time—especially at quarterback. Future Pro Football Hall of Famer Roger Staubach was still in top form. After the 1977 regular season, Staubach helped the Cowboys win their second Super Bowl title in franchise history. And the Cowboys also had a talented young backup quarterback in Danny White. Regardless, Wooten was confident that drafting Moon would have been a boon for the Cowboys.

"Our draft philosophy with the Cowboys was that you go take the best players available. One thing coach Landry would always say is that you can never have too many good players," Wooten said. "If you drafted him, you could have traded him. But looking ahead [to the draft], with the kinds of grades we had on him, I just felt you couldn't let this guy sit on the board."

Moon's name never came off the Cowboys' draft board, or that of any other team: Moon went undrafted during a process in which 334 players were chosen over 12 rounds. Had Moon been willing to change positions, he would have been drafted, many NFL talent evaluators said years later. Moon, though, had no interest in switching. In his heart and mind, he was a quarterback. Nothing would move him from that position. And if the NFL saw things differently and spurned him as a result of his conviction, well, so be it. Moon was willing to die on that hill.

To dissuade some teams from drafting him at another position, Moon intentionally ran slowly while being timed by scouts in the 40-yard dash, a test to measure a player's speed. Moon feared that if he ran as fast as he could, clubs would fall back on drafting him as a defensive back or receiver and remove him from consideration as being a quarterback.

In that draft, Doug Williams, another star quarterback from historically Black powerhouse Grambling State University in Grambling, Louisiana, became the first Black passer selected in the first round. Williams's ascent to new territory for Black quarterbacks was a sign of progress. However, the excitement among Black quarterbacks about that step forward was tempered by the NFL's mistreatment of Moon. The NFL's decision to bypass Moon in the 1978 draft stunned Tony Dungy. Then a defensive back with the Pittsburgh Steelers, Dungy, who dueled with Moon when they were both top college quarterbacks, figured Moon was too good for the NFL to ignore.

"He was the [co]-MVP of the Pac-8 and the MVP of the Rose Bowl. And he didn't get drafted. Just crazy."

Moon didn't wait to be shunned by the NFL. Before the draft, he signed with the Edmonton Eskimos. In the Canadian Football League, Moon became a superstar, amassing eye-opening statistics and winning championships. After his record-setting career in Canada, Moon was a prized free agent. In 1984, the Houston Oilers won a bidding war to sign Moon, who went on to become one of the most productive passers in NFL history and was inducted into the Pro Football Hall of Fame in 2006. It's natural to wonder how things might have been different if Moon had entered the league as a quarterback straight from college, said C. Keith Harrison, a professor of sports business management at the University of Central Florida.

"Some people try to argue that what happened to Warren Moon, and what happened to so many other Black quarterbacks who were unfairly denied opportunities in the NFL, is all in the past and doesn't matter today," Harrison said. "But on an individual level, what it cost Warren Moon was the chance to possibly have the greatest career ever in the NFL. If he was in the NFL all those years instead of in Canada, maybe he winds up not just being high on the [passing] lists. Maybe his name winds up being the first. And then on a societal level, think about what it could have meant to young Black men to see Warren Moon succeeding the way he did in the NFL much earlier. Think about the impact those images could have had."

Although Wooten, who was a Cowboys scout in 1978, recognized that Moon could have potentially inspired many in the Black community, the former player was primarily focused on helping Dallas win football games. In that endeavor, Wooten knew Moon could have helped.

"It just wasn't the right time," Wooten said. "And it wasn't only the Cowboys. No other team picked him, and it was just the way things were. But Doug was picked. Some progress was being made. And a lot more would be coming."

[6]

1968

IT WAS JANUARY 31, 1988, and Marlin Briscoe would have much rather been in different company. The television was a problem, too–the picture and sound were awful. Even so, Briscoe couldn't have been happier. On that monumental day in Black history, Briscoe was Doug Williams's biggest fan as Washington's quarterback became the first African American signal-caller to start in a Super Bowl and win the game's Most Valuable Player Award. While Williams, in the signature performance of his career, took a sledgehammer to the racist myth that Black men lacked the physical ability, intellect, and leadership skills to excel at professional sports' most important position, Briscoe applauded, laughed, jumped out of his chair, danced, and, ultimately, cried tears of joy. The scoreboard summarized so much more than the outcome of a single NFL game: Washington 42, Denver 10.

Twenty years earlier, Briscoe, as a Denver Broncos rookie, was major professional football's first full-time starting Black passer in the game's modern era. He chipped away at the prejudice that prevented generations of Black men from playing quarterback in the United States' top leagues. And while celebrating Williams's iconic achievement, Briscoe almost forgot where he was: behind bars.

"I watched the game in jail. It was the drugs," Briscoe said, the pain still evident in his voice more than 30 years later. "I was in a dark place. What happened . . . it cost me a lot. But I felt I was a part of what Doug did. I felt like what I did all those years ago helped Doug. It was the best feeling I had had in a long time."

Briscoe's unprecedented rise from the bottom to the top of the Broncos' quarterback depth chart in 1968, his reinvention as a Pro Bowl wide receiver and two-time Super Bowl champion after racism ended his career as a passer, and, in retirement, his downward spiral into drug addiction and subsequent rise in therapy is worth more than merely a footnote in history. Briscoe's story is integral to explaining the rise of Black quarterbacks in the NFL. Warren Moon knows it almost as well as he knows his own.

Moon, the only African American quarterback enshrined in the Pro Football Hall of Fame, said he and many others stood on Briscoe's shoulders.

"Whenever an African American, or anyone, does something for the first time, it should be documented the right way," Moon said. "Marlin opened doors for me and a whole lot of people like me. There are some who know about Marlin, but there are a lot who don't know about what he did. The strength and courage Marlin showed . . . that's important. And it's part of our history."

Briscoe, who was born on September 10, 1945, has gone on to live a quiet life in Long Beach, California, enjoying his family, friends, golf–a whole lot of golf–and an occasional burger and fries, though he's quick to point out he's only a little above his playing weight. Retired for several years from his position as the director of a Long Beach Boys & Girls Club, Briscoe also volunteers as a football coach for a high school near his home. The players know little about their soft-spoken coach's background as a pioneer.

"I went through a decade of drug use," Briscoe said. "I lost everything. It felt kind of lonely out there. I thought everyone had forgotten about me."

One could certainly say life has been hard on Briscoe. Denied the chance to fulfill his potential at quarterback because of the institutional racism standard during the era in which he played, Briscoe, like all Black athletes, rode in the back of the bus in professional sports. And who's to say that lingering resentment about the bigotry Briscoe faced wasn't at least partly responsible for his substance abuse? Although it's impossible to draw a straight line from Briscoe twice being briefly locked up in the late 1980s for cocaine possession (he said he hasn't used an illegal substance in more than 30 years) to his painful experience in football essentially a lifetime ago, this much is true: Briscoe was wronged and struggled to cope with what happened to him. The stench of that betrayal has stayed with him. Briscoe, though, doesn't believe in blaming others. He owns his failures as much as he does his victories.

"What happened made me angry," Briscoe said. "I proved I could do it, and it didn't matter. They took it away from me anyway. But I wasn't going to give up and just walk away. I was a product of the '60s. Back then, you knew you had to be three times better to just have the chance to compete with white people. Yeah, it didn't work out for me. But I feel what I did helped the guys who came after me. And I'll always be proud of that."

—

In the history of the United States, 1968 was among the most tumultuous years. The horrors of the unpopular Vietnam war, the assassinations of civil rights icon Martin Luther King Jr. and Senator Robert F. Kennedy little more than two months apart, clashes between protestors and police at the Chicago Democratic National Convention, racial unrest in cities–the nation was ripped apart daily.

And in the United States in 1968, you were more likely to see a unicorn than a Black man under center in pro football. African American quarterbacks fared better in the more progressive Canadian Football League. In terms of prestige, however, the CFL ranked far below the American Football League, which was founded in 1960 as a competitor to the venerable National Football League and operated for 10 seasons until it merged with the NFL in 1970. As for comparing the CFL to the NFL in those days, well, let's put it this way: They were in totally different leagues. AFL owners, officials, and coaches weren't as open-minded as their counter-parts in the CFL about permitting Black players to fill certain positions, but they were much more liberal on the subject than those who ran the NFL.

Even as late as the late 1960s, NFL clubs preferred to draft Black players from colleges and universities whose enrollments were overwhelmingly white. Quarterback was off-limits to Blacks. With few exceptions, Blacks also were prohibited from playing center on offense and middle linebacker on defense–the so-called "thinking-man positions"–because decision-makers believed Blacks lacked the intellect to call plays and make pre-snap adjustments. What's more, the white men who led the NFL viewed football programs at Historically Black Colleges and Universities as being inferior. The NFL, of course, got it completely wrong, as evidenced by the fact that about 10 percent of players in the Pro Football Hall of Fame played at HBCUs.

The AFL definitely benefitted from the NFL's error. Because the NFL had a 40-year jump on the AFL, the AFL couldn't afford to be as racist in drafting players while battling the NFL for football fans' dollars. That was the environment in which Briscoe shattered the glass ceiling that existed in both the NFL and AFL. Yet in 1968,

Briscoe wasn't the Black quarterback expected to do it. Eldridge Dickey was supposed to be that guy.

The Oakland Raiders shocked the football world with an unprecedented move: They made Dickey the first Black quarterback selected in the first round of either the AFL or NFL draft. With the 25th overall pick, the third to last in the opening round of the 1968 combined common draft, the second year in which both leagues drafted college players jointly, the Raiders selected Dickey from HBCU powerhouse Tennessee State, located in Nashville, Tennessee. Nicknamed "the Lord's Prayer," Dickey, who had a booming voice, would lead Tennessee State in team prayer before games. But Dickey, who signed with Tennessee State after an intense recruiting battle among elite HBCU programs, was also the answer to the prayers of the Tigers' coaching staff.

In the 14th round, 332 picks after the Raiders selected Dickey, the Broncos chose Briscoe from Omaha University (now University of Nebraska-Omaha). The Broncos never intended to let Briscoe, who was nicknamed "the Magician" for his ability to elude would-be tacklers, get anywhere close to playing QB for them. They had him slotted as a future cornerback. Having made such a radical move in drafting Dickey so high (pre-draft buzz about the Kansas Chiefs' supposed interest in Dickey likely contributed to Oakland picking him in the first round), the Raiders appeared to be more willing to give him a legitimate shot at competing at quarterback.

"He felt really secure," LaCanas Casselle, Dickey's college sweetheart and ex-wife, said. "There was no pressure because he was given that talent. He was gifted."[68]

A three-time HBCU All-American, Dickey, born and reared in Houston, Texas, was listed at 6 foot 2 and about 200 pounds. His size couldn't be used against him. Dickey also displayed uncommon ambidexterity: On any routes, he could connect with receivers using both his right and left arms. Both were equally strong, too, though he was most accurate with his right passing arm. Dickey was said to have a high IQ. And he was a winner: In 1966, Dickey led Tennessee State to its first undefeated season and the Tigers' second consecutive Black college national championship. Dickey consistently made big plays from the pocket and on the move. He oozed talent. The fact that the Raiders used a first-round pick to get Dickey inspired many Black players in both the AFL and NFL to believe he would be the first Black passer to play–and potentially start early in his career–in a major professional football league in the United States. It figured that the Raiders would be the franchise to attempt the potential game changer.

Under the guidance of Al Davis, then a minority owner and the head of the franchise's football operation, the Raiders were among the AFL's leaders at pursuing top players from HBCUs. Davis, who died at 82 in 2011, was also at the forefront of inclusive hiring in the pro game. He employed the league's first Latino head coach to win a Super Bowl (Tom Flores) and the first Black head coach in the NFL's modern era (Art Shell). Former Raiders executive Amy Trask was among the highest-ranking women in professional sports.

"That's what Al Davis did. He always wanted the Raiders to be the first in football history. And he liked to shake up things," Briscoe said. "He didn't care about Dickey's skin color. Al Davis liked quarterbacks who could throw the ball deep and quarterbacks who won. He cared about Dickey's talent. And, man, he was talented."

Dickey's talent wasn't enough to overcome an awful situation for any rookie quarterback, regardless of race. And being Black only compounded Dickey's problems with the Raiders.

The team was loaded at quarterback. In 1967, the season before Dickey's rookie year, Oakland starter Daryle Lamonica went 13–1 in the regular season. Oakland routed the Houston Oilers in the AFL championship game and lost to the Green Bay Packers in the second Super Bowl. Lamonica was selected the Associated Press 1967 AFL

Player of the Year. Future Pro Football Hall of Famer George Blanda was one of Lamonica's backups. In the second round of the 1968 draft, the Raiders selected Ken Stabler, who quarterbacked perennial college football power Alabama to an 11–0 record as a junior in 1966. Stabler, a backup on Alabama's 1965 national championship team, would go on to become a Pro Football Hall of Famer.

In addition to having accomplished white pro passers ahead of him on the depth chart, Dickey had to battle Stabler, another high-round pick at his position. During training camp, Dickey performed much differently than the Raiders' other quarterbacks. He improvised more. He was apt to make as many plays with his feet as with his arms. He excited Raiders players. He scared the hell out of Raiders coaches. In decades to come, athletic quarterbacks would be rewarded for producing big "off-schedule" plays with their legs. But not in 1968.

"I'd never seen a guy who could do what Dickey did with both hands and both feet. It was just amazing," said former Raiders tackle Gene Upshaw, who played his entire 15-year career with the team, was enshrined in the Pro Football Hall of Fame in 1987, and served as the executive director of the National Football League Players Association for 25 years.

"He didn't go to Alabama. But when he went out on the field and started throwing the ball, you could see he had more ability than Stabler. He shows up, and he's got these white shoes. And he's doing his shit, making it look easy. Blocking for him was hard because he was always moving around. All of a sudden, he'd be out of the pocket. Gone! Nowadays . . . it's okay to leave the pocket, but not then. We were used to Daryle Lamonica, who was a statue–just stood back there. There was no way in the world to know where Dickey was going to be. What we did know was that he was breaking down barriers, and we [Black players] worked our asses off to make sure he succeeded. That's the one thing I got to say about Al Davis:

He would not tolerate racism. In fact, Stabler believed that Davis was giving Dickey the better chance to succeed."[69]

Davis's iconic motto spoke to his philosophy on team building: "Just win, baby." Black, white, or whatever, former Raiders players under Davis say, he truly put winning first, which meant putting the better player first, period, regardless of race. Early during the battle for the Raiders' starting QB job before Dickey's rookie year, it appears Davis was high on Dickey. The coaching staff, however, had other ideas. Raiders head coach John Rauch moved the athletic Dickey to wide receiver. Again, another Black man denied the opportunity to play quarterback in the pros after starring at the position in college.

Though Davis was color-blind in the limited sense of putting winning above all else, in the story of Dickey's fall, Davis doesn't wear a white hat. At best, it's gray.

Notoriously meddlesome in the coaching staff's plans during his long tenure leading the franchise, Davis could have insisted that Dickey be given more opportunities in Oakland under Rauch, who abruptly resigned after the 1968 season because of Davis's incessant interference, and Rauch's successor, John Madden. Through the decades, Davis definitely wasn't shy about putting his thumb on the scale both for and against players. The coaching staff had no interest in building around Dickey. Ultimately, Davis was down with that thinking, too.

The fact that Dickey's style of play, a source of angst within the organization, frustrated Oakland's decision-makers is stunning. How could the Raiders not have known what they were getting? Truth is, Dickey's style probably didn't matter to them. The coaches figured that he'd either conform into being "their type of quarterback," or they would move him to another position. Problem was, the Raiders made history in selecting Dickey, yet had no plan to maximize their sizeable investment in him—or get any return on it at all. They squandered a first-round pick, the most valuable commodity in roster construction, partly because no one in authority proactively tried to help Dickey as he attempted to blaze a new path in professional football.

That's not to suggest Davis should have elevated Dickey above the team's other quarterbacks simply because of his race. Davis was a businessman and a fierce competitor. At some point early in Oakland's experiment with Dickey, Davis also determined that Dickey would not provide the team with the best chance to win. For Davis, it wasn't personal. It was strictly business. It's also probable that concerns were raised within the organization about how fans would react to seeing Dickey under center in the regular season. Drafting Dickey in the first round was one thing. To actually hand him the keys in 1968 or during ensuing seasons, however, was likely a bridge too far for Davis and his underlings, regardless of how Dickey performed.

NFL fans today would excoriate a franchise that used a first-round pick to draft a prolific college quarterback only to let him wither on the vine. They would take to social media, demanding the firing of everyone involved with mishandling the situation. We're talking pitchforks-and-torches stuff, metaphorically speaking. Fans would be at the gates for Davis, too. But back then, the inner workings of NFL squad building weren't obsessively covered, 24/7, by the sports talk media, and the echo chamber of the Twitterverse was yet to hand individual fans a gigantic megaphone.

There's also an argument to be made that Dickey could have–or should have–done more to help himself. As Dickey's standing in Oakland worsened, his level of engagement in the meeting room and on the practice field waned. Mentally and physically, Dickey "checked out." He was still being paid to do a job and didn't hold up his end. There's no way to sugarcoat that. But ask yourself this: Could you maintain an acceptable level of professionalism in your field while coping with a broken spirit?

Later in life, Rauch defended the way Dickey was handled.

"Eldridge Dickey had great athletic skills," Rauch said. "If we needed a quarterback, he could play quarterback. If we needed a running back, he could play running back, If we needed a wide receiver, he could play wide receiver–any skilled position on offense. And that's mainly why Dickey was drafted by the Raiders."[70]

Except Dickey was a quarterback. Except he was more than good enough to play quarterback in the AFL and later in the NFL. Except Black men kept having to adjust because of racism–or walk away from pro football in the United States. When given an opportunity to practice at quarterback, Dickey bristled at the notion he had to remain in the pocket to succeed in the NFL. The louder coaches barked at Dickey to stay put, the more determined he became to remain unleashed. A crystal ball wasn't required to foresee that the Raiders-Dickey union would likely end badly.

"It started going bad because the coaches wanted Dickey to stay in the pocket.... They wanted to make him a prototype quarterback," Upshaw said. "Dickey would stay in there for a while, then he'd say, 'Shit, I'm gone.' They tried to make him a wide receiver. He was too goddam big, number one. And number two, he had too much ability. He could throw [from one end] to the other end of the field."[71]

Not everyone is capable of changing positions successfully, especially moving from quarterback to another spot as a professional. While Dickey was struggling in training camp with the Raiders, former Michigan State quarterback Jimmy Raye was having a rough time trying to make the transition to safety in camp with the NFL's Los Angeles Rams.

"It takes a whole different approach to go from being the quarterback, the leader everyone looks to, to playing wide receiver," Briscoe said. "It's hard. Believe me, I know. And being put in that position, when he knew how good he was, had to be very hard on him."

Dickey didn't make it as a wide receiver. He played in 11 games as rookie and finished with only one catch for 34 yards. Sidelined by injuries, Dickey sat out the next two seasons. In 1971, his final season in pro football, Dickey had four catches for 78 yards with one touchdown. The Raiders released Dickey after he dropped a potential touchdown in their seventh game.

"He never really had a chance, because in those days, they didn't give you a chance," Upshaw said. "You're in the moment, and you don't have a point of reference because there's no one else in front of you. Being a pioneer is a bitch."[72]

Out of football, Dickey also turned to drugs and alcohol. Fortunately for him, though, he got his life turned around and became a minister. He died in 2000 at 54.

"There were a lot of things we all went through because of what was taken from us," Briscoe said. "I saw what was happening with Dickey. But I really believed it would be different for me. And at the start, it was."

From his first day in youth football in Omaha, Nebraska, Briscoe had played quarterback. The diminutive, strong-armed passer with sprinter's speed became a college star in his hometown. At only 5 foot 10, 177 pounds, Briscoe lacked the prototypical size of a top AFL or NFL quarterback prospect. At that time in the NFL, the Minnesota Vikings' Fran Tarkenton, who is listed at 6 feet, ran or "scrambled" often. But Tarkenton, who is white, was the exception to the rule. Of course, it wouldn't have mattered if Briscoe had stood 6 foot 4 and weighed 220 pounds: The NFL and AFL didn't draft Black men to throw passes.

But the fourteenth-round draft pick, knowing the Broncos planned to move him to cornerback, refused to sign with Denver unless management agreed to include him in a three-day quarterback tryout at the start of training camp.

"They thought I was crazy," Briscoe said. "Here I am a fourteenth-round draft pick and I'm Black, and I put a condition on signing. But I felt I had to do it. I had to try to play quarterback. I knew what I could do. I always had confidence in my ability. And the tryout was open [to reporters and fans]. I thought that the more people saw me, the harder it would be for them to ignore me. But I didn't fool myself. No matter what I did, I knew I didn't have much of a chance."

Actually, Briscoe had no chance. As he recalled, he got the fewest reps of any of the quarterbacks vying for roster spots. Responding to reporters' questions about Briscoe's impressive deep balls during drills and his ability to throw accurately on the run, Broncos head coach Lou Saban played down the rookie's performance. Briscoe was headed to the secondary. Fate, however, intervened.

After suffering a hamstring injury, Briscoe was out of the mix on defense to start the season. Meanwhile, the Broncos were struggling– they started 0–3–and their quarterback situation was a mess. Saban had no interest in helping advance the cause of civil rights. But with no better options, Saban finally gave the best passer on the team an opportunity he deserved. On September 29, 1968, Saban turned to Briscoe early in the fourth quarter of the home opener with the Broncos trailing, 17–10, to the Boston Patriots. Briscoe completed his first pass for 22 yards. The next drive, he guided the Broncos 80 yards, covering the last 12 on a highlight-worthy touchdown run. Denver still lost, 20–17. But the score wasn't the headline.

"The thing I remember is the support I got from my teammates and fans . . . that was amazing," Briscoe said. "Fans came up to me after the game. They were great. Back in those days, the fear was that white players wouldn't follow a Black quarterback and fans would be [angry]. That didn't happen. I understood the significance. I knew that I was the first and what that meant. If I did well, it would make it easier on other guys. But you have to understand: I had always been a quarterback. It's what I was meant to do. It wasn't a surprise to me. I just wanted to keep doing it."

The Broncos were awful. But Briscoe inspired his teammates to think they could be better—which is exactly what the best quarterbacks do.

"Marlin was electrifying," former Broncos receiver Al Denson said. "They couldn't touch him because he was so good in the backfield—better than Fran Tarkenton. Marlin was short, and it was hard for him to throw over the linemen, but he was accurate."[73]

Said former Broncos running back Floyd Little, "He was incredible. Running the ball, he was like Barry Sanders. . . . You look at Michael Vick, and you see Marlin Briscoe, forty years removed. Marlin wasn't as quick as Vick, but he had a better arm."[74]

A week after his first appearance at quarterback, Briscoe made his first start. He wound up playing in 11 games, including five starts, and passed for 1,589 yards with 14 touchdown passes—still a Broncos rookie record for touchdown throws. The elusive runner also rushed for 308 yards (with an impressive 7.5-yard average) and three touchdowns. By any criteria, Briscoe, who finished second in voting for AFL Rookie of the Year, had a smashing first season. Briscoe also shredded the argument that white players would not follow Black quarterbacks.

"We were football players. As long as we won, we didn't care about the color of the quarterback," Little said. "Marlin was the best we had. We rallied around him—everybody on the team. We were competitive. Shit, we were moving the ball, getting in the end zone. We had coaches off our asses. The greatest thing in the world was giving Marlin the opportunity to be the quarterback. We all thought he'd be our quarterback the next season. But the coach had different plans. . . . If Lou had stayed with Marlin, our chances would have been better. But I don't think the league was ready for a Black quarterback."[75]

Confident in his standing on the team, Briscoe returned to Omaha to work toward finishing his degree. Briscoe also let down his guard. No matter the era, a Black man can't do that. Briscoe was having the time of his life. Already a rock star in Omaha from his days a sandlot legend, high school hotshot, and big man on campus, his celebrity reached new heights. "The thing was, my family and friends were so proud," Briscoe said. "It was like a dream."

One day in the off-season, Briscoe received a phone call from a cousin who had moved to Denver with him. Then Briscoe's dream became a nightmare.

"I found out they were having quarterback meetings," Briscoe said. "I thought it had to be a mistake. How could they have quarterback meetings and I wasn't there?" Briscoe quickly returned to Denver. Saban confirmed it: Briscoe was out. "He never really explained it. But he didn't have to," Briscoe said. "Later, I heard there was some talk about fans being upset and not going to the games. I just wanted to get out of there."

Saban explained it this way: Despite Briscoe's success, he just wasn't his type of quarterback.

"Marlin was an exceptional athlete, but he didn't have great size. He was always throwing out of a well," Saban said. "I figured his best position was receiver, but we were searching for a quarterback. The four and a half years I was with the Broncos, we never found a guy who could take over the position. We brought in quarterbacks by the dozen."[76]

Except the Broncos in 1968 had a quarterback who produced and inspired his teammates, which Saban chose to ignore because Briscoe didn't fit into his box. The decision to dump Briscoe was all on Saban, Little said, and it was an awful one.

"Marlin didn't have a problem with management—he had a problem with Saban. He bumped heads with a goat," Little said. "Coach Saban ruled with an iron hand. He would grab guys by the face mask. He was always screaming, 'My grandmother's better than you.' One time, he fired the whole kickoff team. . . . I liked Saban. He and I had the same personality. But he was a bastard, a slave master. He made all the decisions."[77]

The Broncos wound up suffering because of Saban's rigidity. Granted, Saban was a coach of his time, and coaches in 1968 did not envision a pro football future in which athletic quarterbacks would rise to the top of the game while heavily utilizing run-pass options. But despite having no better choices, Saban turned away from Briscoe.

—

Saban agreed to release Briscoe, who figured he would have many potential landing spots. Yes, Briscoe was Black. And it was still the late 1960s in America. Surely though, Briscoe reassured himself, there had to be some teams that would focus less on his skin color and more on his ability to help them win. After Briscoe was released, however, his phone didn't ring.

"I found out that Saban called around to stop me from getting picked up," Briscoe said. For teams back then, it would have been risky enough to sign a Black man specifically to play quarterback. Factor in that Briscoe had been unfairly cast as a locker-room agitator, and his days at the position in the United States were over.

Briscoe went north. The CFL welcomed African Americans who were prohibited from playing quarterback in the AFL and NFL. "It just wasn't for me," said Briscoe, who was in Canada only briefly. After returning to Omaha, Briscoe soon got a tryout with the Buffalo Bills. Former Raiders head coach John Rauch, Eldridge Dickey's first coach in Oakland, grew tired of owner Al Davis, whose incessant meddling with the coaching staff became a source of daily frustration for Rauch. In a surprising move, Rauch resigned from one of the AFL's top franchises to helm one of its worst.

Rauch inherited a roster that needed an infusion of youth at quarterback. Entering the 1969 season, Jack Kemp, who would go on to become a successful politician, was past his prime at 34. Backup Tom Flores (later a two-time winning Super Bowl coach with the Oakland/Los Angeles Raiders) was 32. James "Shack"

Harris was only 22 and in his rookie season. In a phone call with Briscoe before his tryout, Rauch explained he was high on Harris–who would become the first to kick open several doors for Black quarterbacks–and wanted Briscoe to play wideout. No other NFL teams were keeping Briscoe busy on the phone, so he agreed to switch to a position he hadn't played at any level.

In preparation for what Briscoe hoped would be a career-saving move, he devoured game film of the best at the position. Briscoe studied route running, blocking, hand positioning on catches–anything to help him stay in the game. He did. His first season in Buffalo, Briscoe had 32 receptions for 532 yards (a 16.6-yard average) and five touchdowns. The next season, Briscoe was selected first team all-conference and second team All-Pro after finishing second in the NFL with 57 catches and setting career-highs with 1,036 yards (an 18.2-yard average) and eight touchdowns. At wide receiver, Briscoe had made it to the top of the game. Still, his success was bittersweet. Briscoe was supposed to be the one throwing the passes, not catching them. During this time, Briscoe roomed with Harris, who was trying to become established in a league that didn't want him playing where he was born to play, either.

"My rookie year, Marlin was a big help to me," Harris said. "He was the only person on the team who understood what I was going through, because he had been through it the year before."

Saban, who forced out Briscoe in Denver, never got the Broncos untracked. He resigned during the 1971 season. In Saban's time leading Denver, the Broncos went 20-42-3. After two awful seasons and battles with Buffalo's owner, Rauch resigned before the start of the 1971 season. Saban was named the head coach of the Bills for the 1972 season, rejoining the franchise he led to consecutive AFL titles after the 1964 and 1965 seasons. Briscoe knew what that meant.

"I was out," he said. "I knew he wouldn't want me there. But I had already proven myself. I showed not only that I could make the switch–but I was good at it. I knew other teams would want me as a receiver."

The Bills traded Briscoe to Miami for a first-round pick in 1971. Briscoe had a team-high four touchdown receptions for the Dolphins in 1972, helping them become the only team in NFL history to go undefeated in the regular season and postseason. In today's pass-happy NFL, a receiver leading a team with only four touchdown receptions wouldn't be impressive. But back in the 1970s, most teams were run-centric on offense–and the talented Dolphins were second to none in the running game.

The 1972 Dolphins led the league in both rushing yards and rushing touchdowns. Future Pro Football Hall of Fame running back Larry Csonka was joined in Miami's backfield by fellow talented runners Mercury Morris and Jim Kiick. And future Pro Football Hall of Fame wide receiver Paul Warfield, who had one fewer touchdown reception than Briscoe in 1972, was the top target of Dolphins quarterback Bob Griese, who also wound up being enshrined in Canton, Ohio. The fact that Briscoe emerged as a statistical leader in that star-studded lineup, especially considering the Dolphins' style of play, was actually quite an accomplishment.

Briscoe won his second Super Bowl ring with Miami the following season and had a nine-year career with six teams.

"Marlin was not only a good pass receiver, but he also had the ability to advance the ball considerably after the catch," Warfield said. "You'd throw him a short pass, and the defense would come up to the line immediately. The coaching staff saw that we could use this to put maximum pressure on the defense. Today, you see quarterbacks flip a quick pass to a receiver to give him a chance to show his running ability. The special play the coaching staff devised for Marlin was similar."[78]

—

After he retired from the NFL at 31 in 1976, Briscoe began a lucrative career as a financial broker in Los Angeles. "I was always good with numbers," Briscoe said. "I had saved money when I played. And I was making good money [in the bond market]."

Then his problems began. In LA in the late 1970s, cocaine was everywhere. Briscoe was flush with cash. For him, that proved to be a disastrous combination.

"I started hanging out with the wrong people. I went on a ten-year downward spiral," Briscoe said. "I had houses and investments. I got married. I had a daughter. But I had that demon. It took me away from who I was."

At his lowest point, Briscoe was addicted to cocaine and living on the streets. Once, Briscoe said, he was robbed at gunpoint by drug dealers. "Then they threw me out [of the car]," Briscoe said. Struggling to survive, he used the two Super Bowl rings he won with the Dolphins as collateral for a loan to keep a roof over his head and eat. When Briscoe defaulted on the loan, he lost the rings. Williams's performance in the Super Bowl inspired Briscoe to fight to regain his life from the drugs.

"The great thing is that Marlin got himself better," said Harris, who remains close with Briscoe.

With the help of $500 from a friend who owed him money, Briscoe started the long road back after being released from jail in San Diego in 1989. He said he quit using without the assistance of formal rehab. What finally prompted a recovery he said has lasted more than 30 years? "I just didn't want to live that way anymore," Briscoe said.

Briscoe said he has worked diligently to repair many personal relationships he wrecked while he was getting high. He reunited with his two adult daughters from a previous relationship.

"No one thought I would ever succumb to the fortunes of evil like I did. It not only shocked other people, it shocked me, too," Briscoe said. "You let your family down. You let your friends down. Your mentors, who led you on a path to success, you let them down. But you can find your way out of the darkness."

Briscoe knocked down a barrier for all the Black quarterbacks who followed and contributed mightily to the NFL's stunning success. And the next time you see Patrick Mahomes, Jackson, Deshaun Watson, Russell Wilson, Dak Prescott, Murray, and others whipping the ball around the field amid cheers and thunderous applause, remember that Briscoe is part of their story, too.

[7]

THE GRAMBLING GUY

ON A SUN-SPLASHED AFTERNOON in August 2019, two distinguished Black men stood on an NFL practice field for hours at Ashburn, Virginia, conferring about Washington's performance. Doug Williams, a high-ranking official with the same franchise that he had led to Super Bowl glory as a younger man, could have evaluated things just fine on his own. But after spending much of his life learning from James "Shack" Harris, Williams saw no need to stop now.

From his days at historically Black powerhouse Grambling State University in Grambling, Louisiana, through his groundbreaking NFL career, Williams followed in Harris's giant footsteps. Many know that Williams, in an MVP-winning performance, was the first African American to quarterback a team to a Super Bowl victory. Harris, however, also had a major role in dismantling racist myths about the ability of Black men to thrive at football's most important position. Harris, Williams said, wielded a big hammer even before Williams held one.

"Let me tell you about James Harris," Williams said. "I have an older brother, but James Harris served as my other older brother. And it's unfortunate that Shack has not gotten the recognition he so rightly deserves. Because when we talk about pioneers at the quarterback position, and a lot of people are quick to give me that title, I say that the James Harrises of the world are the true pioneers."

Williams nailed it. In his 10-year career, Harris kicked down the following doors:

- *He became the first Black quarterback to start a season opener in the modern era of major professional football in the United States.*

- *He became the first Black quarterback to start and win a playoff game.*

- *He became the first Black quarterback to play in the Pro Bowl.*

- *He became the first Black quarterback to be selected Pro Bowl MVP.*

And to think that the Black quarterback who first defied the odds in the NFL briefly declined to bet on himself.

—

After a stellar career at Grambling, which he led to three Southwestern Athletic Conference championships, Harris was eager to prove he had the chops to make it big as an NFL passer. In many ways, he appeared perfectly suited for the job.

At 6 foot 4 and 210 pounds, Harris—whose nickname is short for Meshach, the biblical figure who never wavered in faith of his beliefs—looked as if he arrived straight from Central Casting for the role of NFL quarterback. Well, except for one problem: Harris entered the draft in 1969. In that year, a Black man was more likely to participate in the Apollo 11 moon landing than be selected to line up under center in the NFL. In the college game, Harris had a passing arm second to none among his peers–regardless of race. Sharp with heart, Harris was a born leader. But pro scouts were most interested in what their stopwatches revealed about Harris: He was fast.

It was the same old story–if Harris changed positions, teams told him, he could count on being selected high in the draft. Harris wasn't buying it. If the NFL didn't want Harris as a quarterback, Harris said, then the NFL didn't want him. Harris made it known he would not change positions. That was his proverbial line in the sand.

"I kept my word by not switching," Harris said. "And they kept their word: They didn't draft me on the first day."

Finally, in the eighth round, the Buffalo Bills selected Harris with the 192nd overall pick. That was the same draft in which the Bills used the No. 1 overall selection to acquire O. J. Simpson, the Heisman Trophy–winning running back from the University of Southern California.

Disgusted about being passed over so many times, Harris considered walking away from the game he loved. He kicked around the idea of becoming a football coach. But famed Grambling head coach Eddie Robinson wouldn't let Harris go out like that. Robinson had arrived at a small Black college in northern Louisiana in 1941. Over the next 56 years, he would develop more than 200 future professional football players and champion the cause of equal rights. Although Robinson understood Harris was wounded, he knew there was still plenty of fight left in the young man. Robinson just had to convince Harris to soldier on. Robinson pleaded with Harris to go to Buffalo and fight for not only himself, but also for the Black quarterbacks who would follow him. Robinson challenged his protégé to scale towering walls previously untouched by Black quarterbacks.

"He said, 'James, obviously, the decision is yours. But I just want to let you know that if guys like you don't go to the NFL and play quarterback, it's going to hurt the opportunities for others and it's going to be that much longer before someone gets the opportunity to play,'" Harris said. And Robinson punctuated his pitch with this: "'Now, James, if you decide to go and you don't make it, don't come back and say that the reason you didn't make it was because you're Black. You know it's not going to be fair. You've just got to be better and leave them no choice but to let you play.'"

Message received.

Harris vowed he wouldn't cower. He promised his mentor he would do all he could to overcome the racism they both knew Harris would face.

—

Every day during Buffalo Bills training camp at Niagara University in the town of Lewiston in Niagara County, New York, players battled for hours during grueling practices under a merciless July sun and lived in spartan dorm rooms. The Bills' daily mail call was among the players' few pleasures. But not for Harris.

The hate mail he received was stunning—in both volume and depravity. Typically, players were just handed letters and care packages from family and friends. Not Harris. He received so much mail, the Bills' staff delivered multiple large packages to him. Born and reared in Monroe, Louisiana, Harris came of age in the Jim Crow South. Even the pain of that experience, though, didn't prepare him for the words written on those pages he received in camp.

"I rode on the back of the bus and we could only drink from the colored water fountain, not the white one. So I knew about racism. But hate mail . . . I had never thought about hate mail. That was something different," Harris said. "Here I am, twenty-one, twenty-two years old, and I'm getting all this hate mail about what's going to happen to me, people saying they want to kill me. Now, I didn't take all of it seriously. But there was so much of it. It just wasn't something I expected. I don't know how anyone could expect something like that. And there were other things."

The Bills' training camp provided Harris's first large-scale exposure to white people. He grew up in the segregated South and attended an HBCU. He had few reasons to interact much with other races.

"One of the things that was significant was when I had to step in the huddle the first time [at practice] and all of the offensive linemen were white. I had to make sure I got the play right and did everything right," Harris said. "I had to show them I could do it."

Harris did just that, impressing the coaching staff throughout practice and the preseason. Especially John Rauch, Buffalo's head coach.

"He really liked my arm. He really liked the way I threw the ball," Harris said. "Johnny Rauch was the guy who kept me there. As long as I performed, I felt he would give me a shot."

Word of Harris's strong performance traveled to the NFL league office in New York City. Although the AFL-NFL merger would not be completed until the start of the 1970s, NFL commissioner Pete Rozelle in 1969 was the de facto chief executive of both leagues. Rozelle understood the significance of what was occurring in Buffalo. Before the Bills' third preseason game, Rozelle dispatched Buddy Young to let Harris know that the commissioner was watching and pleased. A star college running back at the University of Illinois and a Pro Bowler with the Baltimore Colts, Young was one of the first Black players in the NFL. He also was the first Black executive in NFL history. Young's words strengthened Harris's resolve.

"They got me out of the locker room before the game to talk to him, and he told me that the commissioner and everyone in the league [office] was aware of the training camp I was having," Harris said. "He said I had a chance to do something special and help the guys behind me if I kept it going. He wanted to let me know what the commissioner thought, but he also wanted me to know I had his support."

By the middle of the AFL preseason, Black America had rallied around Harris. His quest to become the Bills' starting quarterback inspired Black folk. They came out to support Harris in Buffalo, on the road–wherever the Bills played, a throng of Harris's Black supporters followed.

"At the hotels, when I went out on the field before games, after games–Blacks showed up everywhere I went," Harris said. "I had a lot of support because I was the only one."

Harris not only earned a spot on the opening roster; the former quarterback from Grambling who was passed over for 191 other players was the Bills' No. 1 quarterback. Harris started in Buffalo's first regular season game, making him the first Black passer to start a season opener in the modern era of major professional football in the United States. For Harris, though, the euphoria was short-lived.

Harris's debut against Joe Namath and the defending Super Bowl champion Jets didn't go well. He suffered an injury in the first half of a 33–19 loss. Harris wouldn't start again that season and wound up playing in only four games. Things quickly went downhill from there as Harris was unable to overcome his multiple injuries and the Bills' ineptitude (in his three years with the Bills, they were a combined 8–33–1).

Because of a knee injury, Harris was slowed for much of the 1970 season, playing in only seven games. In 1971, Harris made two starts and played in seven games. When Lou Saban, who ran off Marlin Briscoe in Denver years earlier, became the Bills' head coach after the '71 season, he cut Harris, who wasn't offered a contract by another team. Harris, just 25, was out of football in 1972. Just like that.

In the early 1970s, NFL players had not yet reaped the financial windfall of mega television contracts and massive endorsement deals that their successors would receive. For most, wallet-stuffing paydays were still decades away. It wasn't uncommon for players to have nine-to-five jobs in the off-season. During the 1971 off-season,

Harris worked for the United States Department of Commerce, which promotes economic growth at the federal level. Potentially needing to begin a new full-time career, Harris reached out to his contacts in the government agency and was offered a position. He continued to work out while on desk duty the entire 1972 season, remaining ready for a call that finally came in 1973 from Rams head coach Chuck Knox.

Knox saw past Harris's color and his injury-tainted stats to his talent. He asked if Harris was still interested in football. Harris was all in at "Hello."

The Rams offered Harris a chance to compete for the backup job behind starter John Hadl. Harris shook off the rust and proved himself in training camp. Despite a season away from the game, Harris could still sling the ball with the best of them. After being mostly on full-time clipboard duty in 1973, Harris replaced the struggling Hadl early in the 1974 season. He came off the bench to lead the team to seven wins in its final nine games. He also directed the Rams to their first playoff victory in 23 seasons. Harris earned the only Pro Bowl appearance of his career and won the game's MVP award.

Harris had another strong season in 1975, going 11–2 as a starter. However, the Rams' front office was never fully behind Harris, faulting him for the team losing three straight conference championship games during his tenure. The team's decision-makers were always in search of a quarterback that could take them all the way to a Super Bowl. That's not the way they saw Harris, and Harris knew it. "You have to block out all the outside stuff, the things you hear going on behind the scenes, and just play, which is what I did," Harris said. "But when you're winning, which is the most important thing, and you hear you're not wanted . . . it's tough."

By the 1976 season, the Rams were playing musical chairs at quarterback. You can't win that way.

Harris was traded to the San Diego Chargers. As the Rams'

starter, he went 21–6 in the regular season and 1–2 in the playoffs. Harris played three seasons with the Chargers, appearing in 26 games with 11 starts. The relentless pressure to prove himself, to prove that a Black man could excel as an NFL quarterback, was wearing him down. As a Charger, he had a 4–7 record. Harris proved a lot, but alone under the microscope because of his color, he was never at his best as a professional QB.

"Back in those days, we truly were Black quarterbacks. And we knew since that's the way we were looked at, we almost had to play perfectly," Harris said. "For a lot of years, there was nobody in the league starting but me, I was the only one, and there was always this [undercurrent in the media] that someone else should be starting ahead of me. So I felt I couldn't make mistakes. But to play that position the best, like I did in high school and college, you have to be able to move on from a mistake, like an interception, and just put it up some more. And I just didn't feel that way in the pros."

Even not at his best, Harris left no doubt he belonged. And just as Eddie Robinson, who coached and mentored Harris at Grambling, envisioned, Harris kicked open doors for others.

"James used to come back [to Grambling] . . . and tell me how the league worked as far as being a quarterback," Williams said. "He told me what I needed to do, what I needed to work on. All he did was encourage me. He never told me about how hard he had it—and he went through a lot. Some of what he had to deal with, things he told me about years later, it just . . . it just wasn't right. But he didn't want to discourage me. I've always appreciated that. Even today, we talk three or four times a week."

Harris, in turn, is still grateful for the encouragement supplied by his Grambling coach and mentor, Robinson, a half century ago.

"Coach Robinson would say, 'You're just going to get one opportunity. You have to be ready for it,'" Harris said. "That worked out for me. Doug also had a role to play, and he played his role. Along the way, with what we and others did, it has improved for so many other QBs.

"My biggest regret is for all those guys who came before me. There were so many guys who came before me who could really, really play. But they never got a chance. That's one of the saddest things for me."

Guys like Eldridge Dickey, the great HBCU quarterback who was drafted in the first round by the Oakland Raiders only to be switched to wide receiver in his brief and disappointing pro career.

"I played against Eldridge Dickey. I felt very strongly that Eldridge Dickey would be the first Black to play quarterback in the NFL. He was a great player," Harris said. "When he got drafted in the first round, I jumped for joy.

"I knew he could play. There was no doubt in my mind that he would make it. Then they drafted him in the first round, so they're not going to cut him [as a rookie]. You draft someone in the first round, you're supposed to give him a chance. But then they moved him to wide receiver. It was business as usual. He could have made it. They just didn't give him a chance. I got a chance. He didn't."

Although Harris's playing days ended in 1979, he still had many years ahead of him as a trailblazer. In his next act, he became a successful NFL player-personnel official.

Steadily, Harris made the long climb from being a scout to a front-office executive for several clubs. Harris helped build the Baltimore Ravens' 2001 Super Bowl championship team. He was the vice president of player personnel for the Jacksonville Jaguars. In early January 2015, Harris retired from his role as a senior personnel adviser with the Detroit Lions. Harris has challenged the NFL to improve its poor record on inclusive hiring, especially at the general manager level.

"There's no question that there are a lot of talented guys out there who are ready [for the jobs]," Harris said. "There's no question they're qualified. We've just got to continue to put these young guys in position. And then they've got to get the opportunity."

It's common for former professional athletes to reenter the workforce in the leagues they helped to make successful. After retirement, many former NFL players seek to remain close to the sport they've played, in most cases, for more than half their lives. They mostly occupy positions in scouting and coaching, applying their hands-on expertise in helping teams to identify and develop new talent. But few former Black players reach the highest rungs in football operations. That's why the second half of Harris's career story is compelling, too.

[8]

JEFFERSON STREET JOE AND THE PITTSBURGH STEELERS

KNOWING THAT HBCU POWERHOUSE Tennessee State University put on quite a show during pregame warmups, a wide-eyed high school quarterback arrived early on October 30, 1971, for the team's road game against Southern University at Baton Rouge, Louisiana. And Doug Williams did not leave disappointed.

Williams, a Louisiana native who was being recruited by both Southern and Tennessee State, watched in awe as Tennessee State star passer "Jefferson Street Joe" Gilliam rifled passes all over the field to receivers who ran precise, innovative routes. Gilliam capped the performance by whipping the ball behind his back for pinpoint completions to running backs coming out of the backfield. Williams had seen enough. In fact, for Williams, Tennessee State's 27–16 victory over Southern was akin to a boring encore to a thrilling concert. Watching Jefferson Street work before kickoff was worth the price of admission alone.

"Tennessee State was one of those fancy teams during warmups. Just the stuff that he did with the football during drills, his arm strength, his touch, and that behind-the-back stuff, I was like, 'Dang!'" Williams said, still shaking his head in disbelief almost 50 years later.

"His arm was like rubber. He could do whatever he wanted to do with it. He also had the wits to do whatever they wanted to do on offense, and passing is what they did. I'll tell ya, that Jefferson Street, now he was something."

—

Willie Thrower, the first Black quarterback to play in a game during the NFL's modern era, had the coolest name. But no signal-caller has ever had a smoother nickname than Joseph Wiley Gilliam Jr. Jefferson Street is the main boulevard of Black Nashville that runs by Tennessee State. White folk had "Broadway Joe" Namath, the charismatic New York Jets star QB who boldly predicted the team's surprising victory over the heavily favored Baltimore Colts in Super Bowl III. Black folk in Tennessee had HBCU star Jefferson Street Joe, who led the Tigers to consecutive Black college national championships during the 1970 and 1971 seasons.

Gilliam grew up in the Tigers' program, his father the school's longtime defensive coordinator under legendary head coach John Merritt, who, in a 20-year span, led the team to four undefeated seasons and claimed seven Black college national championships. If the younger Gilliam wasn't wowing high school sports spectators in

Nashville in the 1960s, he was most likely with the Tigers, soaking up football knowledge from his father, Joe Sr., Merritt, and star signal-caller Eldridge Dickey.

When it was Jefferson Street's turn to take the program's reins, he kept the good times rolling. The Pittsburgh Steelers noticed. The Steelers weren't in the market for another young quarterback, having selected Terry Hanratty in the second round (30th overall) of the 1969 draft and Terry Bradshaw with the first overall pick the following year. But as the 1972 draft progressed and Gilliam remained on the board, longtime Steelers scout Bill Nunn convinced head coach Chuck Noll that the chance to acquire Gilliam as a late-round pick was an opportunity too good to pass up.

"Joe was accepted as a quarterback, but our thing going into that draft was that we already had quarterbacks," said Nunn, who scouted and recommended many of the players who helped provide the foundation of the franchise's Super Bowl dynasty of the 1970s. "We had Bradshaw. We had Hanratty. We thought we were set."

But as the draft progressed the Pittsburgh brain trust couldn't help noticing that, round after round, Gilliam remained available.

"After a while," Nunn recalled, "he was so high up on our board, we had to take him. I gave him a fourth-round rating because he was really thin, didn't have much weight, but everything else was there. And he had played against big-time competition. By the eleventh round, I said that the only thing preventing him from being accepted in the National Football League was him being Black. That's when Chuck Noll said, 'Let's take him.'"[79]

Gilliam made the opening roster in the 1972 season, but he was stuck behind Bradshaw and Hanratty. Although Bradshaw started every game and helped the Steelers win the AFC Central division, he didn't exactly put a stranglehold on the position. With a berth in the Super Bowl at stake, Bradshaw passed for only 80 yards with a touchdown and two interceptions as Pittsburgh lost to the Miami

Dolphins in the AFC championship game, 21–17. As a rookie, Gilliam attempted only 11 passes.

By 1973, the Steelers were on the cusp of beginning their dynastic run of winning four Super Bowl titles in a span of six seasons. They were loaded with young talent throughout their roster, but Noll had concerns about Bradshaw. Without a doubt, Bradshaw had a great passing arm. His gunslinger approach and propensity to throw interceptions, however, didn't inspire confidence. Hanratty was a leader and predictable. He also was far less physically gifted than Bradshaw. Then there was Gilliam. In the Steelers' quarterback room, no one had a better arm than Gilliam. The second-year pro was a polished passer, too. The Steelers' coaching staff only questioned whether Gilliam, listed at 187 pounds during his playing days, had enough weight and strength to withstand the pain NFL quarterbacks must endure to make it through the season. A quarterback controversy was brewing.

Bradshaw suffered a shoulder injury in the 1973 season, the Steelers slipped to second in the AFC Central, and they were blown out in the playoffs by the Oakland Raiders. Those factors contributed to creating an opening for Gilliam. In late November, Gilliam came off the bench and flashed his talent during a 21–16 road loss to the Cleveland Browns, passing for 197 yards with one touchdown pass and one interception. Although Gilliam fared poorly a week later while making his only start of the season—in seven attempts, he failed to complete a pass and had three intercepted as visiting Pittsburgh fell to the Miami Dolphins, 30–26—he had shown enough in practice and during five games to improve his standing on the depth chart. Suddenly, Noll viewed Gilliam as a viable option to lead the rising Steelers. The stage was set for the team to make a change at quarterback in 1974. Gilliam reported to camp determined to win the starting job. On the practice field and in preseason games, Gilliam clearly outshined Bradshaw.

Before Pittsburgh kicked off the regular season against the

Baltimore Colts, Noll declared Gilliam the team's No. 1 QB. Gilliam shined in the Steelers' 30–0 victory, passing for 257 yards and two touchdowns while becoming the first Black signal-caller to start a season opener after the 1970 AFL-NFL merger. A picture of Gilliam in action against Baltimore appeared on the cover of *Sports Illustrated* under the headline "Pittsburgh's Black Quarterback." The deck headline read, "Joe Gilliam bombs the Colts." Jefferson Street Joe was on his way.

"Joe was performing well. He was energetic, he made practices," former Steelers defensive lineman Dwight White said. "In terms of the playbook, he did everything he was supposed to do. We were winning."[80]

Gilliam was tightening his hold on the starting job just as Shack Harris was beginning his second season as a backup in the Los Angeles Rams, the season in which Harris would rise to the top of the Rams' depth chart and break barriers as a Pro Bowler. But despite the progress Black quarterbacks made in 1974, racism remained a formidable barrier to their continued advancement. Off the field in Pittsburgh, Gilliam had a horrible experience.

"I remember one time my wife Ruth and I went to visit," the elder Gilliam said. "The weather was cold up there. It was between games, during the week, and we were with him in his apartment. He said, 'Come here, Daddy. Look in here.' He opens the closet, and there's a huge cardboard box in there—must've been three by three—filled with letters to the very top. He said, 'Read these letters, Daddy. Read some of them.' I pick one up, and it's a death threat. I throw one down. I pick up another one: a death threat. I said, 'Joey, what's in here?' He said, 'Dad, the whole box is full of death threats.' I said, 'I'm going to call Chuck Noll.' He said, 'No, Dad, he's on top of it. There's a guy down on the sidelines staking me out, because they say they're going to shoot me from the stands.' None of his teammates would stand next to him."[81]

Pittsburgh continued to win, improving to 4–1–1 in its first six games, but Gilliam wasn't directing the offense as well as Noll expected. Sure, at times Gilliam was Jefferson Street Joe, an exciting passer capable of producing a big-time play at any moment. But too often, he was just an average Joe. Or worse. He was making too many mistakes.

Gilliam believed he had to play perfectly to hold off Bradshaw. The pressure was getting to him. The death threats weighed on him. Gilliam's completion percentage steadily dropped. His turnovers piled up. In an era when quarterbacks had much more latitude in play calling, Noll was displeased that Gilliam called his own number too often.

"Noll never really wanted a wide-open passing attack," former Steelers linebacker Andy Russell said. "He was of the belief that when you pass the ball, three things can happen [a completion, an incompletion, or an interception], and two of them are bad. So he wanted to have a running attack. Third and five, he'd give the ball to Franco Harris. His idea of a passing down was third and seven, third and eight. Gilliam was not doing what Chuck Noll wanted him to do, which was give the ball to the running backs. He was checking off to passing plays. Bradshaw wanted to throw the ball, too, but he handed it off."[82]

Fans called for Noll to reinstate Bradshaw. In Week 7 against the Atlanta Falcons, Noll made the switch. Although Bradshaw completed only 9 of 21 pass attempts for 130 yards with no touchdowns and two interceptions, the Steelers won, 24–17. Bradshaw was back in there. Gilliam took his strong record with him to the bench. The situation was unusual.

"Not taking anything away from Bradshaw, but there's no way in the world, in today's time, that you bench a quarterback if he's four-one-one," Doug Williams said. "Mentally, I think that was a big blow to Jefferson Street, to have the job taken away when he was succeeding. I think it really hurt him, and rightfully so.

"You work your tail off to get where you are, to earn the job, and you're four-one-one and you get benched? You can't even understand that. It's not explainable. You can talk about what was going on with the offense and how maybe the coaches wanted some things to be different. But at the end of the day you're winning. You can understand what that did to Joe that season."

Bradshaw was a No. 1 overall draft pick. When a franchise selects a player in the draft's top spot, especially a quarterback, it's difficult to completely cut the cord after not even five full seasons. Noll never acknowledged that Bradshaw's draft position was a factor in his decision to turn back to Bradshaw. However, it wouldn't be surprising if, in Noll's assessment of the situation, the high amount of draft capital the Steelers used to acquire Bradshaw gave the former Louisiana Tech standout an edge over Gilliam. Regardless, the rest, as they say, is history.

With Bradshaw finally entrenched as QB No. 1, the Steelers that season began their run of four world championships over the next six seasons. Bradshaw would wind up being among 10 Steelers players from the 1970s enshrined in the Pro Football Hall of Fame.

Meanwhile, Gilliam began a tragic fall.

He won two Super Bowl rings with the Steelers as a backup but could never overcome the pain of being benched. Gilliam descended into heavy drug use.

"He'd been into marijuana. After the job got transferred back to Terry, that's when the drug use escalated," former Steelers defensive lineman Ernie Holmes said. "It went from coke to speed to heroin, he was experimenting with everything. Receiver Ron Shanklin, myself, Joe Greene, defensive end L. C. Greenwood, all of us tried to talk with him."[83]

It did no good. The 1975 season would be Gilliam's last on an NFL roster.

In 1976, Gilliam signed with the New Orleans Saints, but he

was cut quickly because of disciplinary reasons. Unable to shake his demons, Gilliam was homeless for a stretch and pawned his Super Bowl rings to buy drugs. Through the help of his family, especially his father, Gilliam recovered. He died in 2000 at only 49.

Super Bowl–winning coach and star college quarterback Tony Dungy was a defensive back on the Steelers' 1978 championship team. Some of Dungy's Steelers teammates who also lined up with Gilliam in Pittsburgh often told Dungy that the franchise's history could have wound up being much different.

"What fans today don't understand, or they just don't know the history of it, is that he [Gilliam] won the job," Dungy said. "Terry Bradshaw was there before him and [Gilliam] went in there and got the job. He beat out Bradshaw, so that tells you the type of talent he had. Now could he have stayed healthy and done all that [quarterback the Steelers to four Super Bowl titles] with that frame [slightly built for a starting QB]? Who knows?

"But talent-wise, as far as just throwing the ball and commanding the position, all those veteran guys said he was the guy and he had as much talent as any quarterback in the league. Bradshaw is in the Hall of Fame and he beat him out. That's hard for people to fathom and really understand that this guy was the starting quarterback when the Super Bowl dynasty started. Now, are there a lot of factors and a lot of reasons why it all didn't materialize for him? Well, yes, there are. But talent-wise, yeah, he was a Hall of Fame talent."

[9]

FEELING THE DRAFT

ON A WARM SPRING day in 1978 a fellow Grambling State University student tracked down Doug Williams on the Grambling, Louisiana, campus and delivered an important message: Head coach Eddie Robinson needed to speak with him immediately. It wasn't unusual for Robinson to summon the school's star quarterback to his office for impromptu X's-and-O's sessions or to catch up on how things were going for the young man in the classroom, but Williams had recently completed his senior year. For a moment, Williams wondered what Coach Rob, as Grambling's players affectionately referred to the legendary taskmaster, wanted to discuss. Then Williams quickly remembered the NFL draft was scheduled to start that day. He figured Robinson may have some news to share.

Actually, Robinson was eager to reveal a blockbuster–and a potential game changer for Black quarterbacks.

After making his way to Robinson's office, Williams was surprised by the look of excitement on his mentor's face, which he had not seen before. Robinson jumped up from his chair, rushed from behind his desk, and hugged his groundbreaking protégé: Williams had just become the first African American quarterback selected in the opening round of the NFL draft. On May 2, 1978, the Tampa Bay Buccaneers chose Williams with the 17th overall pick. Every year since 1936, the NFL has conducted a draft of college football players. In the 42nd iteration of the process, a Black quarterback was finally deemed worthy of being chosen with one of the most valuable picks. Yet another longstanding barrier for Black quarterbacks in professional football was toppled by a Grambling man.

Robinson, who assumed head coaching duties at Grambling in 1941, had spent decades waiting for the NFL to finally acknowledge what he had known for so long: There were many Black quarterbacks through the years who possessed first-round talent, and franchises were foolishly wasting opportunities to build around players who could help them win. Robinson also realized that by expending so much draft capital to acquire Williams, the Buccaneers likely would give him a legitimate opportunity to be their starting signal-caller—a rare occurrence for Black quarterbacks to that point in NFL history. That Williams was worthy of that opportunity, Robinson had no doubts. Williams would fly high. Williams had it all.

At 6 foot 4 and a muscular 220 pounds with a booming voice, Williams looked as if he had been designed to command an NFL huddle. Then there was his arm strength, which was off the charts. If someone in the NFL possessed a stronger passing arm than that of Williams, Robinson wanted to meet the man. Williams got it done in the classroom, too: Before the NFL draft, Williams graduated from Grambling with a bachelor's degree in education and began work on a master's degree. As a senior, Williams led the NCAA in several offensive categories. He finished fourth in the 1978 Heisman Trophy voting (University of Texas All-American running back Earl Campbell won the award)—no small feat for an HBCU quarterback.

Now that Tampa Bay had proven they'd recognized what was crystal clear to Robinson, the Grambling coach was ecstatic. Williams had made history in the first round of the draft, and Robinson had no doubt he would go on to make history as a great NFL quarterback.

Williams was happy to see his coach floating around the room, but he was considerably less exuberant. Then 22, Williams's eyes were open. He'd seen how Black men hit a wall in their attempts to play the sport's most important position. Williams didn't trust that he'd really get a fair shot. He had even considered passing on the NFL if no team drafted him in the top three rounds. After learning so much from Coach Rob, Williams thought he would make a good football coach as well. Since he'd been picked in the first round, he decided to give the NFL a shot, but with his feet planted firmly on the ground.

"Back then, the draft wasn't like it is today, with a big show on TV and all the guys having their family and friends and coaches around," Williams said. "And you didn't have all these TV stations and radio stations predicting where everyone might go. I was kept in the dark. I didn't know what was going to happen. And I knew that for teams looking for a quarterback, I wasn't going to be their first choice on a lot of [draft] boards.

"So when the Tampa Bay Buccaneers called Coach Rob and then he called me in to let me know, yeah, I was happy about it. But when I see guys go in the first round now, it's such a celebration. But it wasn't a great big deal at that particular time. It was more of a sense of just being thankful. It was gratitude that you were going to play in the National Football League and you were drafted in the first round. And as far as making history, you have to understand that I knew about Eldridge Dickey.

"I just looked at it from the standpoint that there was another Black quarterback drafted in the first round before me," Williams said. "For all those reasons, that day just wasn't that big of a deal for me. But once I got to the league, the first time I dressed out with that Tampa Bay uniform on, yeah, it became a big deal."

—

Running backs coach Joe Gibbs sprinted the length of the Tampa Bay Buccaneers' practice field to invade the personal space of his colleague, quarterbacks coach Bill Nelsen. Gibbs had heard enough of Nelsen berating the team's rookie signal-caller. One way or another, Gibbs planned to put a stop to it.

Williams was in his first practice with Tampa Bay, and Nelsen had been riding him all day long. It wasn't in Gibbs's nature to confront another assistant on head coach John McKay's staff, but Nelsen was out of bounds. Gibbs made that clear.

"I did something wrong, and he just hollered at me. All of a sudden, I looked down the field, and Joe Gibbs is just running at us. Coach Gibbs told him, 'Don't holler at him one more time! He's got to learn like everybody else!' They almost came to blows."

Gibbs was fiercely protective of Williams, whose pre-draft assessment of the HBCU standout played a big part in Tampa Bay's decision to trade their number one draft pick–a consolation prize for finishing an abysmal 2–12 in the 1977 season–to the Houston Oilers in exchange for talented tight end Jimmie Giles and first- and second-round picks in the 1978 draft, and third- and fifth-round picks in the 1979 draft. Tampa Bay used the first-round pick it received from Houston in 1978, the seventeenth overall, to select Williams.

"Coach McKay told me we needed to find out everything we could about this quarterback at Grambling," Gibbs said. "He sent me there to spend some time with Doug. I got to know him a little. I told Coach McKay that Doug is a great person, and he's really football smart. And gosh, he could throw the football. We took him in the first round."

Gibbs understood the significance of Tampa Bay's historic move. He took pride in the fact that McKay entrusted him with such a pivotal role in the process. Gibbs befriended Williams and was instrumental in Williams's transition to the NFL, which was bumpy. In a contract dispute, Williams sat out the first week of practice his rookie season. Williams's holdout was so brief that white fans and the white press didn't have time to get all in a lather about it publicly, though one would imagine that many in both groups viewed Williams as being ungrateful for the opportunity the Buccaneers bestowed upon him. Once Williams agreed to contract terms with Tampa Bay, Gibbs helped him play catch-up on the team's playbook.

"My rookie year, Coach Gibbs came by the hotel and picked me up every night to go over to his house," Williams said. "We'd go over the playbook, and I'd eat dinner with his family. Every night."

Over those meals at Gibbs's dining room table, a bond was formed that provided the foundation for Williams's star turn in the Super Bowl nine years into the future. Head coach McKay also was Williams's ally. Before becoming the first coach of the expansion Buccaneers in 1976, McKay was one of the most successful coaches in college football history while at the University of Southern California. And McKay was ahead of the curve in understanding that Black men were not only capable of playing quarterback at HBCUs. Jimmy Jones was a three-year Trojans starter and Rose Bowl winner under McKay. Vince Evans got his start under McKay and also went on to win a Rose Bowl.

"Because of coach McKay's history with Black quarterbacks at USC and my relationship with coach Gibbs, I knew I would get a fair shot," Williams said. "Now people outside of the organization, well, that was a different story."

Williams grew up just outside of Zachary, Louisiana. By the time he arrived in Tampa Bay, Williams was well versed in the subject of racism. And while leading the Buccaneers, he encountered a lot of it.

"In every newspaper article, it was either Tampa's Black quarterback or Doug Williams, Tampa Bay's Black quarterback. They wanted people to know I'm Black," Williams said. "You just knew they were looking at you differently. You'd hear people shouting things at the games. You'd get hate mail."

On the field, Williams was a winner. In only his second season, Williams helped lead Tampa Bay to its first division title and first playoff victory. The team finished one step short of the Super Bowl, losing to the Los Angeles Rams in the NFC championship game. Over the next three seasons, the Buccaneers would earn two more playoff berths. Tampa Bay was winning with Williams as its signal-caller. But fans and many within the media downgraded his performance on style points. In his first five seasons, Williams completed more than 50 percent of his passes only twice. But Tampa Bay's offense wasn't structured for Williams to complete a high percentage of his passes.

"Offensively, we did what USC did when coach McKay was there. On the first couple of downs, you pitched left, you pitched right, or you handed it up the middle. Then, on third down, you'd take a seven-step drop and hope someone got open," Williams said. "It's hard to [be efficient] in that type of offense. I mean, I didn't worry about it. I just wanted to win. But it wasn't like it is for today's guys. They take shorter drops and get rid of the ball quicker for two- and three-yard passes."

Despite Williams's success in the win-loss column—the only one that matters—he continued to butt heads with Tampa Bay owner Hugh Culverhouse. After the 1982 season, Culverhouse refused to meet Williams's contract demands. Frustrated about being one of the NFL's lowest-paid QBs, Williams sat out the 1983 season. In 1984, Williams joined the Oklahoma/Arizona Outlaws of the upstart United States Football League, which was founded in 1982. In 1983, Tampa Bay's first season without Williams, the Buccaneers went 2–14. They would go another 14 seasons before qualifying for the playoffs again. During that bleak stretch, Tampa Bay lost at least 10 games in every season except one. As for Williams, he had the best season of his career statistically in the USFL in 1985. But the league folded in 1986. Again, Williams was out of work.

—

Williams answered the phone and instantly recognized the voice on the other end. "Hello, Douglas. How you doing?"

Joe Jackson Gibbs was the only person who referred to Williams by his full given name. Continuing his rise in the NFL's coaching ranks, Gibbs left the Buccaneers after Williams's rookie season. By 1981, he was a head coach, Washington's NFL franchise turning to Gibbs to rebuild a team that had missed the playoffs four consecutive seasons. In only his second season, Gibbs led the team to a Super Bowl championship. Gibbs called Williams because he was in the market for a veteran quarterback to play behind Washington starter Jay Schroeder.

"Now at this point, I don't have a job," Williams said. "I told him, 'Coach, I can be any type of backup you want me to be.' He started laughing," Williams said.

When Williams landed in Washington, his teammates quickly understood he had a special bond with Gibbs.

"You could tell how much Doug respected Coach Gibbs," former wide receiver Ricky Sanders said. "We all respected Coach Gibbs. He was, well, Coach Gibbs. But he and Doug went way back. Doug definitely appreciated everything Coach Gibbs did for him after the USFL."

Still, despite the strength of his relationship with Gibbs, Williams, after his first season with Washington, was frustrated: He appeared in only one game, he attempted only one pass—and he wanted out.

"When I got off the plane after our final preseason game the next season, Coach Gibbs pulled me off to the side. I didn't know what he was going to say," Williams said. "He told me they traded me to the [Los Angeles] Raiders, who had tried to get me when I was in Tampa. I was ready to go. I packed up my apartment. I called everyone back home [in Zachary, Louisiana] to tell them: I'm headed to the Raiders."

Throughout Washington's locker room, word of the trade spread quickly. Many of Williams's teammates were not pleased.

"That first year, everyone knew that Doug was good enough to play and win. No one ever doubted that," former center Jeff Bostic said. "Each day in practice, you could see it. I tell everyone I know that watching Doug that first year [in practice], I had never been around anyone who threw a prettier deep ball. You don't trade someone like that."

Shortly after informing Williams of the trade, Gibbs had second thoughts. Washington called the Raiders–the deal was off. There's an adage in sports: Sometimes the best moves are the ones that aren't made.

"Yeah . . . I changed my mind," Gibbs said. "I thought about it, and I just didn't think that [trading Williams] was best for [Washington]. And I had to do what was best for [Washington]."

Williams was not pleased.

"Coach called me to come to his office. When he finally shows up, he starts smiling. 'Douglas, I changed my mind,' he said. There was no smile on my face. I told Coach he couldn't change his mind. I was ready to go to the Raiders. He got a look on his face I had never seen before and said, 'I don't work for the Raiders. I work for Washington. I changed my mind.'

"Here I'm thinking I'm going to the Raiders, and then I'm back in the same position as before. I didn't have any control. I just had to roll with it. I wasn't happy about it. But right before I left his office, Coach told me he had a feeling that somewhere during the season I was gonna get in and 'we're gonna win this thing.'"

Blah, blah, blah. Williams didn't want to hear it. He wanted an opportunity to play.

Said Gibbs, "I know that was kind of a tough deal. But I had a feeling that during the season, Doug was going to get his chance. I really believed that."

Schroeder, Washington's starting quarterback, provided an opening for Williams.

"Jay had a great year in '86," Bostic said. "He was the concrete starter, and then they [renegotiated] his contract. All of a sudden, it went from 'we' to 'me.' It was pretty apparent to most of the guys on the team that the whole team concept had gone off course with him. Not many teammates had a lot of respect for Jay at that time."

Washington's locker room united behind Williams. "Everybody on the team really respected Doug," Sanders said. "Doug was all about our team. Everybody would tell you that."

Gibbs noticed, too. Williams played well behind Schroeder in 1987. In five games, including two starts, Williams passed for 1,156 yards. He had 11 touchdown passes and five interceptions. With players having responded better to Williams during the regular season, Gibbs made a quarterback change before the playoffs. And the rest, as they say, is history.

"Obviously, if coach Gibbs hadn't stopped that trade, a whole lot could be different today," Williams said. "But I really feel everything I had been through to that point prepared me for what we did that day in the Super Bowl, and for that whole week leading up to it."

—

In Super Bowl XXII, Williams directed the greatest offensive performance during a single quarter in NFL postseason history. He threw four touchdown passes as part of a 35-point, 356-yard second-quarter barrage in Washington's 42–10 victory over Denver. Williams, in the process, became a hero to Black America.

That day in San Diego, with the weight of an entire race on his shoulders, Williams stood on the game's biggest stage and displayed all the skill, intellect, and heart that Black signal-callers supposedly lacked.

"No matter what happened, I was going to be a part of Black history. For me, the best way to be talked about in Black history was for the team to win the game," Williams said. "I didn't want to be a part of Black history and get my ass kicked. That's why I always remembered the fact that [Washington] didn't bring me to San Diego just to show off its Black quarterback. I went to San Diego as [Washington's] starting quarterback. And I went there to win."

In the second quarter, Williams went 9 for 11. He passed for 228 yards and the four touchdowns. Overall, he completed 18 of 29 passes for 340 yards with one interception. Wide receiver Ricky Sanders (four receptions for 168 yards and two touchdowns in the second quarter) and rookie running back Timmy Smith (five rushes for 122 yards and one touchdown) also made indelible marks during Washington's stunning 15-minute run. Williams, however, was the story. Former Washington head coach Joe Gibbs couldn't agree more.

"Obviously, what he did that day . . . Doug really played great," said the Hall of Famer, who led Washington to three Super Bowl championships. "Our offense played great and our defense played great. Our defense doesn't get enough credit for what it did, and I've always felt badly about that. But it was just something about [that day]. I could have closed my eyes, stuck my finger on that play chart, called whatever was there, and it would have gone for eight yards. Every play . . . it was just amazing. I've never experienced anything like that, before or since."

With tears in his eyes after the game, Grambling head coach Eddie Robinson met Williams in the Jack Murphy Stadium tunnel to share another groundbreaking moment. They embraced even longer than they did when Williams was drafted years earlier in the first round by Tampa Bay. And this time, Williams was in lockstep with Coach Rob about the significance of the moment. "We both were crying," Williams said. "Coach Rob said to me, 'Man, you ain't old enough to understand this, but today is like Joe Louis knocking out Max Schmeling [in a 1938 heavyweight bout].' I went back and read about how much that meant to America. The whole country was talking about it. And that's what coach Robinson likened it to."

Williams played two more seasons for Washington. Then he returned to his alma mater to replace Robinson as head coach and had two stints at the school, leading Grambling to three straight Southwestern Athletic Conference titles in the early 2000s and another in 2011. Williams also served as a player-personnel executive with Tampa Bay, the team that drafted him in the first round. Since 2014, he has been a senior official with Washington.

Even more than 30 years later, reminiscing about the best day of his professional career still brings a smile to Williams's face.

"There's not a day that goes by that I don't think about it," Williams said. "Not for what it meant to Doug Williams but because it was about much more than Doug Williams. It meant a lot to a whole lot of other people. All the political angles, what people would say depending on what I did, I knew all of that going into the game. But I tried not to put myself above the team and make it all about Doug Williams."

[10]

THE HALL OF FAMER

ODDLY, UNIVERSITY OF WASHINGTON fans booed throughout home games for three straight seasons in the 1970s. They did it in unison, showering the school's football team in disapproval in 60,000-seat Husky Stadium. The storm of negativity had little to do with the quality of the play on the field, or for that matter the team. An overwhelming majority of Huskies ticket holders disapproved of just a single player: starting quarterback Warren Moon.

And when a Black QB is the target of a fan base's ire, a lengthy investigation isn't required to get to the bottom of things.

"From the time the offense would step on the field during the change of possession, that was all you heard," Moon said. "I'd be the last one to run into the huddle because I'd have to get the plays from the coach. When you go inside that huddle as a quarterback, the most important thing is that all those players are looking at your eyes. You better show in your eyes that you have the confidence that you're going to take the offense down the field and score.

"When your home crowd is against you like that and it's so loud, when those guys looked into my eyes, they had to know how much it was bothering me. And years later, they told me how much it bothered them. But I was the best actor in the world. Even though it was tearing me up inside, when those guys looked into my eyes they had confidence in me. They knew I could do it, even though probably eighty percent of the people in the stadium didn't want me out there."

Huskies fans kept it up through Moon's senior season–until he delivered down the stretch with a Rose Bowl berth at stake. After his impressive performance in a key late-season victory over visiting USC, the boos finally turned to cheers. But Moon couldn't forgive that easily. Who could blame him?

"I broke a seventy-one-yard touchdown run as we were trying to [put the game away], and the crowd was going crazy, chanting my name, 'War-ren, War-ren, War-ren,'" Moon said. "Should have been a great moment for me and my teammates, a great feeling, right? Well, I just wanted to flip the bird all the way around the stadium. I knew I couldn't do that. I knew I was better than that. But that was the feeling inside of me after all that abuse."

Moon was voted the co–Pacific-8 Conference Player of the Year, led Washington to a Rose Bowl victory over the University of Michigan and was selected the Rose Bowl Most Valuable Player. He overcame the racism he encountered in college and was able to win over the Huskies' fans, albeit after suffering way more than he should have, because of his competence. Moon proved he should be judged by his performance on the field rather than the color of his skin. He planned to do the same in the NFL. As it turned out, though, Moon would have to wait much longer than he expected to clear the next hurdle.

—

In NFL history, the 1978 draft was the most significant for Black quarterbacks for two reasons: Doug Williams became the first Black passer selected in the first round, and Warren Moon–who later would become the only one to be enshrined in the Pro Football Hall of Fame–went undrafted. Their individual stories illustrated that the league was making progress in breaking from its racist thinking, but it was still far from the finish line. Moon wasn't surprised that the NFL passed on him.

"I found out prior to the draft that I probably wasn't going to get drafted as a quarterback, that other teams wanted to draft me at another position. But I had never played another position, and I felt like I could play quarterback at anyone's level," Moon said. "I had just shown that I could do it on one of the biggest stages in college football, in the Rose Bowl, being the MVP of that game. I played in one of the top conferences in the country and was the [co-]player of the year of that conference.

"I at least deserved an opportunity to show what I could do at the next level. Did I need to be a first round draft pick? Probably not. But even Doug, who was clearly the best player in that draft at the quarterback position, had to wait seventeen picks to get drafted by the Tampa Bay Buccaneers. [Buccaneers head coach] John McKay had African American quarterbacks when he was at USC. If Tampa Bay hadn't taken Doug, who knows if he gets drafted? But I believed in myself, and I was always willing to work hard to get to where I wanted to be."

Moon never shied away from a challenge, partly because he had many early in life. At only seven, Moon lost his father, also named Harold Warren Moon, who had died from liver and heart ailments. Moon's mother, Pat, was a nurse who worked long hours while raising Moon and his six sisters in Los Angeles, California. Moon was in the middle, with three sisters older than him and three sisters younger. In an effort to ease the load on his mom at home, Moon helped her cook, sew, iron, and housekeep. In high school, Moon maintained his commitment to his family first, deciding he would only play one sport because he had to work to help his mom financially.

For Moon, there was no doubt about it: Football would be that sport. Beginning in youth ball, it was clear to adults that Moon possessed extraordinary "arm talent," natural leadership skills, and the smarts to execute his coaches' vision. Moon knew it, too.

"I just enjoyed the position because of the leadership of it, because of everybody relying on you to make the right decision, to make the big play," Moon said. "I was blessed with a very good arm at a very young age. You know how they line kids up, and who's the fastest is going to be the running back, and who catches the best is going to be the receiver, and who throws the ball the best has a chance to be the quarterback? Well, that was me at quarterback when I was eleven. I gravitated to the position and embraced it."

While juggling his duties in the household and on the football field, Moon emerged as an all-city quarterback at Alexander Hamilton High in Los Angeles. He also stayed clear of the emerging gang culture in Los Angeles in the early 1970s. Moon had big plans for a bright future in football that didn't involve either the Crips or the Bloods.

But in the college recruiting process as a senior, Moon first tasted the disappointment he would experience on a much larger scale years later in the NFL draft. There just weren't as many opportunities as Moon figured there would be for him to play QB at major football powers.

"It was a disappointment, you know? I was wondering, 'What was it going to take?'" Moon said. "I put the work in. I got the accolades. I had proven I was good enough to get an opportunity to play quarterback at the next level. But it just wasn't happening for me.

"A lot of it had to do with the color of my skin and just the stereotypes that went along with African Americans playing quarterback at that time. You had to find the right situation and the right coach who believed in you."

After high school, Moon in 1974 enrolled at West Los Angeles community college. Promised the freedom to play quarterback and showcase his skills for college recruiters at the two-year institution located in Culver City, California, Moon hoped to draw more interest from NCAA programs. Moon, however, had no interest in playing for a community college for two years. He was determined to be one and done.

To spread the word that he was available, he mailed out his own game tapes to four-year colleges. He had a job in the athletic department, and when no one was around, he "borrowed" the coaching staff's game tapes, sending them out with the message that "it is important this tape be returned as soon as possible."[84]

In 1974, the football program at the University of Washington was moribund. The school had not appeared in a bowl game in 11 consecutive seasons.

Washington handed the ball to a new coach, Don James, who brought a fresh perspective. When one of his new assistant coaches, Jim Mora, told him about this great, overlooked quarterback playing at a community college in California, James listened. Washington was the first school to express interest, assuring Moon he would have a fair chance to win the quarterback job as soon as he hit campus. This was not a lie. Before the team had finished double sessions in his first weeks of practice, Moon was the starter.[85]

The problem was that he won the job over Chris Rowland–an incumbent, a senior, and, worse yet, a Washington native. The Huskies were still perennially low in the Pac-8 standings, doomed to extending their run of failure before James's rebuilding program could take hold. Shouldn't the local kid at least have a chance to play? Amid the bad feelings it became easy to put Moon's face on the team's failure. An easy target, a Black face.[86]

During the hard times, and Moon had many in Seattle, James kept his word: Moon was his guy. Without James's support, Moon's football story likely would have ended far short of the Pro Football Hall of Fame.

"He was the coach I needed, especially at that time," Moon said. "I believed I could play major college football, and he believed it, too. Although I wasn't the biggest guy or the fastest guy, I could throw the football. I could lead. Don James saw that.

"He saw something in me that a lot of other people didn't see. He stuck with me through some really hard times, a really rough stretch, early in my career at the University of Washington. His confidence in me helped me persevere and go on to have a pretty successful career in this game."

All quarterbacks would prefer to play under head coaches who believe in them as much as James believed in Moon. Having an ally in the boss is never a bad thing. Such relationships, however, are rare. Often, quarterbacks and assistant coaches, especially QB coaches, form the strongest bonds. They work closest with passers while head coaches, effectively CEOs, are involved in every aspect of preparing teams weekly. At all levels of football and especially in the NFL, many head coach–QB relationships could be described as strained at best. While leading the Pittsburgh Steelers to four Super Bowl titles in the 1970s, head coach Chuck Noll and quarterback Terry Bradshaw, both members of the Pro Football Hall of Fame, were at loggerheads throughout the franchise's dynastic run. The Steelers excelled despite their friction, the team having left an indelible mark on NFL history. At the University of Washington, James was the advocate Moon needed in college. But entering the draft after his senior season with the Huskies, Moon needed a powerful NFL rabbi. He didn't have one.

—

Moon didn't wait for the NFL to shun him. Before the 1978 draft, he signed with the Edmonton Eskimos, heading to Canada like so many Black quarterbacks before him. Eventually, he would leave the Canadian Football League as its all-time most accomplished passer.

The quarterback who supposedly wasn't good enough to play in the NFL racked up unheard-of passing numbers while helping Edmonton, located in the capital city of the Canadian province of Alberta, win five consecutive league championships. In 1982, Moon became the first professional QB to pass for at least 5,000 yards in a single season. Moon was having the time of his life. Sort of.

"There were two things running through my mind," Moon said. "I mean, I loved the situation. I was in a city where we're winning, we had a great football team, great atmosphere, and the people loved us. Was there some homesickness? Yeah, there was. I was up there alone my first three years. I wasn't married at the time. You're in another country and learning a new culture, and all those things that go along with it.

"On the other hand, as I started to really be successful in Canada, I'm thinking, 'I can play with those guys in the NFL and I'm not getting the chance.' And every time I watched a game on television, I was thinking the same thing, 'I'm good enough to play in that league.' But the only way you can really prove that is by actually playing against the best players in the world. And the best players were in the NFL."

The second time Moon showed interest in the NFL, the feeling was mutual. His availability entering the 1984 season ignited a bidding war. The Houston Oilers emerged victorious, luring Moon to the Lone Star State with a five-year contract for about $6 million–at the time the richest deal in league history. Moon's first three seasons with the Oilers were rough. Despite possessing exceptional arm strength and a work ethic second to none, Moon had a new league to learn. Each season, Moon had more interceptions than touchdowns, including a league-high 26 in 1986. In his first 45 starts, Moon had an awful record of 12–33.

Once he made the transition, though, Moon proved he was worth the money.

During both the 1990 and 1991 seasons, Moon led the NFL in passing yards, producing almost 9,400 combined. In 1990, Moon was chosen the Associated Press Offensive Player of the Year. He was selected to nine Pro Bowl teams. For a long stretch in the 1990s, Moon was as good as any passer in the game.

"Man, Warren was a great quarterback," said Doug Williams, Moon's close friend. "He didn't get a chance to come right into the league, but once he finally got in, there was no doubt about how good he was.

"You couldn't deny it because he went out there and did it. You saw it with your own eyes. And I'll tell you this: You better believe there were a lot of teams that wished they hadn't passed on Warren the first time."

In Texas, however, success didn't immunize Moon from facing racism.

Even as Moon led the Oilers to six playoff appearances during a seven-year stretch–he was a Pro Bowler each of those seasons as well–in the late 1980s and early 1990s, the tension was omnipresent. If the team won and Moon played well, he was the Oilers' quarterback. If Moon played poorly and Houston lost, he was its Black quarterback. Or worse. Much worse.

"I couldn't hear most of it because I was playing, but my wife and kids would hear things in the stands," Moon said. "It's tough when you're winning, and when you're doing things in the community, to have your family hear you being called the N-word after a bad play. But you use it as an opportunity to teach your children about life. And you never let it stop you."

Moon kept on rolling through a 17-year NFL career with Houston, Minnesota, Seattle, and Kansas City. With Minnesota, Moon made his final Pro Bowl team at 41. Moon's critics point to his lack of a

Super Bowl title as evidence he shouldn't be considered as one of the NFL's all-time greats. Winning a Super Bowl is the pinnacle of team success in the NFL. For a quarterback, a team's on-field leader, reaching that milestone is a legacy-defining achievement. In the minds of many NFL observers, earning a Super Bowl ring is the most important metric in determining the greatness of a QB. The ring, as it goes, is the thing. It's interesting that many of those same people are quick to laud other Pro Football Hall of Fame QBs who also lack Super Bowl-winning credentials. One wonders: What differentiates Moon from Dan Marino, Fran Tarkenton, and Dan Fouts?

"Teams win playoff games, teams lose playoff games. Teams win Super Bowls, and teams lose Super Bowls," Moon said. "But as a quarterback, you carry a lot of that blame. You carry a lot of that glory, just because of the position you play. I understand that part of it.

"And if people want to be critics and try and pick something out of your career, that's about the only thing they can really pick out of my career. But other than that, I did everything that was expected of me and more, and I'm really proud of my career, except for the fact that I don't have that ring on my finger that I would have loved to have had."

—

The gold jacket looked good on Moon. That's what the other Black quarterback trailblazers thought as they watched their friend step to the lectern on August 6, 2006, in Canton, Ohio, preparing to deliver his Pro Football Hall of Fame enshrinement speech. Moon and the other members of that year's class donned the jackets that signify those who receive them are the "gold standard" in the game of football. As far as Moon is concerned, Marlin Briscoe, James "Shack" Harris, and Doug Williams are worthy of wearing the iconic blazer, too.

Briscoe, Harris, and Williams had each played key roles in the rise of Black quarterbacks in major professional football in the United States. And although none were as prolific as Moon in their professional careers, they all shared a bond of achieving in the face of racism. During Moon's speech, he made sure the world knew what those three meant to him.

"A lot has been said about me as being the first African American quarterback into the Pro Football Hall of Fame," Moon said that day. "It's a subject that I'm very uncomfortable about sometimes only because I've always wanted to be judged as just a quarterback. But because I am the first and because significance does come with that, I accept that. I accept the fact that I am the first.

"But I also remember all the guys before me who blazed that trail to give me the inspiration and the motivation to keep going forward, like Willie Thrower, the first Black quarterback to play in an NFL game, like Marlin Briscoe, who is here today, the first to start in an NFL game. Like James Harris, who is here today, the first to lead his teams to the playoffs. . . . All of us did what we had to do to make the game a little bit better for the guys coming after us."

More than 15 years later, Moon still counts his relationships with Briscoe, Harris, and Williams among his most important.

"I'm very proud of them and just so glad that they've become really, really close friends," Moon said. "We've all gone through things, and we've all tried to help the guys who have come up behind us."

There's no doubt about it: Today's superstar Black quarterbacks have benefitted immensely because Briscoe, Harris, Williams, and Moon never took one step backward in the face of soul-crushing racism during their eras. And the NFL as a whole is better off because they shouldered so much so well. Without the accomplishments of Briscoe, Harris, Williams, and Moon, the NFL would have remained stuck on stupid even longer in its racist thinking about Black quarterbacks. With each achievement by a member of the group, the door was pushed open a little further for the Black QBs behind them. They eventually rushed through it. Now not only are

Black quarterbacks generating new excitement and fans for the league, they are helping to shoulder aside hoary prejudices that have lingered for centuries. Highly visible examples of Black excellence, be it in professional sports or other arenas, pound away at persistent notions about the supposed racial superiority of whites.

[11]

THE ULTIMATE WEAPON

IN REAL TIME, NEW York Giants linebacker Carl Banks told himself the play was over. He did his job. Of that much, Banks was certain. The rest of it? Well, Banks had no idea.

And no matter how often Banks replayed the events in his mind on October 10, 1988, he came to the same conclusion: Philadelphia Eagles quarterback Randall Cunningham should have gone down. Any quarterback whom he hit so hard shouldn't have been able to extend the play. Well, as it turned out, almost any.

Trailing 3–0 in the second quarter on their home field, the Eagles were at the Giants' 5-yard line. Cunningham took the snap, rolled right, and was pursued by Banks, who was among the best tacklers in the game. Banks slammed into Cunningham at about the 9–yet Cunningham didn't go down. Surprisingly, Cunningham, whose feet landed at the 12, placed his left hand on Veteran Stadium's artificial surface to stabilize himself while he firmly gripped the football in his right, popped up, and tossed a touchdown pass to tight end Jimmie Giles. Cunningham's stunner capped a 12-play, 80-yard drive. The most athletic quarterback the NFL had ever seen pulled off one of the most iconic plays in the history of Monday Night Football, which was the water-cooler topic the next morning. Banks, who was briefly frozen in disbelief on his knees while the Eagles celebrated, became a reluctant costar in the signature play of Cunningham's career that has been memorialized on the internet.

"He went back, like, three yards. Three yards. It was a pretty damn good tackle. He was just better," said Banks, who more than 30 years later still shakes his head in disbelief while recalling the absurdity of it all. "I mean, that's not supposed to happen. But with Randall . . . he did a lot of things that weren't supposed to happen."

—

Randall Wade Cunningham was the NFL's first superstar dual-threat quarterback, a prolific runner and passer whose game highlights have withstood the test of time. During a 16-year career, Cunningham, 6 foot 4 and deceptively strong despite his lanky frame, accumulated victories and oh-wow plays in bunches. Long before Michael Vick– who in 2001 became the first Black quarterback selected No. 1 overall in the NFL draft–Russell Wilson, Cam Newton, Colin Kaepernick, and Lamar Jackson would connect with receivers on picturesque deep balls and leave would-be tacklers grasping at air, Cunningham established that there may be benefits to having the best athlete on the field occupy the most important position. Cunningham was an outside-of-the-box player who established that the NFL needed to rethink its position on the QB "box."

Back in the late 1980s and early 1990s, when Banks was one of the game's best linebackers with the Giants and Cunningham was causing fits for opponents with the Eagles, the NFC East was the baddest division in professional sports. And whenever the Giants played the Eagles, Banks knew he would face the ultimate test in trying to contain Cunningham.

"When they would say he was 'the Ultimate Weapon,' he was truly the ultimate weapon," Banks said. "I don't think there was ever a quarterback who was harder to prepare for, or gave defensive players individually more problems or more concerns before the game even started. He was the guy you wanted to play against, but you also hated to play against because you knew he was just an incredible football player. I've played against Doug [Williams], I played against Warren [Moon], I played against Joe [Montana]. I don't think any one of those guys brought to a game the fear that Randall Cunningham put in a defense."

In the evolution of the Black NFL quarterback, Cunningham marked something new. For decades, the NFL dismissed the notion that Black men could be competent NFL starting quarterbacks, let alone elite signal-callers, because they supposedly lacked the smarts, heart, and leadership qualities needed to make it in professional football's best league. Then as a few Black men slowly broke through at the position in the late 1960s and mid-1970s, a new stereotype emerged: Black QBs were exceptional athletes, it was said, but they couldn't pass the ball to the right spots on the field. The knock on their passing ability was criticism of their intelligence writ large, the inference being that all Black quarterbacks weren't smart enough to decipher an opponent's defensive strategy.

Decision-makers used that racist excuse to pass on Black quarterbacks in the NFL draft unless they adhered to the long-standing practice of agreeing to switch positions after being drafted.

Former Minnesota Vikings and New York Giants quarterback Fran Tarkenton is widely credited with being the first successful dual-threat NFL passer. The Pro Football Hall of Fame member extended plays with his legs. But Tarkenton, who's white, wasn't summarily rejected by the NFL because he played in a manner not traditionally accepted at the position in the league. And he certainly never faced the specter of a potential position switch merely because of the color of his skin. But Tarkenton on his best days couldn't produce the type of on-field magic Cunningham could on his worst.

If receivers were well covered, it was common for Cunningham to take off for 20- and 30-yard runs. If there were holes in coverage, Cunningham regularly found them. He kept the pressure on. And within the pocket, Cunningham was a master of deception.

"He was a guy who was really successful with his legs, but he also had a cannon for an arm," said Moon. "He really was the first dual-threat quarterback.

"Some people would say Fran Tarkenton, but he was just more of a scrambler. Randall could scramble, but he could also run. Then after him you had Steve Young, Michael Vick, and the guys who came along later. But Randall really was the first to get that started."

—

The Eagles selected Cunningham in the second round (37th overall) of the 1985 NFL draft. He was the first quarterback chosen in the draft class. Cunningham had been a standout quarterback and All-American punter at the University of Nevada, Las Vegas. Born and reared in Santa Barbara, California, Cunningham strongly considered attending the University of Southern California. Sam Cunningham, Randall's older brother, was an All-American fullback for the Trojans in the 1970s and then a Pro Bowler for the New England Patriots. Beginning with Willie Wood in 1957, USC had a long history of permitting Black men to play quarterback.

Wood was the first starting African American passer in what is today the Pac-12 Conference. After being switched to defensive back in the NFL, Wood became one of the greatest safeties in NFL history and is enshrined in the Pro Football Hall of Fame. Wood opened the door for USC's Jimmy Jones, who in 1969 became the first Black quarterback to appear on the cover of *Sports Illustrated.*

So Cunningham, who had been a star quarterback at Santa Barbara High and was set on playing that position in college, would have been following an established line at USC. Although USC coaches thought they had recruited well at quarterback during that period, none of the school's passers were in Cunningham's class. He believed them when they promised he would have a legitimate shot to earn the starting job eventually, which even during the early 1980s wasn't the case for Black quarterbacks at all or maybe even most schools, but he was convinced that playing time would come earlier at UNLV.

"In high school, I think I was kind of in denial about it, just the whole thing about being Black and playing quarterback at a time when there weren't really a lot of Black quarterbacks," Cunningham said. "I didn't want to look at the color of my skin and say that I can't do something just because other people believe that you don't fit a certain role. I never really became [concerned] about it or worried about having a lack of opportunities. I just figured, 'Hey, let me just work hard enough so that I can achieve.' When USC started to recruit me, I was head over heels for USC. My brother went there, I wanted to go there.

"But I had to use wisdom. UNLV had an African American quarterback who called his own plays. The school had a great coach, and there were three senior quarterbacks. I saw a real opportunity there. Not just to play early at UNLV, but also to have the freedom to really grow and become the best player I could be. As soon as I saw what I could do at UNLV, USC was no longer an option for me. And the way the people treated me in Nevada was great. Most people gave me respect. It wasn't about my color. And so I was able to make a wise decision back then, which would catapult me to being the first quarterback selected in my [draft] year."

While leading the Rebels, Cunningham had his first experience with overt racism.

"When I got into college and we were at a [road] game, someone called out the N-word as I was walking. I wasn't accustomed to that in Santa Barbara. I was like, 'Wow. That's weird,'" Cunningham said. "Most of the time back home, I just didn't think about it [racism]. I turned a blind eye to it. And, again, with being a quarterback, I just made up my mind that it wasn't going to be something that stopped me from getting to where I wanted to be. That's the way my parents brought me up. I always heard their voices, 'If you want something in life, you have to go earn it.' You just do the work and prove yourself."

He did, making it to the NFL. And just as in college, Cunningham in the NFL would continue to experience issues because of the combination of his race and the position he played.

"When I got to the NFL it was: 'How do you feel being a Black quarterback in the NFL?'" Cunningham said. "I kind of wanted to push that question off to the side, because I really didn't want to deal with it.

"I wasn't the breakthrough person for African Americans. I was just another person trying to get the job done. So I basically told them [reporters], I said, 'Well, being in South Philadelphia, I thought I was Italian.' And they laughed, but that was kind of the end of that. Then everything else basically was based on my play and how I did things. . . . That's always the way I wanted it. Judge me on my performance."

That's a wonderful notion in theory. But in reality, in Philadelphia during the 1980s, Cunningham knew most Eagles fans would view his performance, at least partly, through the prism of race. His race could no more be overlooked than could his sprinter's speed or ability to throw pinpoint passes with a flick of his right wrist. All of it made Cunningham, well, Cunningham. And if US history tells us anything, Black men, and people of color in general, don't get to determine how they're defined.

Unlike James "Shack" Harris and Doug Williams, Cunningham didn't grow up in the Jim Crow South. In Santa Barbara, Cunningham didn't encounter the Los Angeles inner-city issues that Moon navigated. Cunningham's big brother starred at one of the nation's traditional football powers and was a longtime NFL player. Although it would be unfair to say Cunningham had a sheltered childhood on matters of race, he did not experience the same struggles as the Black quarterback pioneers who came before him. Cunningham would be the first to acknowledge he had a lot to learn about what Williams and others faced. Williams was happy to show him.

The 1987 season was Cunningham's first as the Eagles' starter. Williams capped the season with his historic Super Bowl performance in leading Washington to a blowout victory over the Denver Broncos. Cunningham attended the game at Jack Murphy Stadium. He stuck around following all of the post-Super Bowl hoopla, seeking to shake Williams's hand and give him an "attaboy." The meeting launched a 30-plus-year friendship and provided Cunningham with a new frame of reference about the struggles of Black quarterbacks through the years. After sharing a moment at the Super Bowl, the two men bonded. Williams invited Cunningham to spend some time with his family in Williams's hometown of Zachary, Louisiana. It was one of the best trips of Cunningham's life.

"When I met his people and saw his upbringing, I was like, 'Man, this is different,'" Cunningham said. "And he told me stories. So he paved the way for me in more ways than just playing. Just by actually taking me to his hometown, and getting to see and hear about how he grew up, it really helped me understand a lot of what he had to deal with. He was paving the way for me and guys after me, not just in the NFL but also in college.

"The things that a lot of African Americans went through and what they saw with their families in the South . . . They went through things that were a whole lot more difficult than anything I faced. That's why I would never claim I paved the way. There were people who came before me, so I could never take the credit for that. What Doug did before me helped me get to Philadelphia. He was a pioneer. Not me."

Black quarterbacks are not monolithic. The have varied life experiences, which are influenced by events where they're reared. Being a kid from Southern California, who was not scarred by the overt racism encountered by so many Black passers who came of age in the Jim Crow South, Cunningham never viewed his skin color as a sword or a shield in the perpetual battle for racial equality. And it wasn't necessarily a fight he felt qualified to participate in. The pioneers from the 1960s–Eldridge Dickey, Marlin Briscoe, and James Harris–shouldered the burden for generations of Black passers denied opportunities before them and for the QBs who would come after them. They viewed it as their calling. By the time Cunningham reached the NFL in the mid-1980s, he was not a trailblazer. Cunningham did not feel pressure to uplift an entire race, which could be viewed as progress. A modicum of it anyway.

—

Throughout Cunningham's tenure in Philadelphia, the Eagles had strong teams. In three consecutive seasons from 1988 through 1990, they finished either first or second in the NFC East and qualified for the postseason. Unfortunately for Cunningham and the Eagles, they went 0–3 in the playoffs during that span. Eagles fans were also frustrated that during Cunningham's 11 seasons in Philadelphia (1985–95), the Eagles' division rivals–the Dallas Cowboys, the New York Giants, and Washington–won six Super Bowl championships.

As is usually the case for players toward the end of their time with a franchise, Cunningham battled injuries and was benched for performance. The team's fans never fully appreciated Cunningham's contributions. Cunningham retired after the '95 season. It seemed

Marlin Briscoe *(Born September 10, 1945. Played in the AFL/NFL from 1968 through 1976.)* As a rookie with the Denver Broncos in 1968, Briscoe became first starting Black quarterback in the game's modern era. After racism ended his career as a QB, Briscoe became a top wide receiver. He was a member of two Miami Dolphins Super Bowl-winning teams, including the franchise's 1972 team–the only team in league history to win all its games.

Randall Cunningham *(Born March 27, 1963. Played in the NFL from 1985 through 1995. After sitting out the 1995 season in retirement, Cunningham returned to the NFL in 1997 and played again until 2001.)* Nicknamed "the Ultimate Weapon," Cunningham was both a star passer and runner. During the 1990 season, Cunningham passed for nearly 3,500 yards with 30 touchdown passes and rushed for 942 yards with five touchdowns while leading the NFL with an 8.0-yard rushing average. At 35, Cunningham was selected as a first-team All-Pro for the only time in his career.

Eldridge Dickey *(Born December 24, 1945. Died May 22, 2000. Played in a total of 18 games, starting two, over four seasons in the AFL/NFL.)* The first Black quarterback chosen in the first round of professional football's modern draft, Dickey was selected 25th overall by the AFL's Oakland Raiders in the 1968 NFL/AFL common draft. The Raiders moved Dickey, a star signal-caller in college at HBCU Tennessee State, to wide receiver. That was a common practice during that era, because Black men were not considered capable of playing QB in the pros. His spirit broken by the move, Dickey never fulfilled his immense promise.

Joseph Gilliam Jr. *(Born December 29, 1950. Died December 25, 2000. Played in the NFL from 1972 through 1975.)* Gilliam was a prolific passer and showman at HBCU Tennessee State. He had a great nickname: "Jefferson Street Joe." In Nashville, Jefferson Street, a boulevard near the Tennessee State campus, is considered the historic center of the city's Black community. Selected by the Pittsburgh Steelers in the eleventh round of the 1972 NFL draft, Gilliam went 4-1-1 as the team's starting QB early during the 1974 season. Benched after running afoul of head coach Chuck Noll over his play-calling and substance abuse, Gilliam was replaced by Terry Bradshaw, who went on to help Pittsburgh win four Super Bowl titles. Gilliam was a backup on the Steelers' 1974 and '75 Super Bowl championship teams. Released after the '75 season, Gilliam never again played in the NFL.

James "Shack" Harris (*Born July 20, 1947. Played in the AFL/NFL from 1969 through 1981.*) Harris's nickname is short for Meshach, the biblical figure who maintained his faith under dire circumstances. Selected in the eighth round of the 1969 AFL/NFL common draft, Harris was the first Black quarterback to start a season opener. He was the first Black quarterback to start and win an NFL playoff game, the first Black quarterback to play in the Pro Bowl, and the first Black quarterback to be selected Pro Bowl MVP. After his playing career ended, Harris became a successful player-personnel executive.

Lamar Jackson *(Born January 7, 1997.)* Selected by the Baltimore Ravens with the final pick in the first round of the 2018 NFL draft, Jackson quickly made his mark in the league as both a runner and a passer. In 2019, Jackson finished his breakthrough sophomore season with a haul of major hardware: He won both the Associated Press and Pro Bowl most valuable player awards. Jackson–selected the 2017 Heisman Trophy winner while at the University of Louisville–became only the second player to win the AP MVP award unanimously, as well as the second-youngest player ever to be given the honor.

Colin Kaepernick *(Born November 3, 1987. Played in the NFL from 2011 through 2016.)* A successful passer and runner, Kaepernick is best known for reigniting the protest movement in sports and having his playing career cut short because of it. While with the San Francisco 49ers during the 2016 NFL season, Kaepernick first sat on the bench and then kneeled during the playing of "The Star-Spangled Banner" before games to shine a light on systemic oppression and police brutality. After that season, no teams signed Kaepernick, who helped San Francisco reach Super Bowl XLVII and ranks among the league's best passers ever in touchdown-to-interception ratio. Kaepernick alleged that owners conspired to end his playing career because of political beliefs. In 2019, the civil rights icon settled his collusion grievance against the NFL.

Patrick Mahomes *(Born September 17, 1995.)* Mahomes, selected by the Kansas City Chiefs in the first round of the 2017 NFL draft, has set a new standard for young quarterbacks. He holds the distinction of being the youngest passer to have a Super Bowl title, a Super Bowl MVP award–having accomplished both of those feats at 24–and a league MVP award. He was selected the 2018 winner by the Associated Press. He's also the youngest quarterback to start in four AFC title games, as well as four in a row.

Donovan McNabb *(Born November 25, 1976. Played in the NFL from 1999 through 2011.)* The Philadelphia Eagles selected McNabb with the second overall pick in the 1999 NFL draft. A six-time Pro Bowler, McNabb led Philadelphia to five NFC championship games and Super Bowl XXXIX.

Warren Moon *(Born November 18, 1956. Played in the NFL from 1984 through 2000.)* The only Black quarterback enshrined in the Pro Football Hall of Fame, Moon wasn't selected in the 1978 NFL draft. Despite being the co-player of the year in his college conference and leading the University of Washington to a Rose Bowl victory as a senior, Moon still had to prove himself in the Canadian Football League. After his prolific career in Canada, Moon joined the NFL's then-Houston Oilers. Following a transition period, Moon became one of the NFL's most productive passers. In 2006, the nine-time Pro Bowler was inducted into the Hall of Fame. He's also a member of the Canadian Football Hall of Fame.

Kyler Murray *(Born August 7, 1997.)* The Arizona Cardinals selected Murray first overall in the 2019 NFL draft. After winning the 2018 Heisman Trophy while starring for the University of Oklahoma, Murray was selected the 2019 Associated Press Offensive Rookie of the Year. He's a two-time Pro Bowler.

Fritz Pollard *(Born January 27, 1894. Died May 11, 1986. Played in the NFL from 1920 through 1926.)* Pollard was an NFL pioneer in many roles. He was the league's first Black player, first Black quarterback, first Black All-Pro, and first Black coach. Chosen as an All-Pro running back after the league's inaugural season, Pollard was enshrined posthumously into the Pro Football Hall of Fame in 2005.

George Taliaferro *(Born January 8, 1927. Died October 8, 2018. Played in the NFL from 1949 through 1955.)* In seven NFL seasons, Taliaferro played seven positions: quarterback, running back, wide receiver, punter, kick returner, punt returner, and defensive back.

Willie Thrower *(Born March 22, 1930. Died February 20, 2002. Played in the NFL in 1953.)* No quarterback ever had a cooler name: Willie Thrower. On October 18, 1953, Thrower became the first African American to play quarterback exclusively following the unofficial 12-year ban on Black players from 1934 to 1946. Then a Chicago Bears rookie, Thrower replaced starting quarterback and future Hall of Famer George Blanda in a 35–28 loss to the San Francisco 49ers. Thrower completed 3 of 8 passes for 27 yards. He played only one season in the league.

Michael Vick *(Born June 26, 1980. Played in the NFL from 2001 through 2006. After being released from jail, he returned to the NFL from 2009 through 2015.)* In the 2001 NFL draft, the Atlanta Falcons made Vick the first Black quarterback selected first overall in the history of the process. A dual-threat star for most of his first six seasons with the Falcons, Vick missed the 2007 and 2008 seasons while incarcerated for 18 months in a federal prison for a dogfighting charge. Once the game's highest-paid player, Vick revived his NFL career after being released from prison. While with the Philadelphia Eagles, Vick won the Associated Press 2010 NFL Comeback Player of the Year award.

Doug Williams (*Born August 9, 1955. Played in the NFL from 1978 through 1982. Played in the USFL in the 1984 and '85 seasons. Returned to the NFL in 1986 and played through 1989.*) In 1978, the Tampa Bay Buccaneers made Williams the first Black quarterback to be selected in the first round by an NFL team. While with the Washington Commanders in Super Bowl XXII, Williams took a sledgehammer to the racist myth that Black men lacked the intellect and leadership skills to help a team win a Super Bowl championship. In Washington's 42-10 rout of the Denver Broncos, Williams completed 18 of 29 passes for 340 yards with four touchdowns and one interception. He became the first Black quarterback to win a Super Bowl and the game's most valuable player award.

his football days were finished. Then Minnesota Vikings head coach Dennis Green called. Green believed that Cunningham, though clearly no longer the dominant athlete of his youth, still had something to offer. If Cunningham wanted a shot at a second act, Green was prepared to offer one. After sitting out the 1996 season, Cunningham joined the Vikings in 1997.

The 1998 season was the best of Cunningham's career. He led the league in passer rating and threw 34 touchdown passes with only 10 interceptions. The Vikings, with a top-notch receiving corps that included two future Pro Football Hall of Fame members—Cris Carter and then-rookie Randy Moss—went 15-1 in the regular season. Again, though, Cunningham experienced playoff disappointment: The heavily favored Vikings lost to the Atlanta Falcons in the NFC championship game. The next season, Cunningham struggled and was benched. He moved on to play for Dallas in 2000 and the Baltimore Ravens in 2001. Then he walked away for good. Cunningham isn't in the Hall of Fame. But he should be.

"Absolutely, one hundred percent, he should be in," said Banks, the New York Giants great. "The voters just don't give him the credit he deserves. He has never been appreciated by those people who never played against him. But people who played against him know how great he was. If you combine Cam Newton and Michael Vick, both of their skill sets, you still don't get Randall Cunningham."

[12]

THE 1990S AND THE ROAD TO NO. 1

THE PHONE CONVERSATIONS OCCURRED weekly during Steve McNair's senior year at Alcorn State University, Doug Williams continuing to make all the right calls long after his NFL playing days were over. Williams offered nothing more than whatever McNair needed–a sympathetic ear, a sounding board, or an advocate–one legendary HBCU passer supporting another still writing his story.

In the history of the NFL draft, no quarterback from an HBCU had been a top-10 overall selection. But as the 1995 event drew near, the buzz was that Steve "Air" McNair, Alcorn State's prolific passer, would break another barrier for Black quarterbacks. McNair placed third in balloting for the 1994 Heisman Trophy. Only one other HBCU quarterback has been a finalist for the prestigious award presented annually to college football's most outstanding player: Grambling State's Williams, in 1977.

Williams was the first Black QB selected in the draft's first round. After attending a game during McNair's freshman year at Alcorn State and then following his career closely, Williams predicted McNair would set a new mark in the draft–and leave a big one on the NFL.

"He wasn't the starter. That day, he came off the bench. But as soon as he got into that game, you knew right then that you had something special," Williams said. "I mean, you can just tell with certain guys.

"You can tell by the way they throw the ball. You can tell by the toughness they show. You can tell by how they respond to pressure. And you can tell by the way guys [teammates] respond to them. With Steve McNair, you could tell by it all."

___

On April 22, 1995, the Houston Oilers chose McNair with the draft's third overall pick. In the history of the NFL draft, which began in 1936, McNair became the then-highest-drafted Black quarterback. To this day, he remains the highest drafted offensive player from an HBCU. (In the 1974 draft, the Dallas Cowboys drafted star Tennessee State defensive end Ed "Too Tall" Jones first overall. Jones is the only player from an HBCU to be drafted higher than McNair.)

"Near from the moment I first saw him play, I was enthralled with him," former Oilers executive vice president and general manager Floyd Reese said.[87]

By 1994, the Oilers, who after the 1996 season would relocate to Tennessee and become the Titans, had a canyon-sized hole at quarterback. Believing Warren Moon's best days were behind him at 38, and that he could be adequately replaced by the other passers on their roster, the Oilers traded the perennial Pro Bowler to the Minnesota Vikings before the start of the 1994 season. The Oilers chose poorly.

Relying on a trio of ineffective signal-callers, Houston missed the playoffs for the first time since the 1986 season. They finished 2–14.

In his first season with the Vikings, Moon ranked third in the

NFL with 4,264 yards passing and eighth with a 61.7 completion percentage. He helped Minnesota reach the NFC playoffs and was named to his seventh consecutive Pro Bowl team, including his first representing the NFC. The next season, at 39, Moon kept rolling: He ranked third in the league with 4,228 yards passing, second with 33 touchdown passes, and completed 62.2 percent of his passes, ranking seventh. Again, Moon was named to the NFC Pro Bowl squad–his eighth straight Pro Bowl selection. As a member of the Seattle Seahawks in 1997, Moon, at 41, was named to his ninth Pro Bowl team.

The Oilers believed McNair was the right quarterback to redeem their bad judgment in pulling the plug on Moon too early and lead them back to the playoffs. As it turned out, that was sound thinking.

By his third season, the franchise's first in Tennessee, McNair was the starter. Just as he did at Alcorn State, McNair in the NFL quickly displayed the toughness and leadership qualities that inspired teammates to follow him. Strong at 6 foot 2 and 230 pounds, McNair stood firm in the pocket against the pass rush.

"First of all, he might have been the strongest quarterback to ever play this game," said Williams. "He played hurt, but you never knew it by the way he played. He wasn't a runner. He was a pure pocket quarterback who could run the football when things got tough. There's a big difference there. And the fact that he played in the pocket, but could also get out and make a play if he absolutely needed to, made him a hard guy for defenses to deal with."

In 1999, Tennessee reached the playoffs. The Titans advanced to the Super Bowl against the St. Louis Rams and were driving for a potential game-winning touchdown late in the fourth quarter.

On the game's penultimate play, with the Titans needing five yards for a first down on third down, McNair displayed all the qualities Williams first noticed when the then-teenager came off the bench as a freshman for Alcorn State. McNair made some nifty moves in the pocket to evade the Rams' pass rush, escaped the clutches of two would-be Rams tacklers, and completed a 16-yard pass to wide receiver Kevin Dyson for a first down on the Rams' 10-yard line. On the final play, with only six seconds remaining on the game clock, McNair completed another pass to Dyson at about the 5-yard line on the right side of the field. Running toward the middle of the field, Dyson stretched to break the plane of the goal line while being tackled but came up short as time expired. Final score: Rams 23, Titans 16.

Since 1957, the Associated Press NFL MVP award has been presented to the league's top player. Until 2003, no Black QB had received the honor. McNair, who, despite that heartbreaking near-miss loss, shared the award for that season with quarterback Peyton Manning of the Indianapolis Colts, wowed voters by leading the league in several statistical categories, including passer rating, which measures a passer's overall performance based on four metrics: completion percentage, yards per passing attempt, touchdown percentage, and interception percentage. McNair also established a personal-best with 24 touchdown passes while leading the Titans to a 12-4 record and an AFC wild-card playoff berth.

"Steve was one of a kind," said Reese, the former Houston Oilers' executive. "He meant everything in the world to us."[88]

During 11 seasons with the Oilers/Titans, McNair led the franchise to four playoff appearances and was selected to three Pro Bowl teams. With McNair on the back side of his career by 2006, the Titans traded him to the Baltimore Ravens, with whom he enjoyed a renaissance season. He played well and Baltimore finished 13-3 in winning the AFC North division, but McNair had a disappointing performance in a playoff loss to Indianapolis. At 34 heading into the 2007 NFL season, his body battered from 12 years of withering punishment, McNair could no longer hide his pain and excel as he once did. McNair played in only six games and announced his retirement following the season. In retirement, McNair struggled like so many players before him, unable to fill a void that results from missing the game and the fulfillment it provides on many levels.

McNair's life ended tragically: in a murder-suicide on Independence Day in July 2009. He was shot in his sleep by his mistress, who then took her own life. Some NFL observers believe that McNair's unseemly ending has hurt his candidacy for the Pro Football Hall of Fame. The theory being that voters are reluctant to honor McNair, despite his undeniable bona fides as a winner and a trailblazer, because honoring him would dredge up the unsettling circumstances surrounding his demise. However, at least one person enshrined in Canton, Ohio, believes McNair deserves to have a bronze bust in the building as well.

"He definitely should be in," said Moon. "That's how good he was when he played.

"He took a team to a Super Bowl, he shared an MVP, and his teams were [often] in contention at the end of the season. He won. I know the stuff off the field probably hurts him, but it shouldn't. It shouldn't even be a part of the discussion. His career was over when that happened."

———

Three young quarterbacks sat together during the final week before the 1999 NFL draft, reveling in having a rare moment of free time. A scheduling glitch had put them all in the same place for the first time in a long stretch, and Donovan McNabb, Akili Smith, and Daunte Culpepper seized the moment.

There was catching up to do. They shared stories about their experiences interviewing with clubs throughout the pre-draft process, about their never-ending media commitments, and, most important, about their hopes and dreams. But what made this meeting different was what came next: a discussion about how, together, they could help change the NFL for the better.

"I remember we were all kind of sitting there, laughing and joking, and the question was brought up: 'What if we all go high in the draft?'" McNabb said. "We just started talking about what that would mean for all of us to be [first-round picks]. We thought it could mean something. For the NFL, and for a lot of young African American players who wanted to play the position, and were told for so long that they couldn't, we thought it would mean something."

The 1999 draft marked the first time in NFL history that three Black quarterbacks–McNabb, Smith, and Culpepper–were selected in the opening round of the event. That seminal occasion signaled to the world that Black quarterbacks had overcome a narrative that never fit the facts.

Warren Moon recalled how he swelled with pride while hearing the names of McNabb, Smith, and Culpepper called out in the first round. He sensed something significant had changed.

"You can really point to 1999 as a year when you knew something was different," said Moon. "You've got to understand: It was unheard of to have three Black quarterbacks go in the first round. So to have teams invest so much in us, at the top of the draft . . . it was definitely a new day."

In the run-up to the draft, McNabb, Smith, and Culpepper were all considered top-rated prospects. McNabb was the biggest star of the group. A three-time Big East Conference Offensive Player of the Year at Syracuse, McNabb was taken second overall by the Philadelphia Eagles. Smith–the Pacific-10 Conference's 1998 Offensive Player of the Year–was in the running to be selected first by the Cleveland Browns despite playing only two seasons at Oregon. The Browns selected Kentucky's Tim Couch instead, and Smith wound up going third to the Cincinnati Bengals. Then there was Culpepper, from the University of Central Florida. Although not as highly rated as McNabb and Smith, Culpepper nonetheless went 11th to the Minnesota Vikings.

"It was definitely special, no doubt," McNabb said. "Once our names were called, we were very excited. Obviously, we were excited for each other, but also for so many of those kids who were coming behind us. They saw the three of us all go in the first round. What do you think that did for kids who looked like us?"

According to Jason Campbell, it did a whole lot. Then a 17-year-old quarterback at Taylorsville High in Taylorsville, Mississippi, Campbell had a keen interest in the 1999 draft.

"It was just really encouraging to see all those guys go that high," said Campbell, a 2005 first-round pick who started 79 games for five NFL teams over nine seasons. "You knew that the NFL saw they had the potential to play the game at a high level. That was the only thing that mattered. And it was three. Three guys who were like me."

Ultimately, McNabb had the best career of the group. A six-time Pro Bowler, McNabb led Philadelphia to five NFC championship games and Super Bowl XXXIX under then–Eagles head coach Andy Reid, who played a key role in drafting McNabb.

In Cincinnati, Smith never found a good match. Out of the league by 2002, Smith finished his NFL career with a record of 3-14.

"Back then, [NFL coaches] were really adamant about developing the pocket passer, keeping everyone in the pocket," Smith said. "None of us were running 4.2 [in the 40-yard dash] like [Baltimore QB] Lamar [Jackson]. But we could have been doing the RPO stuff [run-pass option], some of the zone-read stuff way back in 1999. All of the time, I think about how things could have been different if [coaches] would have done for me what I see Baltimore did for Lamar."

Culpepper fared better. A three-time Pro Bowler with the Vikings, Culpepper led Minnesota to the playoffs twice and had a few big seasons statistically. He went on to have an 11-year career but never regained top form after leading the league in completions and yards passing during the 2004 season.

Williams, who had an outsize role in changing much of the thinking, albeit slowly, about whether Black men could win from the pocket in the NFL, said the varying degrees of success McNabb, Smith, and Culpepper experienced in the league doesn't diminish the overall importance of their impact as a group.

"What those guys did, what they showed, was that the NFL was looking at things with more of an open mind," Williams said. "So now you look at it, these teams won't hesitate to draft [multiple Black quarterbacks] in the first round.

"It's about guys getting opportunities, some guys succeeding and some guys not, but getting the same opportunities as other people to try. That's a good feeling. It shows we've come a long, long way."

——

The first haymaker connected on the opening play from scrimmage: Philadelphia Eagles quarterback Michael Vick launching a perfect deep ball to wide receiver DeSean Jackson that covered almost 61 yards in the air. Jackson did the rest on an 88-yard touchdown pass. And Vick wasn't even warmed up yet.

The Eagles scored touchdowns on their next four possessions, including two passing and one rushing by Vick. Stunned on its home field on November 15, 2010, Washington fell behind, 35–0, during a humiliating 59–28 loss. Vick finished with sparkling statistics in the signature performance of his career, passing for 333 yards and four touchdowns with no interceptions and rushing for 80 yards and another two touchdowns on only eight carries. Vick's six-touchdown showstopper on Monday Night Football was the talk of the league for weeks. His improbable comeback was complete: Not only was Vick back—he was better than ever.

Less than 18 months after serving 548 days in a federal prison for his role in a dogfighting operation, Vick once again terrorized opponents and wowed crowds with his powerful left passing arm and electrifying athleticism. Before his slide, Vick had led the Atlanta Falcons to the 2004 NFC championship game. He was the highest-paid player in the NFL. His stunning fall from grace led to an even greater feat. After his release from prison and signing with the Philadelphia Eagles and briefly serving as a backup to starter Donovan McNabb, who was traded to Washington before the 2010 season, he not only regained his pre-prison form, but exceeded it in the best season of his career, capped by being selected the Associated Press 2010 NFL Comeback Player of the Year. No player in the history of the award had previously returned from prison to win it. Again, Vick broke new ground, albeit he would rather not have been in the position to accomplish the Comeback Player of the Year feat.

"There are some things I went through, some things I would never want to go through again, that helped me to grow and mature as a man," Vick said. "Everybody has a journey, and mine was hard because of decisions I made. I accepted that. Obviously, there were a lot of hard days. I still kept believing in myself that I could [make it all the way back], but did I know I would? I can't honestly say I was always sure I would."

For Vick, the long climb back occurred in stages. He had too far to go to complete his journey in one continuous motion.

"Stage one was accepting it, knowing that, listen, I screwed up, I made a mistake, and somehow, some way this has to be corrected, but as of right now, I don't know how I can do it, but I know it's some challenges ahead that I'm not going to like, but I have to deal with," Vick said in reflection. "Step two was living in it and understanding that, listen, I'm in a place where I don't want to be, it was all self-inflicted and I accept it, and it hurts right now and I'm struggling, but I put my faith in God and not in man.

"Step three was just the whole belief in the people around me and the whole faith thing that I had. And believing in God centered me around people when I came home that gave me a different vision, a different structure, a different outline on what my life could look like in seven years. I looked at it and I accepted, and I said, 'Listen, I've pushed through the toughest parts of my life, and maybe there will be parts of my life that will be tougher. I know what I leaned on. I'm accepting the truth and faith,' and being proactive, making my life a reality in terms of what I wanted, and I did that. And that's where I'm at to this day, and I stand by it."[89]

With good reason, former longtime Washington defensive back DeAngelo Hall also doubted that his good friend would return to stardom.

As a teammate of Vick's in the NFL with the Atlanta Falcons before his stunning fall, Hall rooted for his buddy to get his life back on track. That's what was most important. Hall never entertained the thought of Vick recapturing his past glory, let alone becoming an even better quarterback, because that just didn't seem possible. Hall was never happier about being wrong.

"I was definitely shocked at what he did. It was amazing to watch," Hall said. "To go through the things that he went through, I don't think anyone could have ever expected him to get back to that level and then even surpass it. I mean, you just can't expect anyone to be off that long, with everything that he was dealing with, to get it all back.

"After watching him that first season out [of prison], I was like, 'Man, I don't know if he'll ever be the same guy.' Then watching him that next year, it was . . . it was amazing. A lot of people thought he would never be able to do it. A lot of people thought he was finished. And you can definitely understand why."

Vick's performance earned him selection to his fourth Pro Bowl team and reminded the league of how he initially burst onto the scene with Atlanta.

No Black quarterback had ever been chosen with the No. 1 overall pick until the Falcons traded with the then–San Diego Chargers to move up and select Vick first.

Jason Campbell, who would be a first-round draft pick in 2005 after quarterbacking Auburn University to a perfect 13-0 record as a senior, believes he and others later benefitted from the barrier Vick toppled.

"You've got to understand that, at that time, Mike Vick was the man," said Campbell. "We [younger Black quarterbacks] used to watch him play and be like, 'Man. Look at his game.' Just the way he played."

Said Vick: "I was just playing the way I played. But I knew it was different."

On the field, Vick dazzled while often improvising, playing unapologetically Black. Style, flamboyance, swagger–pick a word. Vick oozed them all. He was also in the right setting to display his full repertoire and have it embraced by fans.

Atlanta has long been a "Black mecca." Best known for being the cradle of the civil rights movement, the city also occupies a position of prominence in Black entertainment, being the home of superstar hip-hop artists and singers. Atlanta is a center of Black wealth, political power, and higher education. Vick knew his audience. He played with flair, gaining yards in chunks on long runs and using his powerful left arm to launch passes to every part of the field.

In doing so, Vick inspired Black folk, including some who lined up alongside him in the NFL.

On August 17, 2020, Jason Wright, a former NFL running back who ascended quickly in the business world after earning his MBA at the University of Chicago, was introduced as the new head of business operations for the Washington Commanders (then known as the Washington Football Team). Exactly one month before the NFL turned 100, Wright became the league's first Black team president. While teammates in Atlanta in 2004, Vick encouraged Wright to pursue his biggest dreams.

"I've been asked in various versions, 'How did you get to your role?' And I don't like answering it, but the question has forced me to think about it. Mike Vick being my quarterback as a rookie and heading into my second year made a big difference," Wright said. "The fact that the star player, the person who is calling the plays in the huddle, who is calling the audibles, literally directing and carrying the team, was a Black man, meant a lot to me. My personal experience was that he was a soft-spoken, gentle leader who knew how to command a huddle when he needed to.

"And as a young rookie who was struggling, he gave immense encouragement. Subconsciously I started to see, 'Oh, like, Black folks belong in and thrive in these roles, these types of leadership roles.' I already had a little bit of that from my parents and that expectation growing up that, 'Hey, you should be in all the spaces white folks are and these types of roles.' My experience in the NFL, starting out with this Black man as my quarterback, reinforced that. It gave me some of the boldness, gumption, et cetera, to jump into this position [leading Washington] without hesitation."

Vick has become a vocal animal rights advocate. He speaks often with children and teenagers, trying to help them stay on the right path. Hall, Wright, and many others who believe in the concept of redemption admire how Vick rebuilt his life and career.

"He went through some things, took responsibility, and tried to learn from it and grow," Hall said. "He got back on the field and tried to make a difference off the field. You have to respect that."

[13]

COLIN KAEPERNICK

NFL MEDIA REPORTER STEVE Wyche settled into his seat in the press box at Levi's Stadium in Santa Clara, California, on August 27, 2016, and prepared to watch the San Francisco 49ers play host to the Green Bay Packers during all-important Week 3 of the NFL's four-week preseason schedule. Traditionally, the league's head coaches structure that week as a dress rehearsal for the regular season. In penultimate preseason matchups, starters—most of whom are held out of the final tune-up to minimize risk of injury before the season kicks off in earnest—play past halftime, coaches declare winners in position battles, and all players are expected to show they're ready for the lid-lifters. With so much to digest and report, Wyche hunkered down for a long evening. It would wind up being longer than he could have ever envisioned. The events Wyche alone chronicled that night would thrust 49ers quarterback Colin Kaepernick into the uncommon position of being both a national hero and a national pariah, rock the NFL to its core, spark a long-running nationwide debate about the meaning of patriotism, inspire athletes to launch a new civil rights movement in sports, and provide the accelerant to ignite a culture war that the nation's next president would eagerly stoke.

An exciting quarterback capable of making big plays both passing the ball and running with it, Kaepernick, who had helped the 49ers reach the Super Bowl after the 2012 season, only his second in the NFL (they lost to the Baltimore Ravens, 34–31), had last been active in a game during November 2015. Placed on the injured reserve list that month because of a season-ending shoulder injury, Kaepernick would subsequently undergo surgeries on his left shoulder, left knee, and right thumb–yet another young worker whose body was battered in professional sports' most violent workplace. Following a long recovery period that included grueling rehab processes, Kaepernick was finally back and expected to play against the Packers. He seemed to be at the starting line of something new off the field, too.

While sidelined, Kaepernick, in a major change for him as well as a stark departure from acceptable behavior for any starting NFL signal-caller, utilized social media to actively weigh in on social justice topics. From January through June on Instagram and Twitter, he posted about civil rights leaders Martin Luther King Jr. and Malcolm X, famed boxing champion and global icon Muhammad Ali, Black Panther cofounder Huey P. Newton, and hip-hop artist Tupac Shakur. After Kaepernick in early June received medical clearance to resume practicing with the 49ers, his commentary that summer often focused on the increasing racial strife in the United States triggered by an alarming spate of high-profile killings of Black people by police, some of which were captured on video. Kaepernick made his position clear about Alton Sterling's death at the hands of two Baton Rouge, Louisiana, police officers; about Philando Castile's killing a day later by a Minnesota police officer in front of Castile's girlfriend and her four-year-old after a traffic stop; about Charles Kinsey–who was on his back on the ground with his hands up–being shot by police in

North Miami, Florida; and about the fact that there were no convictions of Baltimore Police Department officers in the death of Freddie Gray, who was arrested over possessing a knife and died after being injured while in police custody.

Throughout the league's history, quarterbacks have avoided becoming embroiled in controversial topics, especially those involving race. The reason is simple: As the highest-paid players and the faces of the game, they have too much to lose financially, both in their team contracts and endorsement deals. Of course, it's important to note that for the overwhelming majority of NFL history, Black men were prohibited from playing quarterback because of racism. Not that only Blacks are capable or permitted to comment on matters of race. But history proves that Blacks are much more likely than whites to risk speaking out about racial injustice because they have skin in the game. Literally.

It was nonetheless surprising to watch as Kaepernick took a strong, public stand in acknowledging America's history of systemic oppression and police brutality–without question third-rail topics for any NFL player, let alone a starting QB. At the time, Wyche, for one, believed something profound was happening with Kaepernick, who is the biological son of a white mother and an African American father and was adopted by a white couple at five weeks old.

"At the very least," said Wyche, who's also Black, "Kaep was finding his voice."

Actually, Kaepernick was experiencing something even more profound: his own racial awakening. The young man who was reared in Turlock, California, a region known for its dairy farms and a paucity of Black people, was undergoing a metamorphosis. After so many years spent wandering as an adolescent, searching to understand his Blackness while mostly alienated from Black folk, Kaepernick was now eager to raise a clenched fist and make a stand.

"Growing up with white parents, I moved through life with

their audacity of whiteness. I assumed their privilege was mine," Kaepernick said. "I was in for a rude awakening."[90]

Heading into the preseason game in August 2016, Wyche was focused squarely on whether Kaepernick, who was fighting to reclaim the 49ers' first-string spot after having been replaced by Blaine Gabbert, would regain his standing on the field.

"I was thinking about, 'Can Kap get his mojo back?'" Wyche said.

Shortly before kickoff, however, Wyche's perspective changed. Quickly.

—

Wyche's mobile phone rang. The caller had news to share.

Mike Garafolo, Wyche's NFL Media colleague, passed along a tip he received from a 49ers team source: Kaepernick did not stand for the playing of the national anthem, as is customary, before San Francisco's first two preseason games. Immediately, Wyche recalled a conversation he had months earlier while on assignment at a 49ers practice. A different San Francisco team source told Wyche that Kaepernick was taking courses to learn more about the Black experience in America. Then there was Kaepernick's activity on social media, which clearly spoke to Black and brown people who have had negative experiences with law enforcement. For Wyche, a picture was coming into focus: Kaepernick's cultural metamorphosis could have resulted in the passer taking a political stand about the anthem.

With kickoff only minutes away, Wyche's thoughts then turned to former NBA player Mahmoud Abdul-Rauf, who lost millions during the height of his playing career after deciding during the 1995–96 NBA season to not stand for the playing of "The Star-Spangled Banner." Abdul-Rauf viewed the American flag as a symbol of oppression and racism. Wyche wondered whether Kaepernick was embarking on a similar journey. On the lookout for Kaepernick as the anthem played at Levi's Stadium, Wyche, perched high above the field in the press box, struggled to locate the quarterback along the sideline. Then, as the anthem's final note faded, Wyche identified Kaepernick as he rose from the bench. "Okay," Wyche said to himself. "There's something going on here."

With the game just underway, it would be several hours before Wyche could interview Kaepernick about his pregame actions. Wyche had plenty of work to do before then. Formerly an ink-stained wretch on sports staffs at some of the nation's most prominent newspapers, Wyche had been a lead reporter on many major breaking sports stories. In 2000, as a reporter for the *Washington Post*, he covered Michael Jordan's surprising move to become a partial owner of the Washington Wizards. While with the *Atlanta Journal-Constitution* in 2007, he reported extensively on star quarterback Michael Vick's stunning downfall stemming from Vick's role in a dogfighting operation. Increasingly, as the pieces came together that night at Levi's Stadium, Wyche sensed he was on the biggest story of his career. But were any other reporters chasing it as well?

Wyche contacted his editors at NFL Media, telling them to be prepared for him to file a major story. Next on Wyche's to-do list: track down Bob Lange, 49ers vice president of communications. If other reporters observed Kaepernick sitting on the bench, the topic, undoubtedly, would have been raised in the postgame media availability with coaches and players. If no one broached the subject, however, Wyche preferred to interview Kaepernick privately. Lange agreed to the request, partly because of Wyche's relationship with Kaepernick.

Wyche first interviewed Kaepernick back in 2011 at a pre-draft showcase for college players who had completed their eligibility. The 6-foot-4, 230-pound Kaepernick dazzled NFL talent evaluators during weeklong practices leading to the Senior Bowl in Mobile, Alabama, displaying the passing and running skills that enabled him to terrorize opponents while starring at the University of Nevada. Kaepernick's statistics of 10,098 yards passing and 4,112 yards rushing are a testament to his versatility in college. He's the only quarterback in the history of Division I college football, which is comprised of the largest and most competitive schools in the National Collegiate Athletic Association, to reach those levels in a career. Intrigued by the tall QB with the eye-opening numbers, Wyche struck up several conversations with Kaepernick at the Senior Bowl, laying the foundation for a good working relationship that continued after the 49ers selected the two-time Western Athletic Conference Offensive Player of the Year with the fourth pick in the second round (36th overall) in the 2011 draft.

Fortunately for Wyche, Kaepernick was not asked about his decision to sit on the bench during the anthem. After the group news conference in a small auditorium ended, Kaepernick and Wyche walked out of the room together and into a hallway to talk about what happened. Just as Wyche suspected, Kaepernick was protesting during the anthem.

"I am not going to stand up to show pride in a flag for a country that oppresses Black people and people of color," Kaepernick told Wyche in the exclusive interview after the game. "To me, this is bigger than football and it would be selfish on my part to look the other way. There are bodies in the street and people [law enforcement officers] getting paid leave and getting away with murder."[91]

Kaepernick did not inform the 49ers of his plans beforehand or discuss his thinking with coaches or teammates. Angered by what he saw playing out on television, what he considered to be state-sanctioned crimes committed against Black and brown people, Kaepernick believed he had to protest it all in some way. Kaepernick wasn't seeking to draw attention to his protest, as evidenced by the fact that he neither consulted with anyone in the 49ers' organization nor made his intentions known publicly.

Initially, it was just something personal. There's always a right side of history–Kaepernick was determined to be on it.

"Standing there with him, just the two of us, I mean . . . he was very passionate," Wyche said. "I'm not saying it just because he was talking to me. Anyone who asked him, he would have given the same answer, I believe. This has been on his heart."

The 49ers provided Wyche with a statement for his report. It read, "The national anthem is and always will be a special part of the pre-game ceremony. It is an opportunity to honor our country and reflect on the great liberties we are afforded as its citizens. In respecting such American principles as freedom of religion and freedom of expression, we recognize the right of an individual to choose and participate, or not, in our celebration of the national anthem."[92]

The franchise's statement wasn't exactly a full-throated endorsement of Kaepernick's actions, and it made no mention of what the quarterback was protesting, but management at least acknowledged Kaepernick had the right to do what he did. During the opening moments of the ESPYs–an annual awards ceremony in which honorees are recognized for individual and team athletic achievement–broadcast a month prior to Kaepernick's protest, NBA superstars Carmelo Anthony, Chris Paul, Dwyane Wade, and LeBron James urged their fellow athletes to take a stand on social justice issues in response to the high-profile shootings.

"Generations ago, legends like Jesse Owens, Jackie Robinson, Muhammad Ali, John Carlos and Tommie Smith, Kareem Abdul-Jabbar, Jim Brown, Billie Jean King, Arthur Ashe, and countless others, they set a model for what athletes should stand for," Paul, one of the best point guards in NBA history, said on July 13, 2016. "So we choose to follow in their footsteps."

Speaking out onstage at the outset of an awards show, however, is much different than protesting during the national anthem before a major sporting event.

—

Under the rules in place at the time in the NFL's game operations manual, players were not required to stand for the anthem. During the anthem, "players on the field and bench area *should* [emphasis added] stand at attention, face the flag, hold helmets in their left hand and refrain from talking," according to the key passage on the issue in the manual. Moreover, under US labor law, NFL owners could not take retaliatory action against players for demonstrating during the anthem. The right to protest peacefully is protected by the Constitution. For tens of millions of Americans, however, none of that matters. To them, any form of protest during the anthem is considered unpatriotic.

As his lengthy interview with Kaepernick wound down that night at Levi's Stadium, Wyche realized the gravity of the situation of Kaepernick's own making. During the 1995–96 NBA season, Abdul-Rauf's protest initially went unnoticed as well, as he stretched or remained inside the locker room during the playing of "The Star-Spangled Banner." Once a reporter noticed and questioned Abdul-Rauf, the situation, not surprisingly, exploded.

In addition to his concerns about what the United States flag represented to him, Abdul-Rauf, known as Chris Jackson before he converted to Islam, said standing for the anthem would conflict with his Muslim faith. "You can't be for God and for oppression. It's clear in the Quran, Islam is the only way," he said at the time. "I don't criticize those who stand, so don't criticize me for sitting."[93]

On March 12, 1996, the NBA suspended Abdul-Rauf for one game, citing a rule that players must line up in a "dignified posture" for the anthem. It cost him almost $32,000 of his $2.6 million salary.

The players union supported Abdul-Rauf, and he quickly reached a compromise with the league that allowed him to stand and pray with his head down during the anthem. But at the end of the season, the Nuggets traded Abdul-Rauf, who averaged a team-high 19.2 points and 6.8 assists, to the Sacramento Kings. His playing time dropped. He lost his starting spot. After his contract expired in 1998, Abdul-Rauf couldn't get so much as a tryout with any NBA team. He was just 29 years old. After the NBA shunned him, he played a season in Turkey, making about half of the $3.3 million he earned in the last year of his NBA contract. Abdul-Rauf caught on with the NBA's Vancouver Grizzlies in 2000–01 but played only 12 minutes per game. He never got another NBA opportunity, playing another six seasons in Russia, Italy, Greece, Saudi Arabia, and Japan before retiring in 2011.[94]

Although Wyche is a journalist, he's a Black man first. And as a Black man and a father of sons, the eldest of whom is only a few years younger than Kaepernick, Wyche felt almost a paternal obligation to make sure the quarterback fully understood the potential ramifications of his stand. Once Wyche's story was posted on the internet, Kaepernick's life would forever be changed.

Abdul-Rauf's career was destroyed. He received death threats by mail and telephone, and the letters "KKK" were spray-painted on a sign near the construction of his new house, five miles outside his hometown of Gulfport, Mississippi. Abdul-Rauf's then-wife did not want to move into a 2,800-square-foot residence the couple was building, and in 2001, while the structure was vacant and for sale, it was destroyed by fire.[95]

As Wyche and Kaepernick spoke in a corridor in the bowels of Levi's Stadium in 2016, Wyche looked into Kaepernick's eyes and saw pain—and the determination to move to ease it. He listened to Kaepernick's words and heard a young man who, as Wyche surmised, had found his voice and was eager to speak on behalf of the voiceless. Standing only a few feet from Kaepernick and discussing with him the pros and cons of an undertaking that would be perilous for the passer personally, Wyche got it: Kaepernick was all in. Kaepernick understood he was risking losing future earnings from the NFL and potential endorsement deals. Kaepernick realized that he would be accused of being anti-American. And so be it, Kaepernick told Wyche, because having all the money in the world and being respected for toeing the wrong line isn't worth anything if one is ashamed to look in the mirror each day.

"He was like, 'Yeah. I get it.' And at first, I pushed back. I was like, 'No, man. This is going to be big,'" Wyche said. "We talked about Abdul-Rauf, who, at the time, he had not met. I told him that I remembered when Abdul-Rauf did what he did and what happened. Just all of the backlash. When you step into the don't-tread-on-me world in America [people who hold conservative or far-right views and who vociferously oppose actions they view as being anti-American], and you don't honor the flag in a certain way . . . a lot of people feel a certain way about that. And things can get bad. Things can get ugly.

"But he kept saying, 'I get it. I get it.' And I just came to understand that he did. He really did get it. He knew what he would face. He understood that there would be backlash. He understood he was risking a lot. He was definitely risking a lot more than most people would, especially when you think about everything he put on the line; what he could potentially lose. It's just that the backlash didn't matter to him as much as what he potentially could do to help people and, maybe, change the way some people think."

After asking Kaepernick so many important questions, Wyche punctuated the interview, one final time, by reiterating the most salient: "Are you sure about this?" The activist-quarterback didn't take one step backward.

Wyche returned to the press box, wrote his piece, and emailed it to his editors. Then he packed up his computer and began the trek back to his hotel room, where his wife and youngest son were sleeping. Wyche, though, only shut his eyes briefly. He was riding a reporter's wave of adrenaline from a big scoop—as well as the unsettling knowledge that turmoil lay ahead for Kaepernick, the NFL, and America.

At 10:17 a.m. EDT on August 27, 2016, Wyche posted his report to Twitter. Shortly thereafter, predictably, all hell broke loose.

On social media, Kaepernick was roundly condemned as being unpatriotic. Many in the love-America-or-leave-it crowd demanded that the 49ers and the NFL take swift action to punish the ungrateful player who would protest against a country that had given him so much. The NFL took notice.

Being in tune with its fans helped the NFL become the most successful and powerful professional sports league in the known history of human existence. And at 345 Park Avenue, New York, NFL headquarters, the complexities of the problems presented by Kaepernick's protest were clear immediately. For team owners and top league decision-makers, Kaepernick's decision to sit during the anthem was tantamount to an act of betrayal. Among players, quarterbacks reap the lion's share of rewards from the game. On average, they're the highest-paid players and are well positioned to make the most money off the field in endorsements. As such, club owners view "franchise quarterbacks," the most elite players at the position, as their de facto partners in growing the game. In 1940, the NFL adopted a shield-based logo. All players are expected to "protect the shield," but quarterbacks are supposed to provide the first line of defense. NFL power brokers feared that Kaepernick's actions could do irreparable damage to the shield. But for the league, addressing the situation was fraught politically on two fronts.

Although NFL team owners would have preferred to mollify

their outraged fans by prohibiting Kaepernick from protesting, they simply couldn't do that. His form of protest did not violate league rules, and then there was the whole pesky issue about the rights afforded to citizens under the Constitution. Franchise owners also had to consider the myriad thorny issues dealing with matters of race. The NFL's on-field workforce is very Black: At the start of the 2020 season, 57.5 percent of players identified as Black or African American, according to research conducted by the Institute for Diversity and Ethics in Sport at the University of Central Florida. Optically, it would have been horrible for the NFL to attempt to punish a Black quarterback for using his platform to shine a light on killings of Black people. While team owners and top league decision-makers scrambled to chart a new course in the week Kaepernick's protest became public, they would soon have to contend with another major storm.

In the 49ers' fourth and final preseason game, Kaepernick altered his protest, kneeling during the anthem instead of sitting on the bench. Nate Boyer, an Army Green Beret veteran and a former college football player at the University of Texas who briefly played with the Seattle Seahawks during the 2015 preseason, contacted Kaepernick after watching news reports about Kaepernick's protest during the third week of the preseason. Boyer explained that taking a knee would be more respectful than sitting. In the military, soldiers often take a knee when honoring other fallen soldiers and during moments of silence.

Kaepernick agreed and decided that he would kneel during the anthem for the entire 2016 season. For the NFL, Kaepernick's change only made things worse. His fast-expanding legion of critics, presumably unaware of the solemnity associated with kneeling in the military, or merely looking for additional fuel for their anger, were even more outraged by Kaepernick's new approach. On the eve of the 2016 kickoff, it became clear Kaepernick would dominate the regular-season discussion. And just as many of the league's top brass feared, Kaepernick would not remain a lone voice in the wind for long.

San Francisco safety Eric Reid became the first player to kneel alongside Kaepernick. Then other 49ers teammates joined them. Like wildfire, the movement spread from team to team. Much to the frustration of club owners, listing how many players kneeled each week of the 2016 season became as commonplace for media outlets as reporting on the scores of games.

By the middle of the 2016 season, the NFL was immersed in a full-blown crisis. Outrage continued to be directed at Kaepernick for protesting–as well as the NFL for not stopping him. In the right-wing media echo chamber, Kaepernick became the face of all that was wrong with America. Polls indicated that millions of Americans were tuning out the NFL–though support for the protests largely fell along political lines–because of the Kaepernick-inspired movement that had spilled over into other professional sports leagues, the college ranks, and even high school sports. The NFL's television ratings dropped precipitously.

By early October 2016, the league's ratings had fallen 11 percent from the same period during the 2015 season. The significant slide set off alarms among the corner-office television executives in business with the NFL, who dole out billions to the league annually in anticipation of receiving a high rate of return on their investment in the form of boffo ratings. Television ratings are used to set ad rates for advertisers. For the NFL's television partners, the model doesn't work if the league fails to hold up its end. At league headquarters, the ratings drop, and media inquiries about the growing problem, stirred such concern that an internal memo was sent on October 6, 2016, to all 32 clubs, which was obtained by reporters, addressing the situation. And while the memo played down the obvious effects of the player protests–"no one factor can explain the ratings we've seen thus far this season," the memo read–the very existence of the document laid bare the undeniable truth: The Kaepernick-led movement was hurting the NFL.

And the league had another looming problem: president-elect Donald Trump. Fueled by a campaign in which he stoked white grievance, Trump won the Republican Party's nomination and, despite losing the popular vote to Democratic Party nominee Hillary Clinton by almost 2.9 million votes, won the Electoral College vote 304 to 227. On launching his candidacy, Trump said, "When Mexico sends its people [to the United States], they're not sending their best. . . . They're sending people that have lots of problems, and they're bringing those problems with us. They're bringing drugs. They're bringing crime. They're rapists. And some, I assume, are good people."

Yep. For Trump, the NFL protest movement was a gift.

It didn't matter to Trump that many NFL owners were in lockstep with his political views. Seven even donated at least $1 million to Trump's inaugural festivities. Kaepernick put a face on an issue that would enable Trump to rile up his base. And the fact that it was a Black face, well, all the better. Trump and his supporters framed the players' actions as anthem protests. Repeatedly, players explained they were not opposed to the anthem; they were protesting during the anthem to draw attention to their issues. It was definitely a distinction with a difference, which many opposed to the movement chose to ignore.

—

Early in the 2016 season, Kaepernick, having had little time in the preseason to unseat Gabbert as the 49ers' starting signal-caller, was stuck on the bench. But with the team at 1–4 after a four-game losing streak, San Francisco's coaching staff made a switch: Kaepernick would start Week 6 in a road game against the Buffalo Bills. Kaepernick had last started during a regular season game in

Week 8 of the 2015 season. With his only first-team reps that season coming the week the 49ers faced the Bills, Kaepernick looked every bit like someone still taking baby steps.

Kaepernick completed only 13 of 29 passes for 187 yards. On a busted coverage, he linked up with wide receiver Torrey Smith for a 53-yard catch-and-run touchdown. Kaepernick also led the 49ers in rushing with 66 yards and an 8.3-yard average. It made no difference for the woeful 49ers, who were routed, 45–16, in their fifth consecutive loss, part of an ignominious run in which they would lose 13 straight in a 2–14 season. Kaepernick getting back in the game was only a small part of the story.

Dressed like he'd come straight from a protest march, Kaepernick arrived at New Era Field dripping in Black pride. His signature Afro was picked all the way out. Under a black blazer, he wore a shirt adorned with an image of Muhammad Ali. Kaepernick finished the in-your-face outfit with black slacks and a pair of black-and-white Air Jordan high-tops. The Ali shirt brought it all together.

"He was someone who fought a very similar fight and was trying to do what is right," Kaepernick said of Ali that day in 2016. "For me to have someone like that come before me, that is huge. He is someone who helped pave the way for this to happen. What he did, and what he stood for, people remember him more for that than they do as a boxer. I have to try to carry that on. Fight that same fight until we accomplish our goal."

And for what Kaepernick stood for, he remained under siege all day at Orchard Park, New York. Just off of stadium property, vendors sold anti-Kaepernick shirts. In one image depicted on a shirt, Kaepernick was in the crosshairs of a rifle scope, one media outlet reported. Inside the stadium, Kaepernick was booed vociferously, and fans directed chants of "U-S-A, U-S-A" at him. Kaepernick retained San Francisco's No. 1 job for the remainder of the season in which he would endure similar mistreatment on the road.

In a packed room at the stadium after the game, Kaepernick stood in front of reporters and a bank of television cameras, reiterating much of what he told NFL Media's Wyche when they spoke privately two months earlier: He would not back down.

"Like I said from the beginning: I knew the consequences of what could come from this," he said. "I was prepared for that. . . . The message carries weight because people realize what's happening and that it is something that needs to be addressed.

"People's lives [are] being taken and people's lives [are] being affected by this on a daily basis. More and more conversations are happening that need to happen so, ultimately, we can address this issue and create change."

As it turned out, Kaepernick would do most of his work as a change agent in exile.

Under new leadership in the front office and on the field after the 2016 season, the 49ers planned to release Kaepernick, who wasn't ideally suited to direct the incoming coaching staff's style of offense. Kaepernick had the right to opt out of the final, nonguaranteed year of his contract, which he did, hoping to get a jump on finding a new home. One never materialized. The Baltimore Ravens supposedly kicked the tires. Word was the Seattle Seahawks had some interest in Kaepernick. Over the years, there were rumblings that Kaepernick was on several teams' short lists of the best available free-agent passers. But his name never came off of them. Just like that, Kaepernick was gone from the NFL.

—

At only 29 and physically sound, Colin Kaepernick got the boot from the NFL. Let that sink in. A mobile quarterback, who in his last five seasons started in two NFC championship games and one Super Bowl, was shown the door. And it was hermetically sealed behind him.

Kaepernick was not charged with any crimes. He was not accused of violating any aspect of the league's collective bargaining agreement. He did nothing more than exercise his right to protest peacefully, which is protected by the Constitution. Yet, NFL decision-makers, year after year, have found it more palatable to entrust their teams–most desperately in need of a competent quarterback–to guys better suited to be third-stringers than Kaepernick, who at the very least has shown he's capable of being better than any primary backup on the league's 32 teams. Considering the dearth of competent, let alone highly effective, quarterbacks in the NFL, it strains credulity to believe Kaepernick remains unsigned because some other free-agent passers display slightly better touch on their balls in the mid-range passing game. Something else, something insidious, is occurring.

With 58 career starts, Kaepernick has experience. His touchdowns-to-interceptions ratio ranks among the best in NFL history. In that statistic, Kaepernick is better than Steve Young, Peyton Manning, and Tony Romo, to name a few. NFL coaches want quarterbacks with experience who take care of the football. Suddenly, it doesn't seem to matter that Kaepernick can check both boxes.

Even playing for the horrid 49ers in 2016, his final season in the NFL, Kaepernick still displayed big-play ability. San Francisco receivers had the second-highest percentage of dropped passes in the league. Yet, Kaepernick completed almost 60 percent of his passes (59.2). He passed for 16 touchdowns and had only four interceptions. Granted, we're not talking Patrick Mahomes–type numbers. On the other hand, there are NFL backups who have never passed for as many as 16 touchdowns in their careers.

The fact is, except for fans who disagree with Kaepernick's politics and the broadcasters and writers who carry the league's water on the nonsensical Kaepernick-isn't-good-enough-to-be-on-an-NFL-roster argument, it has been as clear as the space between a goalpost's uprights that the NFL has been stiff-arming the talented QB for reasons that have nothing to do with X's and O's. In 2018, the Washington franchise proved that.

After starter Alex Smith suffered a potentially career-ending injury in November, Washington signed failed 32-year-old passer Mark Sanchez. After Sanchez did what Sanchez does, Washington dipped back into the free-agent quarterback market and signed Josh Johnson, who was also 32 and who had not thrown a pass in a regular season NFL game since 2011.

Really?

In the years since Kaepernick has been on the outside looking in, the list of ridiculously ineffective quarterbacks who have been signed is as long as it is laughable. It's as if the league posted a sign in flashing red neon at every stadium that reads, "Don't believe what your eyes are seeing. All of these guys are actually better than Kaepernick."

The Jedi mind trick doesn't work on everyone.

The woeful performances of many players at Kaepernick's position undercut the league's argument every day of the week and twice on Sundays. The NFL finally acknowledged as much in February 2019, settling a collusion grievance in which Kaepernick alleged owners conspired to keep him unemployed because of his political activism. Although terms of the settlement are cloaked in a confidentially agreement, Kaepernick was true to his word, never backing down against the most formidable foe of his career.

——

At a political rally in Huntsville, Alabama, in late September 2017, Trump blasted NFL players for kneeling during the anthem.

"Wouldn't you love to see one of these NFL owners, when somebody disrespects our flag, to say, 'Get that son of a bitch off the field right now,'" Trump said at the rally. "Out. He's fired! He's fired!"

If Trump's intention was to unite many players in the NFL as well as some of the biggest stars in the NBA against him, he succeeded.

Cleveland Cavaliers forward LeBron James, the greatest basketball player of his generation and possibly the most famous athlete in the world, called the president a "bum" for a tweet Trump directed at Golden State Warriors superstar Stephen Curry. In response to Trump's comments in Alabama, Curry, who helped the Golden State Warriors win the 2017 NBA Finals, said he didn't want to participate in the traditional White House visit that championship teams of professional sports leagues make annually.

Initially ripped by many fans, the overwhelming majority of whom are white, and political pundits for not stopping the protests, the NFL steadily faced withering criticism from the Black community for not doing enough to *support* the players. African Americans attend NFL games. They watch them on television. They gripe about their fantasy teams. They buy jerseys. By any metric, Blacks have contributed immensely to the enormous popularity of the NFL's multibillion-dollar business. Both on and off the field, they've helped the NFL become the colossus it is today. The very notion, however, that African Americans also support the NFL was conspicuously absent from the debate about protests during the national anthem.

The NFL became the No. 1 sport in the US by having wide appeal. One doesn't get to the top of the mountain by drawing interest from narrow demographics. The league is spectacularly popular across gender, age, and racial lines. But African Americans have a unique relationship with the NFL.

Almost 60 percent of the league's players are Black. The NFL's so-called "skill positions" of wide receiver and running back, the players who score most of the points, are dominated by African Americans. Besides stirring excitement among fans by producing touchdowns, those players are also the league's greatest showmen.

From Billy "White Shoes" Johnson's "Funky Chicken" dance to Antonio Brown's twerking, the league has been made relevant in popular culture largely because of the influence of Black culture.

Most children aren't likely to become impassioned followers of the NFL because they're enthralled with the complexities of route trees and blitz packages. But they'll remember a great catch or highlight-worthy run by their favorite player. They'll want to wear a jersey featuring that guy's number and team colors. Black players have helped energize generations of fans for the NFL. Through their actions, Kaepernick and the other players who protested spoke directly to people who love the NFL but feel they weren't embraced in return—especially because Kaepernick was disrespected after standing up for them.

Of course, Black people are not monolithic. While it's true there was strong support for protesters among Blacks, it was not unanimous. There are some African American NFL fans, especially Black conservatives, who viewed the players' actions as being wholly inappropriate. Among Blacks, however, that group was very much in the minority.

—

On both sides, the NFL was getting squeezed. By early in the 2017 NFL season, it was painfully obvious to team owners that, somehow, they had to stop the bleeding.

In October, club owners, high-ranking league executives, leaders of the recently formed Players Coalition, the main group of protesting players, and NFL Players Association officials gathered in New York in an effort to both discuss issues that adversely affect African American communities and to bring closure to the biggest public relations disaster in the league's history. Although no specific measures were announced, the tone of several of the meeting's participants strongly indicated that a partnership could be reached.

Players insisted there would be no quid pro quo; they would not relinquish their rights to protest during the national anthem. But the feeling in the negotiating room was that if franchise owners were willing to help Black players address concerns in their communities, especially with substantial financial backing, perhaps players would no longer feel compelled to bring attention to the issues through protest. The fact that owners engaged with players on an unprecedented level to discuss concerns primarily affecting Black and brown bodies proved the effectiveness of the Kaepernick-led protests.

In late November 2017, the NFL and the Players Coalition reached agreement on a landmark seven-year, $89 million deal to effect social justice change. Owners ratified the package during the annual league meetings in March 2018. A little more than two years later, the league expanded its social justice footprint, pledging to commit $250 million and lengthening the deal's term to 10 years. Grants have been provided to nonprofit groups that focus on civil rights and racial justice, helping adults move from minimum wage jobs to employment that can lead to meaningful careers, and empowering students to stay in school. As franchise owners had hoped, their partnership with players effectively ended the protest movement. During the 2019 season, only three players protested. After making a nonsensical revision to the NFL's anthem policy that could have resulted in players facing disciplinary action for protesting, club owners and the league office, with help from the NFL Players Association, settled on language that enables players to remain in the locker room until after the anthem is performed. If players choose to be on the field while the anthem is performed, they "shall stand and show respect for the flag and the anthem," the policy reads.

After the NFL player protests mostly faded from memory, fans outraged by the players' actions came back to the league. Or at least enough of them returned to provide the league with the leverage it revels in wielding in broadcast rights negotiations: In March 2021, the NFL finalized a new round of rights agreements with Amazon, CBS, ESPN/ABC, Fox, and NBC that will pay it $113 billon over an 11-year period, beginning with the 2023 season. The total payout to the NFL will be 80 percent higher than the previous rights deal, providing club owners with much more of their favorite color: green.

By the end of the 2020 season, Kaepernick had not thrown a pass in an NFL game for four seasons. But his influence over the game had never been stronger. The Players Coalition reaped the benefits of the seeds sown by Kaepernick back in 2016. For his part, Kaepernick has continued to back up his talk with action. He made good on his pledge to donate $1 million to charity, providing funds to assist those on the front lines of pushing for social justice change and improving educational opportunities for children.

In 2020, Kaepernick's charity, the Know Your Rights Camp, donated more than $1.75 million to aid Black and brown communities and assist with COVID-19 relief. In addition to using his wealth to spur positive change, Kaepernick remained active working in the field, supporting groups he believes in when no television cameras are present.

Wyche, the reporter who broke the news of Kaepernick's protest in 2016, isn't surprised by what the former quarterback has achieved.

"When you say the name Colin Kaepernick, people get it, and it has nothing to do with football," Wyche said. "He has impacted the thinking of a generation, people who are working to create change in society. When I think about Colin Kaepernick, I think about all the people he has helped and all the people he has inspired."

[14]

KYLER MURRAY

ONE FALL SATURDAY MORNING in 2013, inside a large, dimly lit office located in the Allen (Texas) High School Eagles' $60 million athletic facility, offensive coordinator Jeff Fleener was about to get a blinding flash of football's future. Reviewing game film of the previous evening's 77–37 drubbing of Plano West High, before a somnolent audience of teenage quarterbacks and wide receivers, Fleener abruptly stopped the video. "Murray!" Fleener barked, at once waking and silencing the room. Heavy eyes popped open and turned toward the team's star, junior quarterback Kyler Murray. Instantly, Fleener had the group's full attention.

Regularly throughout the video sessions, Fleener would hit the pause button whenever he identified teachable moments. But this time, Fleener had halted the on-screen action because it was he who needed to be educated. Before the game, Fleener and Murray had had many long discussions about the options available to Murray on a certain play based on myriad factors, including the defense's post-snap adjustments. The teacher and his star pupil determined that if things unfolded as they envisioned, one of Allen's receivers would run uncovered and Murray could easily connect with him for a big gain. As the video made clear, the play had developed just as Fleener and Murray had hoped. Then Murray flipped the script. Instead of attempting the easy pass, Murray connected on a much more difficult one to a player who was well guarded. Of course, the fact that Murray completed the pass was immaterial to Fleener. The coach had only one concern: Why did Murray take the harder road?

"I said, 'Now why in the world would we try to jam that in rather than [attempt the easy pass] that we know is going to be open right there?'" Fleener said. "And the thing is, he doesn't miss a beat. He looks over to me and he says, 'Coach, we're up four touchdowns. You're about to take me out. But in a few weeks in the playoffs, we're going to be playing [one of Allen's powerful rivals]. I have to know if I can make that throw. So why would we not right there, based on the drop I took, see if I can make it rather than [attempt the easy pass]?' I just kind of stood there silent for a second, thinking, 'This kid is playing chess and everybody else is playing checkers.' It was a great answer. I just said, 'Well . . . yeah.' I was totally cool with it. I just started the [tape] again. That's who he is."

—

Kyler Cole Murray was born on August 7, 1997, in Bedford, Texas. From childhood, Murray was schooled in the position with energy and sophistication by his father, Kevin, who was a standout quarterback at Texas A&M University in the mid-1980s and later became a private quarterback coach. Early on, it became evident to Kevin that Kyler was both naturally gifted and dedicated to excelling at a sport he loved—the perfect combination to make it big at the glamour position in a state obsessed with football. In Texas, it has been said, football isn't merely a sport. It's a religion. On Friday nights across the state, businesses close early and whole towns often shut down as fans pack high school stadiums—some with seating capacities approaching 20,000. Successful quarterbacks, even at the youth level, are lionized. The appropriateness of feting children and adolescents for their proficiency in completing passes against a zone defense is a question worthy of debate, but that's the way they do things in the Lone Star State. Under the harsh glare of high expectations, Murray burst onto the scene in youth football, setting himself apart from the other preteen luminaries by both passing the ball and running with it better than the rest.

"There were these YouTube videos of him already up when he was in [youth football]," said Fleener, who's among Kevin Murray's closest confidants. "You really started to hear about him. You started to hear he was good. Then you started to hear he was *really* good."

Becoming a football legend before going through puberty could leave one full of self-importance. Missy Murray made sure the head on her son's shoulders remained a manageable size. Within the Murray household, Kyler wasn't a rock star. He was part of a loving family, which supported his early athletic achievements but also stressed the need for him to fulfill his other familial obligations. The message got through.

When Murray was 14, the family moved to Allen, Texas, a Dallas suburb. In Texas high school football, Allen *is* the biggest stage. Literally. The state's largest public institution based on enrollment, Allen also participates in the top classification for athletics. During Murray's sophomore year, the Allen Independent School District unveiled Eagle Stadium–a sparkling $60 million edifice complete with a towering upper deck, a 38-foot-wide high-definition video screen, and corporate sponsors.

In this big-time edifice, Murray fit like a pearl in an oyster shell. By his sophomore year, Murray was emerging as an outstanding college prospect and, equally important to his family, a grounded teenager and leader.

"Even at fifteen, nothing seemed to bother him [on the football field]," Fleener said. "He was just as cool and collected, in any situation, that you could possibly imagine. No stage was too big for Kyler."

During three seasons as Allen's starting QB, Murray never lost a game in his high school's football palace–or anywhere else for that matter. He finished an astonishing 42–0 (the Eagles were also victorious in the one start Murray missed in his career) and led the school to three state championships. The only thing Texans love more than football is *winning* football. No high school quarterback in the state won more while playing the position as artfully as Murray.

"For a kid everybody considered to be undersized, he saw the field better than any quarterback I've ever been around," Fleener said. "Just as far as understanding where [throwing] windows were going to be, [and] when he had to let the ball go to hit that guy in stride."

As a senior, Murray swept the major state and national awards of consequence for high school athletes, including being named the Gatorade Player of the Year and *USA Today* Offensive Player of the Year. Among the nation's top dual-threat QB recruits, Murray was rated second to none by many recruiting analysts. Murray's high school statistics are staggering. He amassed 10,386 passing yards and had 117 touchdown passes–with only 22 interceptions. As a runner, he accounted for 4,139 yards rushing (with an 8.4-yard average) and added another 69 touchdowns rushing. That all adds up to dizzying combined totals of 14,525 yards and 186 touchdowns. Murray's numbers are all the more impressive considering he often sat out during the fourth quarter of games while Allen, whose roster was loaded with future college players, steamrolled opponents during its stunning streak. Each season, Murray set the tone for the Eagles, demanding the best of himself and, by example, everyone around him.

"If he didn't get pulled out of so many games in the third quarter, there's no telling how many state records he would have broken," Fleener said. "But we were up by thirty, thirty-five points, a lot, in the third quarter. You just don't feel good about leaving the kid in. Still, his numbers, even with being pulled so often, were video-game numbers. And the thing that set him apart, that helped him reach that level and stay there, was not just his God-given talent. It was how hard he worked to develop it. He was never satisfied. He was always working. He was always thinking about ways to get better."

One could make quite a persuasive argument that not only is Murray the greatest high school quarterback in the history of Texas, he also tops the state's all-time list of high school football players. Period. Granted, that's big talk, especially considering that quarter-backs Patrick Mahomes, Drew Brees, and Matthew Stafford spent much of their teenage years thrilling fans under Texas's Friday-night lights. Pro Football Hall of Fame running backs Earl Campbell and Eric Dickerson also are Texans, as are many other greats at every position on a football roster. The fact, though, that Murray never lost a game in high school while facing the best competition in the state, combined with his showstopping performances in Allen's three state title victories (he accounted for 13 total touchdowns) puts him squarely in the discussion to wear the crown.

The thing is, in high school, Murray displayed almost as much talent on the baseball diamond as he did on the football field. A shortstop and second baseman, Murray was the first player selected to play in the prestigious Under Armour All-America games for both football and baseball. On the Eagles' baseball team, Murray displayed all the tools required to be rated as a big-time Major League Baseball prospect.

"He started as a sophomore for us, but I still kind of saw him as a stud football player. But, man, he had some tools," said Paul Coe, Allen's baseball coach during Murray's time on the team. "In his junior year, he just broke out. He hit nine home runs, led our team; led our team in stolen bases. He just took his game to another level that year. There was a point in time when he was doing a lot of the [football] stuff in the summer so he didn't get to play as much baseball. Once he finished football and he started hitting baseballs in January and February every day? His game just took off."[96]

It was widely known, however, that Murray, the object of an intense recruiting battle among the state's traditional college football powers, was sticking with football. Murray signed to play at Texas A&M, where his father was an all-conference signal-caller and led the Aggies to consecutive conference titles. In 1999, Kevin, who while in college suffered a severe ankle injury that contributed to ending his dream of having an NFL career, was inducted into the Texas A&M Athletic Hall of Fame. Following in his father's footsteps with the Aggies, Kyler appeared poised to add another rousing chapter to his storybook athletic journey. For Murray, though, an unwelcome plot twist was forthcoming.

—

After his freshman season, Kyler bolted from Texas A&M. He began the season second on the Aggies' depth chart behind Kyle Allen, who started the first seven games. Murray then supplanted Allen in the team's next three games. Neither Murray nor Allen were pleased with how coaches handled the Aggies' season-long quarterback competition, and both grew especially frustrated because of what they considered to be poor communication from the staff about its plans. Only a week after Allen announced his intention to transfer, Murray followed suit, departing the program despite being a true freshman atop the QB depth chart. For the first time since he took charge of a huddle, Murray hit a bump. Although Murray experienced his first moment of uncertainty in football, he was nonetheless confident about this much: The setback was only a pause, not an ending.

"With Kyle Allen and him, and everything that happened his freshman year, it just wasn't a good fit," Fleener said. "There are some times that these moves need to happen because it's not the right fit, especially at the quarterback position, and Kyler needed to move on."

In search of a place to start over, Murray ultimately transferred to the University of Oklahoma. A brief meeting during Murray's senior year at Allen in 2015 paved his path to Norman, Oklahoma. Shortly after Lincoln Riley was hired to become the Sooners' offensive coordinator, he reached out to Allen's coaching staff. The word in recruiting circles was that Murray was "a lock" to attend Texas A&M. Still, Riley, who would succeed longtime Oklahoma head coach Bob Stoops shortly before the 2017 college football season kicked off, hoped to meet with the young QB in a last-ditch effort to present a case for the Sooners.

"Lincoln Riley got to Oklahoma three weeks before [national] signing day, and I'd known coach Riley since he was a graduate assistant [coach] [at Texas Tech]," Fleener said. "I told him Kyler was pretty sure he was going to A&M, but that he had to at least meet Kyler. We set up a little meeting. Afterwards, I said, 'Well, what'd you think?' And he goes, 'That kid has got to be the most fun kid to coach.' I told him he's a dream. And I asked Kyler the same thing. I said, 'What did you think of coach Riley?' He said, 'Man. He's cool.' They both remembered that, which helped Kyler wind up in the right place for him."

Murray definitely left a lasting impression on Riley.

"You could tell right away he was a football guy. You could tell he loved the game. He had a passion for it," Riley said. "We talked a little bit [about] schematics and you just liked everything about him intangibly [in addition to] what you saw on tape. It was a great first meeting. Unfortunately, we just didn't have time to build enough of a relationship for him to sign with us coming out of a high school."

Under NCAA transfer rules, Murray was ineligible to play in football games for Oklahoma during the 2016 season. Taking a mandatory break from one sport enabled him to refocus on another. In an effort to help Murray maximize his time playing college baseball, Riley and Oklahoma baseball coach Skip Johnson forged a partnership, rare among college head coaches at the same institution, to best accommodate Murray's schedule as he split time between the programs. Often, coaches of different sports are rivals within a school's athletic department. It's common for them to demand that multisport athletes pledge fealty to only one sport. Riley and Johnson realized Murray was, well, different, and adjusted to benefit his development. Murray possessed so much potential in both baseball and football, Riley and Johnson did everything they could to hold open both doors for him.

It would have been remarkable for any prospect, but it's worth remembering that gatekeepers in these two sports, sports that for decades had actively suppressed the Black talent in their midst, were now going out of their way to nurture it.

"You know, he practiced with us as a team less than ten times, show up at 5:35 for a [7:30 p.m.] game, [assistant] coach [Clay] Overcash would throw him batting practice, and [Murray would] go out and play the game and get two hits," Johnson said. "Football and baseball coming together to help an athlete. That was what was more unique than anything, because I think that's a special thing that a lot of people can't say."[97]

Johnson converted Murray from an infielder to an outfielder, believing that's where he could make the biggest impact if he ever played in the majors. During his first season with the Sooners, Murray had a rough transition to the outfield and batted .122 with only six hits, no home runs, and 20 strikeouts in 49 at-bats.

"My first year playing baseball at OU, you would have thought I was garbage," Murray said. "It's really windy in Oklahoma. It's tough to read the ball off the bat. It wasn't easy, so I had to work at that. The next year we made a big jump."[98]

Like an Olympic champion.

As a junior, Murray, playing in 51 games, batted .296 (56 for 189) with 10 home runs, 47 runs batted in, and 10 stolen bases. After failing to produce a hit for extra bases as a sophomore, Murray, in addition to the 10 balls he hit out of stadiums, also had 13 doubles and three triples. Murray's impressive slash line of .296/.398/.556 underscored his overall production as a well-rounded hitter. Baseball scouts noticed. Entering the 2018 MLB draft, the buzz was that Murray had played himself into being a first-round pick. Sure enough, the Athletics selected Murray ninth overall and handed him a $4.66 million signing bonus. A top-10 pick with a fat signing bonus in hand, Murray's future in baseball seemed bright. On the other hand, what awaited him in football was downright blinding.

"He was always confident that he could do it [in football], but the chance for him to catch his breath [after transferring], where he didn't have to be the guy right off the top, helped him," Riley said. "And going through what he did as a freshman [at Texas A&M], he had more of an appreciation for it [what it took to succeed as a college QB]. That no matter how good you are in high school, this is a different level. It's tough. There are new challenges. The downtime . . . that first year was exactly what he needed. He handled it very well."

During his sophomore season on OU's football team, Murray played in seven games while serving as starter Baker Mayfield's primary backup. Murray completed 85.7 percent of his passes (18 for 21) for 359 yards with three touchdowns and no interceptions. He also rushed for 142 yards with a 10.1-yard average. Mayfield had a spectacular season. He won the 2017 Heisman Trophy and went on to be the No. 1 overall pick in the 2018 NFL draft.

"We had another good quarterback at the time. But there was enough to see that, if he did win the starting job, he had a chance to be really unique and really special," Riley said. "He was improving at a high rate. He played very well in the games that he went in. He was a great team guy, but you could tell he was certainly ready to go out there and earn his shot."

The Sooners would again have a talent-rich roster in 2018, and Murray was eager to remind everyone why he had been considered, only a short time ago, one of the best dual-threat QB prospects ever. He wasted no time.

Murray shot out of the gate, passing for 17 touchdowns with only two interceptions and rushing for four touchdowns as Oklahoma started 5–0. By season's end, Murray's stats were almost identical to those that Mayfield posted during his Heisman Trophy–winning season. In 14 games during his final season at Oklahoma, Mayfield completed 70.5 percent of his passes for 4,627 yards with 43 touchdown passes and six interceptions. Over 14 games during the 2018 season, Murray connected on 69 percent of his attempts. He had 4,361 yards passing, 42 touchdown passes, and seven interceptions. Murray was actually much more productive than Mayfield in one key area: rushing. While starting for three seasons at Oklahoma, Mayfield rushed for 895 yards combined. During Murray's final season, he had 1,001 yards (with a 7.2-yard average) and 12 touchdowns. Riley saw it all coming.

"He's such an intense competitor. He's unique because he expects so much out of the people around him, the receivers and the other offensive players," Riley said. "I mean, he really demands it. And he's really on those guys hard. But he can do that because he puts it in [the work] himself and he's so committed to the game and committed to winning. He just expects everybody to be that way. He has a hard time understanding when somebody is not. He sets a great standard for offensive players for winning. That's something that bleeds over to everybody that's around him."

Oklahoma wound up having consecutive Heisman Trophy–winning QBs. In the history of the award, which has been presented annually since 1935, a school has had a Heisman winner in back-to-back years only five times. Oklahoma is the only school to have had consecutive Heisman winners at QB.

Following his spectacular junior season for the Sooners' football team, Murray chose the NFL over MLB. Under his contract terms, Murray was required to either repay or forfeit all but $210,000 of his $4.66 million signing bonus.

Shortly before Murray announced his decision to play football over baseball, Oakland officials met with the two-sport star to make their final pitch. They reportedly offered Murray a package that included another $14 million in guaranteed money on top of his signing bonus. As for Murray's signing bonus, a question immediately comes to mind: Why was he even able to pocket a relatively small part of it? Well, MLB clubs pay big bonuses over time. At the time Murray officially spurned the A's, the franchise had already paid him $1.5 million, of which he was contractually required to repay $1.29 million. Murray forfeited the remaining $3.15 million. Despite the fact Murray never took the field for the Athletics, he kept $210,000. That's real money, of course, but it's also pocket change for MLB owners, even those who operate clubs in small markets such as Oakland.

Not surprisingly, Murray's decision precipitated a tough conversation with the Athletics.

"Yeah, [it was difficult] just because they invested so much in me and honestly, they were the best throughout this whole process," Murray said. "Just letting me be me, letting me do my own thing and then watching me play football from afar. But at the same time letting me know how much I meant to them, and at the same time it's relationships that I'll have forever. At the end of the day, they drafted me. In my heart, I'll always feel like I'll be an A just because they took the time to do that, and obviously it's a dream come true to be drafted No. 9, first round to them. It was definitely tough. It's not like breaking up with a girlfriend, but it was hard to have that conversation for sure."[99]

The Cardinals were in the market for a new quarterback. They thought they had found a great one in the 2018 draft, selecting former UCLA standout Josh Rosen with the 10th overall pick. That's why it was shocking when the Cardinals traded Rosen after only a season and used the draft's first pick in 2019 to acquire Murray. Although Rosen often struggled while starting 13 games for an abysmal Cardinals team during the 2018–19 season, he acquitted himself well enough, especially considering he was sacked 45 times while playing behind a porous offensive line, to continue learning on the job. It seemed hasty, to put it kindly, for management to have cut ties with a 22-year-old quarterback who, less than a year earlier, was viewed within Arizona's organization as a potential franchise savior. As a rule, NFL teams just don't make moves like that. Murray's potential for greatness prompted the Cardinals' unprecedented change in course. Murray was simply too good to pass on, Cardinals officials believed confidently, so the optics of moving on so quickly from Rosen be damned. From his first day in the NFL, Murray validated the Cardinals' faith in him.

As a rookie, Murray completed 64.4 percent of his passes. He had 3,722 yards with 20 touchdown passes and 12 interceptions. Murray also rushed for 544 yards (with a 5.8-yard average) and four touchdowns. The Cardinals, who went 3–13 the season before Murray arrived, improved to 5–10–1. Granted, some would argue that the Cardinals made only moderate progress. But it was progress nonetheless. During many seasons, Murray's statistics would have been good enough for him to be part of the NFC's Pro Bowl team. Not after the 2019–20 season, though, because so many quarterbacks–especially Black quarterbacks–had historic seasons. Seattle's Russell Wilson, whom Murray admired as he rose in high school and college, had one of his best seasons and was among the QBs selected ahead of Murray for the NFC's roster. As it was, Murray had to settle with being voted the Associated Press Offensive Rookie of the Year.

While learning so much that first season about the NFL and his place in it, Murray recalled conversations he had with his father years earlier about the game's history and the legacy of Black quarterbacks—a legacy of which Murray was now a part.

"Guys from my dad's [generation], and definitely before, yeah, they knew they had to deal with . . . a lack of opportunities," Murray said. "Obviously, there were a lot of guys capable of playing quarterback, guys like my dad, but there weren't a lot in the NFL. That's just the way it was. . . . It's great now that every season there are more guys coming in and proving what they can do."

Entering his second season, Murray vowed to take another significant step for himself individually and as the Cardinals' leader, and as he so often had in the past, he made good on his vow. His completion percentage increased to 67.2. Murray also had 3,971 yards passing, 26 touchdowns, and 12 interceptions. As a runner, Murray finished with 819 yards (with a 6.2-yard average) and 11 touchdowns. He set an NFL record for having the most games with at least one passing touchdown and one rushing touchdown and joined Cam Newton—the third Black quarterback to be selected first overall in the NFL draft—as the only players in league history to have at least 25 passing touchdowns and 10 rushing touchdowns in a single season.

Only 11 seconds remained on the clock. It was November 15, 2020, Week 10 of the NFL season, and the visiting Buffalo Bills held a 30–26 lead over the Arizona Cardinals in a game that appeared to be all but over as Kyler Murray, Arizona's gifted second-year quarterback, led his teammates out of the huddle. From the first time Murray lined up behind center as a tyke in football-crazed Texas through his record-setting high school and college careers, he had envisioned succeeding as a pro passer in seemingly insurmountable situations. The best of the best NFL quarterbacks burnished their legacies on late-game heroics. Snatching victory from the jaws of defeat helped to make them legends. Murray embraced the opportunity to be baptized by fire. For his growth, he believed, the experience would be essential. On that day against the Bills in Glendale, Arizona, things couldn't have been hotter. If the Cardinals were to achieve a highly improbable victory, Murray would likely have to be the catalyst for it. To a man, the Cardinals believed the right person occupied the job. With the pressure palpable as Murray barked orders at the line of scrimmage, unanimity inspired confidence. On first and 10 at the Bills' 43-yard line, Murray, in the shotgun formation, received the snap. Quickly surveying the field, his eyes darting right to left as Buffalo's determined pass rushers closed in on him, Murray nimbly scrambled left to evade pressure. At the Cardinals' 46, Murray made a nifty stutter-step move, freezing 6-foot-3, 260-pound Bills defensive end Mario Addison just long enough to break free from his grasp. Then, with another menacing defensive player almost within arm's reach of Murray near the sideline at Buffalo's 49, and the clock winding down to a row of zeroes, he quickly set his feet and launched a deep pass that, from almost every other arm, might have reeked of desperation. But this was Kyler Murray, and the ball took off like a laser-guided missile hell-bent on its target. Superstar wide receiver DeAndre Hopkins did the rest.

After lining up alone wide left in Arizona's four-receiver formation, Hopkins ran straight to the end zone, stopping about three yards in. The Bills were ready: Three defensive backs bracketed him—and it didn't matter. Hopkins has huge hands and his vertical leap has been measured at 36 inches. This is what Murray knew and had counted on. The whizzing ball appeared at exactly the right moment, precisely four feet above Hopkins's head. Hopkins stretched out his massive arms and leapt above the competition. When he returned to earth, the ball was safely sealed in his meat-hook hands, completing one of the most spectacular game-winning plays in NFL history.

Final score: Arizona 32, Buffalo 30, the victory that ultimately would ensure that, for only the second time in five seasons, the Cardinals, with Murray serving as a team captain, would finish without a losing record.

Instantly on social media, the play was dubbed "the Hail Murray." Hopkins's ridiculously difficult contested catch was one for the ages, earning him well-deserved praise. But Murray's rare combination of elite athleticism and superior arm strength sparkled just as brightly. The list of QBs capable of eluding such a formidable pass rush and making a pinpoint throw in that situation is as short as it distinguished. During his long coaching career, Mike Shanahan worked with a few signal-callers in that group, and the Super Bowl winner said that watching Murray that day provided a window into the future of the position.

"He's just one of the most exceptional athletes that I've ever watched [at quarterback] because he can do it all," said Shanahan, who led the Denver Broncos to consecutive Super Bowl titles in the late 1990s. "He's a natural thrower who also has so much ability to run the ball . . . his skill set is just unbelievable. And one of the biggest things is . . . he's an example of how the game has changed. In a lot of ways, he's a perfect example of how the position has changed."

Only the fifth Black quarterback picked No. 1 overall since the draft began in 1936, Murray symbolizes the progress the NFL has made in evaluating signal-callers. Gone for good are the days when NFL decision-makers would require all Blacks who played quarterback in college to change positions after being drafted merely because of the high degree of melanin in their skin. Club owners and their underlings finally came to accept, albeit begrudgingly, that Black players were not only adept at running with or catching the ball. Many could throw it with the best of their white counterparts as well. The sea change actually occurred because of the team owners' favorite color: green. As the league's popularity increased exponentially from the 1980s on, and revenue from ever-ballooning television contracts and corporate sponsorships poured into club coffers, the pressure to win on executives and coaches became commensurate with the NFL's standing in American popular culture. Apparently, the prospect of gargantuan profit can spur one to become more enlightened both on matters of race and X's and O's. In the not-too-distant past, the 5- foot-10 Murray would have been dinged on scouting reports almost as much for his lack of height as his skin color. In not-so-long-gone days, the NFL would rarely give a second glance at QBs shorter than 6 foot 1. The thinking was that college QBs of less stature wouldn't measure up in the pro game while trying to complete passes over hulking offensive linemen. Fortunately for NFL fans, however, that thinking went the way of leather helmets. In the contemporary NFL, star Black quarterbacks are as commonplace as billionaire franchise owners and a passer's height no longer is considered determinative of potential success. Murray is living proof of that.

"It's not what you look like, or really about just one type of quarterback anymore. It's about how you play and if you can help a team win. Period," Murray said. "The league is more open to guys who maybe don't have the [prototypical] size, or what everyone used to think an NFL quarterback should look like, and understanding that there are different ways to win."

On December 21, 2020, Murray, at only 23, became the youngest Cardinals quarterback in franchise history to be selected as a Pro Bowler.

"For me, going into every year, I ask myself, 'How can I be the best me? What can I do to get better?'" Murray said. "I want to be the best ever. I want to win Super Bowls. I want to keep building with this team. I want to keep moving in that direction, making each step of the process. That's what drives me."

All grown up now, the one-time Texas high school phenom has

taken his place alongside the NFL's best passers. And while Murray wasn't the first Black quarterback to change the game, his presence among the league's best today is proof positive of how much the game has changed, in all the right ways, for them.

[15]

LAMAR JACKSON

THE LINE FORMED AT M&T Bank Stadium as soon as time expired on the game clock, the fans readying for autographs while Baltimore Ravens coaches and players exchanged congratulatory handshakes after a 42–21 rout of the visiting New York Jets late in the 2019–20 NFL season. But before the victors could even conclude a chorus of "attaboys," Ravens superstar quarterback Lamar Jackson was back at work, signing jerseys and posing for pictures with his beaming admirers.

Time was of the essence. The Jets had a plane to catch. But Jackson didn't want to give his fans short shrift. These weren't 40-something beer-soaked dudes wearing crow-head hats, or 12-year-olds holding out footballs to sign. They were large sweaty men in shoulder pads who only minutes ago had been unsuccessfully attempting to stop Jackson from making magic on the football field.

In a scene that appeared odd to many onlookers, Jackson gave considerable face time to the Ravens' vanquished opponents, embracing players, sharing laughs, and welcoming their words of encouragement before they finally departed the field in defeat. In the NFL, it's commonplace for opponents to exchange jerseys following games. The act is an acknowledgment of respect for a fellow competitor after an athletic battle. But what occurred that night on the Ravens' home field was, well, different.

During the Ravens' 10th straight victory, Jackson had another virtuoso performance in front of a national-television audience, passing for five touchdowns without an interception while adding another 86 yards rushing. In only his second season in the NFL and first entrenched atop Baltimore's depth chart, Jackson had long since silenced many of his doubters in the league's establishment, who liked to say–both loudly and often–that he had no chance of making it as an NFL quarterback.

On that chilly December night in Baltimore (it was 33 degrees at kickoff), Jackson dominated the Jets throughout the game, yet there they still stood on the field afterward, several of them appearing delighted as they awaited their turns to be closer to greatness. Just as he had done during the game, Jackson came prepared, passing out and signing multiple jerseys bearing his name and number provided to him by Baltimore's equipment manager. With the size of the crowd Jackson was serving, he could have used more. And Jackson worked on a one-way street: For his largesse, Jackson sought nothing in return.

In one news report, a summary of the uncommon encounter read, "It's pretty much standard procedure at this point for players to exchange jerseys on the field after a game. But it was weird seeing several players gathering around an opponent who had just destroyed them on national television and beaming with smiles as he signed a jersey for them. . . . It was reminiscent of the Dream Team at the 1992 Olympics, posing for photos with elated players from faraway countries who never thought they'd end up on the same court as the best players in the world."[100]

What played out among Jackson and those other men–all of

whom are Black–had nothing do with fanboy worship. The respect Jackson received signified the unspoken understanding among Black folk when one of us excels in the face of dog whistles and racist tropes. The Jets' players admired Jackson for stiff-arming the doubters–especially the loudest voices in the run-up to the 2018 draft, who insisted he needed to change positions to even have a shot at an NFL career–and proving he was not only capable of being a starting passer at the game's highest level, but also one of the best.

Immediately, that's what came to mind for ESPN NFL analyst Domonique Foxworth while he watched a video of the Jets' interaction with Jackson. A former NFL cornerback, Foxworth has been there before, too.

"As a Black person, we recognize that anytime a Black person is in a prominent position, it comes to mean so much more to all of society," said Foxworth, who played for the Denver Broncos, Atlanta Falcons, and Ravens during his six-year NFL career. "And when Lamar was entering the draft, the conversation about Lamar meant so much more, and took on so much more. There were so many undertones about what was being said and what was being implied about Lamar. What that was about was . . . we've been there before."

—

The wrongheaded thinking about Jackson as he entered the NFL is as old as the league itself. From the moment Fritz Pollard, the league's first Black QB, took the field in 1923, Black signal-callers have faced doubts–founded in racism, not facts–that they lack the smarts and leadership ability to function successfully in the key role. Through the decades, Black would-be NFL quarterbacks, who were equal parts athletically and cerebrally gifted, were converted to defensive backs and wide receivers, each insulting and economically disenfranchising move adding more broken hearts to a trail of shattered dreams.

As late as the late 1970s, the unwritten rule remained in effect that African Americans who played quarterback in college would have to change positions if they wanted to play in the NFL. A few classic dropback, strong-armed Black QBs managed to break through during that long, shameful period in the league's history. James "Shack" Harris and Doug Williams were the most successful. But teams were so committed to the racist approach that Warren Moon began his career in the Canadian Football League because NFL decision-makers couldn't see past his skin color to his talent during the 1977 draft. Things were even worse for Black quarterbacks assigned the "dual-threat" label, meaning they were highly adept at making plays both passing and running. Rarely did those guys even receive cursory consideration to play behind center in the NFL. They were hurried along to the other position groups where speed and athleticism were valued most. The whole thing seems counterintuitive, that the NFL would stigmatize and cast aside players at any position because of their versatility. At any other position on the field, versatility and exceptional athleticism is valued.

Perhaps the most offensive part of the longtime, unspoken league-wide policy (with so many to pick from, it's hard to choose) is that those who had their hands on the levers of power attempted, with a straight face, to cast themselves in a favorable light for effectively barring Blacks from playing quarterback. They claimed they actually helped Black players by pushing them to play other positions, the twisted thinking being that they "saved" them from the inevitable humiliation of failing in the NFL. Denied the chance to compete for jobs, Black quarterbacks were told, effectively, they should be thankful for being discriminated against. The game can't get more rigged than that.

The coded language evolved through the generations. By the 1980s, the term of art to denigrate African American college quarterbacks was to say they lacked the "passing mechanics" needed to make it in the NFL. The NFL supposedly couldn't find many Black quarterbacks capable of throwing the ball from point A to point B without making a mockery out of the position. Apparently, any NFL team that drafted Jackson and dared to have him line up under center would set back the position decades. That's the drivel that was out there. Even more remarkable: that kind of thinking persisted well into the twenty-first century and even shadowed Jackson into the 2018 NFL draft.

Jackson displayed superior arm strength and rare athletic skills regardless of position while becoming the youngest player to win the Heisman Trophy—the premier award presented annually to college football's most outstanding player—after his sophomore season at the University of Louisville. The Pompano Beach, Florida, native accomplished the feat at only 19 years, 337 days. Jameis Winston, the previous youngest winner, was five days older than Jackson when he received the honor while at Florida State University. Regardless, Jackson was not a viable NFL quarterback prospect, his critics in NFL player-personnel offices and within the media insisted.

Among Jackson's detractors entering the draft, Hall of Famer Bill Polian had the biggest bullhorn. Widely regarded as one of the most astute talent evaluators of his generation, Polian, as general manager of the Buffalo Bills, was the chief architect of teams that lost four consecutive Super Bowls from 1991–94. In his next act as general manager of the Carolina Panthers, Polian constructed a roster that enabled the franchise to reach the NFC championship game in only its second year of existence. Before the curtain dropped on his NFL career, Polian won a Super Bowl while serving as general manager and team president of the Indianapolis Colts. He was voted the NFL's executive of the year so often—a record six times from 1988 to 2009— the award should bear his name.

Before the draft, Polian, then in his role as an ESPN analyst, ignited a social-media firestorm by strongly suggesting that Jackson should move to another position. When Polian speaks, top league decision-makers drop whatever they're doing and listen. His comments about Jackson resonated with the entire NFL community. If the great Bill Polian had already determined that Jackson wouldn't make it as an NFL quarterback, well, Jackson probably wouldn't make it as an NFL quarterback. During a February 19, 2018, appearance on ESPN's *Golic and Wingo* show, Polian made his position on Jackson crystal clear.

"I think wide receiver," Polian said of Jackson. "Exceptional athlete, exceptional ability to make you miss, exceptional acceleration, exceptional instinct with the ball in his hand and that's rare for wide receivers." And Polian added, "Clearly–clearly–not the thrower that the other guys [quarterbacks in the 2018 draft class] are. The accuracy isn't there."

In studying video of Jackson's performance while he rose to national prominence at the University of Louisville, Foxworth saw something much different than what Polian and Jackson's other detractors observed. But Foxworth knew what the doubters had zeroed in on and, more important, why many of them could never recognize Jackson's enormous potential.

"They didn't come right out and say anything about intelligence or leadership, but all that stuff is implied," said Foxworth, who was active in the NFL Players Association throughout his playing career and served as the union's president in 2012. "And that happens anytime a Black person is up for something important, or in any role of significance, and there's no more significant role as a player than quarterback. The Black players saw what happened to Lamar, they know what's happened throughout history, and they see Lamar as one of them."

ESPN NFL analyst Ryan Clark drilled down even deeper.

"What you saw happening there [with Jackson and the Jets' players] was cultural respect as much as football respect," said Clark, a former longtime NFL safety who started on the Pittsburgh Steelers' Super Bowl XLIII championship team in 2009. "They certainly respected who he is as a football player, but they also respected him as a man and what he was doing for the [Black] culture.

"So often, for such a long time [in the United States], Black people have had to come together around injustices. We've had to unite because of things that were wrong and we had to overcome. All of those guys knew about the things that were said about Lamar. They knew he wasn't accepted [by the NFL hierarchy] at first. So to me, what you saw on that field was a celebration–a celebration of an injustice overcome."

—

Lamar Demeatrice Jackson Jr. was born on January 7, 1997, to Felicia Jones and Lamar Jackson Sr. The younger Jackson, who is the eldest sibling to a brother and two sisters, has said his father died of a heart attack when he was eight. Jones raised her son and encouraged his love of football, serving the dual role of being his first cheerleader and year-round coach. Jones, who is fiercely private and does not grant interviews, got Jackson started in football, played a key role in his training through high school, and helped manage his college recruitment. Early on, Jones made sure Jackson understood how hard he would have to work to achieve his dreams.

Jones would take Jackson running on the beach and have him practice his dropbacks in the shallows of the Atlantic Ocean. She took him running on a bridge near their house, and some of his former youth teammates joined in their intense workouts. "She had them vomiting," Jackson said. "She never had me vomit. I always tried to work hard, and I took it serious, trying to better myself."[101]

When Jackson was seven, Michael Vick opened up a new world to him–that of a star NFL quarterback. Jackson came to idolize Vick– the electrifying dual-threat signal-caller who was the first Black passer selected No. 1 overall in the NFL draft–in the same manner as most kids of his generation: digitally.

"My first Madden [video] game was 2003, but I played with Michael Vick in 2004, and he was out of control," Jackson said. "Just watching him on a video game and watching him on TV and seeing what he did, what he brought to the table with his team, winning games for Atlanta, it was like, 'Man, I want to do some of the things he did on the field.' So I would go out there on a little league game on a Saturday and try to do the same things and emulate what he did. He has been a big influence on me."

While trying to imitate Vick's signature moves, as well as beginning to develop many of his own, Jackson became a youth football legend in Pompano Beach. Then at Boynton Beach Community High, Jackson dazzled while emerging as a major college recruit. Quickly, Boynton Beach head coach Rick Swain, who Jackson played under on the school's varsity for two seasons, realized Jackson was a gifted football player–and definitely a quarterback.

"I looked up in the sky and I praised the football gods," Swain said. "I knew I had something special."

At Boynton, coaches and teammates praised Jackson as much for his competitiveness as the weekly highlight-worthy touchdowns he produced. The spectacularly athletic teenage quarterback never cowered from a challenge.

Before Boynton Beach's 2014 spring game against Village Academy of Delray Beach, Florida, the neighboring rival let it be known that it planned to shut down Jackson. In the assessment of Village Academy's players, Jackson was overrated.

"They poked the beast," said Dan Start, who served as a Boynton Beach assistant coach from 2008 to 2014. "We had to sit Lamar the first quarter because of some small disciplinary stuff, and he entered the game in the second quarter. It was like a tornado struck. In the second quarter alone, he had 223 yards of offense and four TDs."[102]

As a high school senior, Jackson, who also was a top track performer in the 100-meter dash, accounted for 18 touchdowns passing and 17 running. He embodied the best traits of a dual-threat passer. Louisville head coach Bobby Petrino noticed.

In an effort to win the recruiting war (not surprisingly, Jackson had multiple scholarship offers from major football schools), Petrino made two promises to Felicia. The first, which got her attention, was that Jackson would play quarterback, exclusively, for the Cardinals. Other college recruiters made a much different pitch.

Petrino's competitors hoped the most influential person in Jackson's life, his protective mama bear, would be open to Jackson playing another position, at least early in his college career, perhaps defensive back or wide receiver. Those coaches explained that changing positions, temporarily, presumably would facilitate Jackson receiving playing time as soon as possible, instead of having to wait his turn behind upperclassmen QBs. With the Cardinals, Petrino assured Felicia, Jackson would never leave the quarterback group. Petrino's first commitment was a great conversation starter. His second closed the deal. If Felicia would entrust Petrino to watch over her son in college and guide his development on and off the football field, Petrino vowed he would put Jackson in the best possible position to succeed from the start. Mama bear liked what she heard.

"The number one thing is we were recruiting him to play quarterback. We weren't recruiting him to another position," Petrino said. "And then I told [his] mom that I would give him the same amount of reps [beginning in summer practice, when the entire incoming freshman class participates] as whoever came out of spring ball as the starter so that he could show his teammates he was the best guy. And even as young and inexperienced as he was, a true freshman, it wasn't hard to give him those reps. Actually, it was easy to keep giving him more and more reps as we went along. He made it easy for us."

—

Louisville athletic director Tom Jurich had heard the buzz about the freshman quarterback and decided to investigate for himself. On the second day of practice before the Cardinals' 2015 football season, Jurich made his way to the field and visited with Petrino on the sideline. As the two men chatted, Petrino said, Jurich received immediate confirmation of everything swirling around campus.

"He stands next to me and says, 'Well, what do you think of this guy?' And I said, 'Tom, this guy's going to be unbelievable. Probably the best we've ever had.'" Right as Jurich was saying that, Jackson smoothly avoided a ferocious rush by sliding right in the pocket and launching a bomb that connected with a deep receiver for a touchdown.

"You just see things," Petrino said. "Even when he was so young that first year . . . he just did things that you could just tell where he was headed.

"At that point, he might not have known the progressions [where a quarterback is supposed to throw the ball based on the alignment of a defense], but he had such vision and instincts, which took over. You just knew that once he got the progressions down and understood the [offensive line] protections and started running the whole thing . . . he would just be unstoppable. It was clear what we had to do."

For Petrino's offensive assistants, the mandate heading into the 2015 season didn't need to be spoken: Do whatever it takes to get Jackson in the lineup as soon as possible.

In that aim, the coaching staff decided to pare down the playbook for Jackson. The move had nothing do with Jackson lacking the intelligence to master the whole thing, which he did eventually. But Petrino had no intention of overwhelming the 18-year-old freshman, who, Petrino was confident, was destined for greatness in the not-too-distant future. Petrino's plan called for the coaches to teach Jackson part of the offense "and see if we can get him good at all those plays" in time for the season opener against highly ranked Auburn University at the Georgia Dome in Atlanta.

In practice, Jackson worked from a playbook of five formations with eight plays per formation. The Cardinals' complete playbook had nine formations and many more plays per formation than eight. What's more, Louisville's staff did everything it could to help Jackson get comfortable in his new role, as much as any freshman quarterback can ease into playing his opening game in front of a national-television audience at a stadium that seats more than 71,000. In high school, Jackson worked from the pistol formation or shotgun formation, in which quarterbacks line up a few yards behind center or several yards behind center, respectively. In those formations, a lot is removed from a quarterback's shoulders in terms of footwork fundamentals, which is a big part of what makes a quarterback a polished passer.

Petrino, a former NFL offensive assistant, is a staunch proponent of the pro-style passing game in which quarterbacks line up under the center, take rhythmic three-, five-, and seven-step drops based on the receivers' route combinations and are required to read the whole field. "We didn't try to make him go [under] the center at that time," Petrino said. "We kept him in the gun or pistol to start because we just really wanted to get him out there."

Throughout practice before the opener, Jackson held up his end. He pleased the coaching staff, learning his package of plays quickly and each day taking a bigger leadership role in practice. Against Auburn, Jackson was listed as the backup quarterback. But everyone in the program knew the freshman who had provided so many thrills in practice was a second-stringer in name only.

"His natural leadership and his love of the game was obvious," Petrino said. "Every day, he came to practice with a smile on his face and did everything full speed. Literally, every time he ran the ball, he ran it all the way to the end zone. When your quarterback has that type of attitude, when he shows that all the time, his teammates will follow. Even then, he just made everyone around him better."

Early in the Cardinals' opener, the rest of college football finally got to see a show that had already been playing for weeks on Louisville's practice field. Not surprisingly, Jackson was overly excited at the start. On the game's first play from scrimmage, Jackson lined up in the backfield behind the starting quarterback, who was under center at the Cardinals' 25-yard line. Before the snap, the quarterback went in motion to the left. Jackson received a direct snap, rolled to his right, and, approaching the sideline and trying to avoid the pass rush, threw a pass that Auburn intercepted at its 39-yard line. An auspicious start to his college career it wasn't.

After Auburn built a 24–0 lead early in the third quarter, Jackson finally got rolling. Trailing 24–3 late in the quarter, the Cardinals had first and goal on the Tigers' 10-yard line. At quarterback, Jackson received the snap, faked a handoff to a running back, juked a defender who was left grasping at air, and sprinted left for a touchdown. With under four minutes to play and the Cardinals down 31–17, Jackson gained 11 yards on a fourth-and-7 run to move his team to the Tigers' 8-yard line. On the drive, Louisville scored another touchdown.

Unfortunately for the Cardinals, time conspired against them in their comeback bid. Final score: Auburn 31, Louisville 24.

For Louisville, however, the game's outcome was secondary. What it confirmed for the coaching staff was paramount: Jackson was on a path to superstardom. And it figured to be a short trip. While sharing time at QB in his college debut, Jackson passed for 100 yards with an interception and rushed for 100 yards with a touchdown. His statistics didn't jump off the page, but Jackson passed the eye test. Auburn's defensive players left the field shaking their heads after trying to tackle Jackson, who made similar ankle-twisting moves in practice to the surprise of his teammates daily.

The opener against Auburn provided a springboard for Jackson's strong freshman year. In 11 games, including seven starts, Jackson performed well while directing the streamlined portion of the offense the staff had tailored to his strengths. On November 28, Louisville completed its regular-season schedule with a 38–24 victory over its in-state rival, the University of Kentucky. In helping the Cardinals rally from a 17-point halftime deficit, Jackson rushed for 186 yards and two touchdowns and passed for 130 yards and another touchdown. With a 7–5 record, Louisville received and accepted a bid to face Texas A&M University in the Music City Bowl in Nashville, Tennessee. As Jackson and the Cardinals enjoyed the break in the schedule before their bowl game, things were going swimmingly, Petrino believed. To say Petrino was pleased with Jackson's development would have been an understatement. But Jackson wasn't satisfied. He should be doing more, he told himself. Jackson needed to be doing more.

———

On his first morning back in the office to start preparing for Texas A&M, Petrino barely had time to settle into his desk chair when he heard a knock on the door. It was Jackson, who had a look of determination on his face his coach had not seen before. Immediately, Petrino realized the ensuing conversation would be unlike any they had previously.

Although Jackson was appreciative of the coaching staff's efforts to enable him to contribute, he understood the Cardinals' offense wasn't operating at full capacity with him at its controls. It was time for that to change, Jackson told Petrino.

"He said, 'I want to be a real quarterback. I want to know what

I need to do to be a real quarterback. Whatever it takes, I'll do it,'"
Petrino said. "We got started right away."

In the month before the bowl game, Jackson had daily 6:00 a.m.
study sessions with coaches. Petrino and his assistants pored over the
entire playbook with Jackson and put him through his paces, testing
Jackson on his knowledge of not only what the quarterback should
do on each play, but what every player on the field–linemen, running
backs, wide receivers–should do as well. The best quarterbacks know
how to utilize all the pieces on the board, and Jackson started to see
things several moves ahead of the questions he was being asked.

"We retaught the entire offense. It was like doing another whole
[playbook] installation from where we started in camp," Petrino
said. "And he got it. Going into the bowl game, that made a huge
difference for him."

Apparently.

Brimming with confidence resulting from his newfound command
of the entire offense, Jackson terrorized Texas A&M in Louisville's 27–21
victory. He had 227 yards passing and two touchdowns with no interceptions and 226 yards rushing with two touchdowns.

Dual threat, indeed.

As a sophomore the next season, Jackson was as close to being
truly unstoppable as a player can be in football. En route to winning
the 2016 Heisman Trophy, Jackson had 3,543 yards passing and 30
touchdown passes against only nine interceptions. He also rushed
for 1,571 yards (with a 6.0-yard average) and 21 touchdowns. In only
13 games, Jackson accounted for a staggering 51 touchdowns. For
Petrino, there was no suspense in anything Jackson accomplished
while leading the Cardinals to a 9–4 record. Petrino expected
Jackson to dominate. Things had been trending in that direction
since Jackson arrived on campus. In the history of college football,
there just weren't many quarterbacks who possessed Jackson's
combination of arm strength to connect with receivers in stride

on any route imaginable as well as the speed to leave elite corner-backs in his dust. In fact, when assessing Jackson's athletic gifts and impact on the game, only one player came to mind: Vick.

The elusive, strong-armed left-hander had burst onto the scene with Virginia Tech University in 1999. Vick spent two seasons making college defensive players look foolish before the Atlanta Falcons selected him No. 1 overall in the 2001 draft. With the Hokies, Vick had 3,299 yards passing with 21 touchdowns and 11 interceptions. He added another 1,299 yards rushing (with a 5.5-yard average) and 17 touchdowns. Vick's statistics, coupled with the athleticism he displayed while accumulating them, resulted in another barrier being toppled in the NFL when he was drafted.

While Jackson was at Louisville, however, he produced statistics Vick could never have dreamed of. Although Jackson failed to repeat as the Heisman Trophy winner in 2017 and finished third (Archie Griffin, who played at Ohio State University, is the only player to win the award twice), he had a better season as a junior. His completion percentage improved from 56.2 to 59.1. His passing yardage increased to 3,660, and Jackson had 27 touchdown passes with 10 interceptions. Jackson also had more yards rushing (1,601) and a higher average per carry (6.9) than in his sophomore season while scoring 18 touchdowns. In 2017, Vick had nothing but praise for his on-field doppelgänger.

"People say he plays a lot like how I played," Vick said. "He plays exactly like I played. Now I know what it must have been like to try to [tackle] me in college."

By the end of Jackson's junior season, it was clear he was ready for the NFL. But was the NFL ready for Jackson?

—

The manner by which players enter the NFL from college has been described as equal parts dehumanizing and anti-capitalistic. At the pre-draft NFL Scouting Combine, players are weighed, measured, and put through a battery of tests to assess their agility, strength, speed, endurance, and intelligence. Some have likened the combine to slave auctions, at which slaves were stripped naked and humiliated as potential buyers pulled open their mouths to see their teeth and pinched their arms and legs in an effort to gauge their strength. Of course, anyone who likens the NFL combine to slave auctions is engaging in hyperbole. There are myriad differences between the two processes, the biggest of which being that slaves had no choice in whether to participate in auctions. And slaves weren't getting offered multimillion-dollar contracts. But at that point in a player's career, the combine makes clear who has the balance of power between them and the billionaire owners of NFL teams.

Following the combine, the NFL, through its annual draft, restricts players' earning ability and freedom of choice in where they start their careers. Both prongs of the operation are antithetical to the free-market beliefs franchise owners hold dear, but that's a matter for another day. The bottom line is that the system is set up for teams to have control over the top college players as they transition into the league. For team owners, the system functions at its best when players fall in line and do what's expected of them. In big ways, Jackson bucked the system.

At the seven-day combine at Indianapolis in 2018, Jackson emerged as the event's most confounding participant. Every night, in conversations that began during dinner at the city's swankiest steak houses and continued over late-night cocktails and cigars in packed bars, NFL general managers, head coaches, and their top player-personnel lieutenants struggled to get a handle on the decorated QB. One would think that a player who launches picturesque deep balls with the flick of his right wrist, is top-of-the-charts fast, and measures up well enough on the QB height chart (at 6 foot 2, Jackson is able to operate just fine within the pocket) wouldn't engender confusion among people paid handsomely to evaluate football players. But with Polian's comments about Jackson still ringing in their ears, many of the people who wielded the most power during the draft didn't have a clue where to slot Jackson on their boards.

Although Jackson's arm strength wasn't at issue, his lack of accuracy concerned many teams. In three seasons at Louisville, Jackson completed 57 percent of his passes, achieving his highest mark of 59.1 as a junior. There was a time in football when Jackson's completion percentage would have been outstanding. In their NFL careers, Hall of Famers Joe Namath and Terry Bradshaw had completion percentages of 50.1 and 51.9, respectively.

But Namath and Bradshaw played during eras before rule changes were instituted in an effort to boost the game's popularity—and television ratings, resulting in the NFL and college leagues receiving fatter contracts from their TV partners—through increased scoring. Nowadays, it almost seems as if cornerbacks will be flagged for so much as even looking at wide receivers the wrong way. In such a quarterback-friendly climate, top quarterbacks are expected to complete at least 60 percent of their passes. Behind the scenes, the word at the combine was that many clubs disliked Jackson's throwing mechanics and doubted they could be improved. Curiously, though, there wasn't widespread consternation about University of Wyoming quarterback Josh Allen's accuracy issues. A mobile quarterback, Allen in three seasons at Wyoming completed 56.2 percent of his passes. Allen is white. Perhaps his race wasn't a factor in teams being less concerned about his errant passes than they were about Jackson's misfires. The optics of the situation, however, weren't great for the league.

—

Many teams had other issues with Jackson as well.

He declined to run the 40-yard dash, traditionally the most

important measurement of speed for NFL players. With all the talk about Jackson potentially switching positions swirling in the media (at the combine, he faced a volley of questions on the subject from reporters), he was determined to plant his flag as a quarterback entering the draft. Jackson figured that if he wowed scouts with a fantastic time, which was probable for the 100-meter-sprint star, the external pressure on him to relent to a position switch would only increase. Jackson never opened the door. He was willing to risk potentially being criticized for his decision while focusing exclusively on displaying his passing skills at the talent showcase. When scouts evaluated Louisville players at the university's pro day in March 2018, Jackson again skipped running speed-test drills.

Moon can relate. Forty years before Jackson, Moon, the former Houston Oilers great, wrestled with a decision on whether to run for scouts. A standout passer for the University of Washington, Moon led the Huskies to a victory over Michigan in the 1978 Rose Bowl and was selected co-player of the year in the then–Pacific-8 Conference. Back in those days, however, NFL owners had as much interest in drafting Black quarterbacks as they did in supporting higher capital gains tax rates.

Moon viewed the 40-yard dash as a potential trap. But unlike Jackson, who realized his decision would merely irritate some team officials, Moon didn't have the option of skipping the test altogether. Scouts would have labeled Moon as being difficult. Such an odious tag in that era, combined with being a Black quarterback, would have ruined Moon's draft prospects. Hence, he had a dilemma. "I knew that if I ran too fast, they would want to change my position, because I had already heard that was the thinking," Moon recalled. "I didn't want to give them any more ammunition. So instead of busting my butt and really accelerating through the tape, I let up, probably the last ten yards, so I wouldn't have that really fast time."

Moon was passed over in the draft. In order to pursue his dreams of a pro football career, Moon traveled north to Canada. He got the last laugh, though: After his record-setting career in the CFL, Moon was the object of a bidding war among NFL teams, which the then–Houston Oilers won. In 1984, the club signed Moon to a contract worth more than $5.5 million–making him the highest-paid player in league history at the time.

"But for Lamar, times had changed enough so he didn't have to run, which is a decision he stuck to," Moon said. "He did what he felt he had to do at a time there was a lot being said about him–a lot that was just totally wrong."

Jackson's mom came under scrutiny as well at the combine after word emerged she had assumed the role of being the passer's de facto agent. It struck many NFL executives as an odd move, considering they were unaware whether Jones had a background in contract negotiations. With so little maneuverability in a player's first contract under the NFL rookie wage scale, Jackson explained, he preferred to pocket the big commission he would have owed an agent. Nevertheless, another negative narrative formed around Jackson, with Jones in the role of a controlling stage mom and Jackson as a son supposedly not strong enough to keep his mother at arm's length for the good of his career. Jones was Jackson's first teammate, and any franchise that drafted Jackson would have to understand that their bond, forged in shared heartache and triumph, couldn't be broken.

"My immediate family is my mom," Jackson said. "Everything goes around her. I'm a mama's boy. That's my baby. That's my mama. . . . She's the one who keeps me motivated no matter what. She's driving me."[103]

All the way to the top, as it turned out.

—

The first round of the 2018 NFL draft was winding down on April 26 at AT&T Stadium in Arlington, Texas, but the most interesting development of the night was unfolding far away in Owings Mills, Maryland.

Hunkered down in the draft room at their franchise headquarters, the Ravens' top brass–led by owner Steve Bisciotti, general manager Ozzie Newsome, head coach John Harbaugh and assistant general manager Eric DeCosta–had a big decision to make. The club had already used its first-round pick, the 25th overall, to select tight end Hayden Hurst from the University of Tennessee. But with only a few picks remaining in the 32-pick opening round, the Ravens zeroed in on another player: Jackson.

Although most clubs, based on their pre-draft evaluations of Jackson, did not have the Heisman Trophy winner rated as an opening-round pick, the Ravens weren't with the pack. In the months before the draft, Baltimore officials were on Louisville's campus early and often. They asked Petrino all the right questions about Lamar. Then they asked more of them. Petrino had two stints in the NFL, first as an assistant for three years under two-time Super Bowl winning coach Tom Coughlin and then as the head coach of the Atlanta Falcons for one season. Based on how the Ravens went about vetting Jackson, Petrino was confident they had serious interest in drafting him.

"They did all their research. They did all the things you need to do," Petrino said. "They spent time with me, spent time with all of our other coaches, spent time with him, and worked him out extra. They did all of their homework and their due diligence."

Yet, as the second round drew near, Jackson remained seated inside AT&T Stadium all dressed up with nowhere to go. Then the Ravens sprang into action.

Confident they had the draft capital required to move back into the first round and nab Jackson, a player whom they believed the rest of the league was missing the boat on, the Ravens worked the phones quickly. In the Philadelphia Eagles, the Ravens found a willing partner to make a deal.

The Eagles agreed to trade their first- and fourth-round selections

(32nd and 132nd) in exchange for the Ravens' second- and fourth-round selections (52nd and 125th) and a second-round selection in 2019. Suddenly, Baltimore was on the clock with the final pick of the first round. And Jackson, finally, was about to join the party.

He had sat with his mother anxiously awaiting his moment onstage, both literally and figuratively, while four other former college quarterbacks in the first round found NFL homes before him that night: Baker Mayfield (University of Oklahoma) went first overall to the Cleveland Browns, the Jets chose Sam Darnold (University of Southern California) with the third pick, the Buffalo Bills picked Josh Allen (Wyoming) with the seventh selection, and Josh Rosen (University of California, Los Angeles) went tenth to the Arizona Cardinals. Among Baltimore's senior leadership group, there was unanimity. The Ravens, they believed, had gotten their next franchise quarterback in the steal of the draft.

"There were some really good quarterbacks in that draft," Newsome said. "Baker went, Sam Darnold went, Josh Allen, Josh Rosen. But there was affection in the room that was started by Steve Bisciotti, our owner, for Lamar.

"Sitting down at the end of the table, having the discussion that we've got all of these picks, and Lamar's still on the board, let's go trade up [and back into the first round] and get him. We're doing something different, we're taking something special. But everybody in the room was in agreement that we should do it."

After being picked, Jackson stepped to the lectern late into the evening in Texas and assured the Ravens they wouldn't be disappointed. He also served notice that the rest of the league would soon realize the error of its ways.

"When my name finally got called, I was like, 'Man, I'm glad I wore this suit,'" Jackson said, his comment punctuated by laughter that belied his profound nervousness only a few minutes earlier.

"[It's] just an honor for the Ravens organization to believe in me.

And all the teams that passed me up . . . there's a lot that's gonna come with that."

—

For veteran Ravens quarterback Joe Flacco, the handwriting on the wall was billboard-sized. Baltimore's decision to draft Jackson in the opening round meant that Flacco's long, distinguished run with the team was officially coming to an end. As a rule, NFL teams don't draft quarterbacks in the first round to keep them on clipboard duty for years.

Baltimore's first-round selection (18th overall) in the 2008 draft, Flacco was a solid, albeit not spectacular, traditional pocket passer. Never selected to the Pro Bowl or first- or second-team All-Pro, Flacco did his part well enough to help Baltimore, which was built on a foundation of defense, win consistently under Harbaugh. With Flacco under center, the Ravens qualified for the AFC playoffs in his first five seasons and in six of his first seven. For his efforts in helping the Ravens win Super Bowl XLVII in 2013, Flacco was selected the game's MVP. But by 2018, the former University of Delaware record-setter was clearly on the back end of his career.

Although the Ravens were eager to begin the transition process from Flacco to Jackson, some issues had to be addressed. The team's offensive approach topped the list.

Flacco was almost 6 foot 7. When Flacco dropped back to read a defense over hulking offensive and defensive linemen engaged in hand-to-hand combat, his height was an asset. For most of his career, Flacco's playing weight had hovered around 245 pounds. His size and strength enabled him to absorb the pounding quarterbacks take (it has been likened to being in multiple car crashes each week) and stay in the game: In his first seven seasons, Flacco didn't miss a potential start. He made every start in 9 of his first 10 seasons.

However, Flacco was not, as they say, fleet of foot. Wisely,

Harbaugh had structured Baltimore's offense to capitalize on Flacco's ability to succeed playing in the pocket exclusively; no need to create a package of designed runs for him. Jackson was one of the best athletes to ever set foot on an NFL field. To get Jackson's best, Harbaugh realized he would have to, eventually, make major changes to Baltimore's offense with Jackson's amazing skill set always being front of mind for him. That established, the future would have to wait. Entering the 2018–19 season, Flacco was still under contract and the Ravens were playing it safe with Jackson, who was only 21 when the season kicked off.

As the season opened, Flacco, as expected, retained the Ravens' No. 1 job. Through their first nine games, the Ravens, who had failed to qualify for the playoffs during the previous three seasons and in four of the past five, were 4–5. It appeared their postseason drought would continue, especially after Flacco, who was having a solid season statistically, was sidelined because of a hip injury. Baltimore had no choice: Ready or not, Jackson got the keys. He was exactly the change of pace the Ravens needed.

The rookie quarterback ignited a stunning turnaround. Jackson revived the moribund team and went 6–1 as a starter. In seven games, Jackson completed 58.2 percent of his passes for 1,201 yards with six touchdowns and three interceptions. He also rushed for 695 yards (with a 4.7-yard average) and five touchdowns.

Jackson played a big role in the Ravens qualifying for postseason play for the first time since the 2014–15 season. At 21 years and 364 days, Jackson became the youngest quarterback to start a playoff game in NFL history. Harbaugh, Baltimore's head coach, had seen enough. It was time to complete the changing of the guard.

In the off-season, the Ravens traded Flacco to the Denver Broncos, thereby averting a potential quarterback controversy beginning the 2019–20 season. Clearing a path for Jackson to be the unquestioned starter, however, was only part of Harbaugh's plan. For the move to Jackson to work, for the Ravens' to reap the full benefit of Jackson's athletic gifts, it was time for them to go all in: tear down the offense and create something new for Jackson. Something that would result in opponents both gasping for breath and grasping for words to describe what had hit them.

▬

Five days after Baltimore lost to the Los Angeles Chargers in the AFC wild-card round, Harbaugh shook up his coaching staff: offensive coordinator Marty Mornhinweg was out and Greg Roman, previously the team's run-game specialist and tight ends coach, was in as the Ravens' top assistant on offense. Then Harbaugh and Roman torched the Ravens' old playbook, rolled up their sleeves, and locked themselves in the lab. In Roman, Harbaugh picked the right man to drive the big project.

Before joining Harbaugh's staff in 2015, Roman was the San Francisco 49ers' offensive play caller from 2011 to 2014. In the role, Roman had quite a good stretch with a dual-threat passer named Colin Kaepernick. Under Roman's guidance, Kaepernick had three strong seasons—San Francisco lost to Baltimore in the Super Bowl after the 2012 season and returned to the NFC championship game the next season—and the 49ers had one of the league's best offenses. Roman helped Harbaugh's younger brother, Jim, who was the then-49ers' head coach, make a smooth transition from quarterback Alex Smith to Kaepernick. The job Roman was tasked with in Baltimore was much more complex. The 49ers only tinkered with their approach, modifying things here and there to utilize plays that best suited Kaepernick.

Essentially, the elder Harbaugh razed the building and told his chief architect to have a new one finished and open for business in nine months, the period between the Ravens' playoff loss and the kickoff of the 2019–2020 season. Roman knew what he had signed up for, and heavy lifting didn't scare him.

"We're literally redefining everything we do as a staff, as a group," Roman said in February 2019. "Literally, everything: every formation, every route, every run, every route concept. How can we make this offense–which up until this point has been good–we're trying to make it as great as we can be."[104]

Additionally, the Ravens added players on offense who would complement Jackson. Two of the most important moves were made at running back and wide receiver. They signed productive free-agent Mark Ingram to be Jackson's main partner in the team's new rushing approach. Then, in the 2019 draft, Baltimore selected wideout Marquise Brown from the University of Oklahoma to be Jackson's top deep threat. Baltimore's coaching staff anticipated that tight end Mark Andrews, part of the team's strong 2018 draft class that included Jackson, would have a breakout season in the team's new way of doing things.

Finally emerging from the lab during organized team activities in May 2019, Harbaugh and Roman unveiled their creation, revolving around Jackson. If all went according to plan, Jackson would switch seamlessly between gaining rushing yards in chunks on college option-style plays and passing yards in bunches against defenses in a perpetual state of confusion. A QB capable of ripping off an 80-yard TD run on one possession and then throwing an 80-yard TD pass on the next, Harbaugh figured, might just keep opponents off-balance.

Jackson would be required to work more from the pocket in the pistol formation, a hybrid of the shotgun and lining up under center, which was his favorite formation in high school and college. In the pistol, quarterbacks line up four yards behind the center, which is much closer than a QB's seven-yard depth in a shotgun formation. The shotgun formation limits what teams can do in the running game because of a quarterback's deep pre-snap depth and the relatively long period of time needed to get a running play going. Based on where running backs line up in the option, the formation also often tips an offensive coordinator's hand in play calling. Harbaugh and Roman figured having Jackson in the pistol, as a staple of the Ravens' offense, was exactly the right foundation to help the Ravens fly.

—

In what would be the first true test of their new offense, the Ravens arrived at Hard Rock Stadium in Miami on September 8, 2019, to open the season against the Miami Dolphins. Throughout off-season workouts and in preseason games, coaches and players at times struggled to familiarize themselves with new plays and new terminology. It was a process that included inevitable growing pains. The team went 4-0 during the preseason, in which first-stringers play little. Against the Dolphins, the Ravens would learn where they stood.

As it turned out, the view was spectacular.

Jackson played flawlessly, leading the Ravens to a 59–10 rout. While helping Baltimore establish new franchise marks for points and total yards with 643, Jackson became the youngest quarterback to have a perfect passer rating, which is calculated by using a player's passing attempts, completions, yards, touchdowns, and interceptions to measure performance on a scale of 0 to 158.3. He had only three incompletions in 20 attempts, 324 yards passing, five touchdown passes, and no interceptions. For the Ravens' coaching staff, the most gratifying part of Jackson's performance was that the southeastern Florida native took a wrecking ball to the Dolphins' defense from the pocket: Jackson had only six yards rushing on three carries.

Beginning with the NFL scouting combine before the 2018 draft, Jackson had mostly deflected reporters' questions about his supposed shortcomings as a passer. But just to make it clear he had been paying attention, Jackson delivered a zinger after his smashing opening act, saying, "Not bad for a running back." Jackson let down his guard, if ever so briefly, to reveal he took offense to all the talk about his supposed inability to make it as an NFL QB.

The boulder-sized chip on Jackson's shoulder left no doubt about his thinking. After leaving the Dolphins in ruins, Jackson embarked on a season-long tour across the league in which he, eagerly through his performance, reminded the Ravens' opponents they all made a huge mistake in passing on him. It was something to see.

Each week, with Roman pushing the correct buttons, Jackson was the talk of the league. Just as Harbaugh had hoped, opponents were always out of sorts because of Jackson's cleverness in the backfield (he mastered faking handoffs and then taking off) and speed and elusiveness in the open field. Linebackers focused so much attention on Jackson, Ingram often went untouched through the line, Andrews had space to roam in the mid-range passing game, and Brown, with safeties playing closer to the line to offer run support against Baltimore, capitalized on one-on-one coverage from cornerbacks. Every Ravens opponent, as the centerpiece of their defensive strategies, focused on trying to corral Jackson in the Ravens' option running game. It didn't matter. Jackson thwarted the best-laid plans.

While directing a 49–13 rout of the Cincinnati Bengals in November, Jackson had his second perfect passer rating of the season. In NFL history, Pittsburgh Steelers quarterback Ben Roethlisberger is the only other player to accomplish the feat multiple times in a single season. Roethlisberger had two such performances in 2007. During the Ravens' blowout of the Bengals in November, Jackson, who seemed to have a did-you-see-that? run each game, produced his signature highlight of the season as a ball carrier. In the third quarter, Jackson faked a handoff to a running back, pulled back the ball, and ran left. He juked the first Bengals player within striking distance of him, making the fellow look silly, then with another taking an angle toward him, Jackson completed a stunning 360-degree spin move and kept rolling for a 47-yard touchdown. Literally and figuratively, the Bengals were spinning.

After Jackson returned to the Ravens' sideline and a procession line formed to praise him, Harbaugh located Jackson and plopped down next to him on the bench. Television cameras captured what happened next:

"Most quarterbacks worry about their stats, but you're a leader," Harbaugh, who was clearly bursting with pride, told Jackson. "I love the way you play. You don't flinch, you just attack. All you do is attack."

"It's all I know," Jackson responded.

"You changed the game, man," Harbaugh said.

The kicker Harbaugh delivered spoke to so much more than just football.

"Do you know how many little kids in this country are going to be wearing No. 8 playing quarterback for the next twenty years?" Harbaugh asked.

Who knows how many young Black boys were inspired that day, or on many others, by Jackson, who in the ultimate leadership position in sports excelled in a manner unlike any superstar quarterback before him. Ryan Clark, the former longtime NFL safety and ESPN analyst, soaked it all in.

"Even though Harbaugh is a white man, he said, 'Do you know what you're doing for little kids? Little kids are going to wear that jersey.' When I heard that, to me it was little Black kids," Clark said. "Little Black kids from where you are from. Little Black kids who look like you and play ball like you play.

"What [Harbaugh] was really saying to him, what came through so clearly, is he was saying you're giving them a reason to say, 'I can play quarterback and succeed at the highest level. And even if I'm not accepted right away, I can look at Lamar Jackson and say, we've seen this before.' What he was saying is that you're going to give them hope."

And Jackson does so on his own terms.

Jackson sports box or wash braids, sometimes a "Cruddy," or perhaps a nappy 'fro and talks like a 22-year-old Black kid from southeastern Florida.[105]

For many Black people, Clark said, Jackson's apparent comfort in his hairstyle and how he speaks is even more important than the highlights he creates. "In terms of what he's doing for the [Black] culture, Lamar even went a step beyond Michael Vick. Black people see Lamar and they see . . . they see themselves."

—

Lamar Jackson sat patiently in the front row of the NFL Honors show on February 1, 2020, at the Adrienne Arsht Center in Miami, Florida. Flanked by Ravens Hall of Fame linebacker Ray Lewis on his right and Felicia Jones, his mother and business partner, on his left, Jackson was close to home. But this wasn't the homecoming he most wanted.

The Baltimore Ravens were the NFL's most dominant team during the 2019–20 regular season. Ravens head coach John Harbaugh and offensive coordinator Greg Roman were rewarded spectacularly for believing in Jackson. They scrapped Baltimore's longtime offense, built back better, and had the league's best record at 14–2. Baltimore, which finished the regular season on a 12-game winning streak, led the NFL in yards rushing, finished second in total offense, and tied an NFL record by having 12 players named to the AFC Pro Bowl roster. Jackson made it all come together.

He topped the NFL with 36 touchdown passes and had only six interceptions. More important, Jackson improved his accuracy significantly from 58.2 percent as a rookie to a sparkling 66.1 percent, tied for eighth in the league. The panel of All-Pro team voters selected Jackson as the first-team quarterback. Again, not bad for a running back. As a ball carrier, Jackson was a record-setter. He sprinted for 1,206 yards (with a dazzling 6.9-yard average) and seven touchdowns. Jackson established a new single-season NFL rushing record for QBs, breaking Vick's mark of 1,039 in 2006. Ingram had one of the best seasons of his career, rushing for 1,018 (with a 5.0-yard average) and 10 touchdowns. Ravens coaches absolutely nailed it on their belief that Andrews would hit it big. The tight end averaged 13.3 yards on 64 catches and had 10 TD receptions. Brown, the rookie wideout, had seven touchdown receptions. Doug Williams, the first Black QB to win a Super Bowl, was thrilled for Jackson. Williams had never seen anything like it.

"Listen, I've been around this league since 1978. When you talk about the history of the NFL, teams don't do that [start over completely on offense] for many guys no matter what color they are," Williams said. "But when you look at the opportunities we were denied through the years, to have the Ravens look at Lamar and believe in him that way . . . it has to make you feel good. And you know what was even better? What he did with the opportunity they gave him."

For the Ravens, however, the story of the 2019–20 season didn't have a Hollywood fairy-tale ending. It was more like the original Brothers Grimm version.

Widely expected to represent the AFC in Super Bowl LIV at Hard Rock Stadium in Miami Gardens, the Ravens stumbled in the divisional round, losing to the Tennessee Titans on their home field, 28–12. The Ravens' flat performance proved yet again that securing the top playoff seeding won't necessarily provide a team with a sure path to the Super Bowl. There's a school of thought in the NFL that receiving a first-round bye, a reward that accompanies having the best record in each conference, can result in top teams losing their rhythm at the worst possible time. Clearly, after their break, the Ravens weren't in a groove in the divisional round.

Bruising Tennessee running back Derrick Henry met little resistance from Baltimore's defense en route to having a spectacular performance: Henry rushed for 195 yards with a 6.5-yard average, outstanding numbers for any game but especially during the season's most important stretch, and tossed a short touchdown pass. The Ravens needed Jackson to be at his best, which he wasn't in his first career playoff game. He passed for 365 yards and rushed for 143, which, on its face, appeared to be a banner outing. On closer inspection, though, Jackson's three turnovers (he had two interceptions and lost a fumble) undermined his other positive numbers. He had a bad day. Many young QBs struggle in their introduction to the playoffs. Pro Football Hall of Famers John Elway, Dan Marino, and Peyton Manning could attest to that.

Here's what made the Ravens' playoff flop even tougher on Jackson: Hard Rock Stadium is located about 25 miles northeast of Pompano Beach, Jackson's hometown. There was no sugarcoating it: Failing to reach the Super Bowl in his home state was an awful closing chapter to an otherwise great story. Jackson, though, would not return to Baltimore empty-handed.

—

As the taping of the NFL Honors broadcast drew to a close, the Ravens had reason to be pleased: Harbaugh was selected the league's coach of the year. The decision was a no-brainer.

Harbaugh identified Jackson's potential, a skill most of his coaching colleagues clearly lacked, then risked making over Baltimore's offense for an inexperienced player. In doing so, Harbaugh displayed great leadership. If that's not what coaching is about, what is?

The Ravens weren't the first team in professional sports history to flop in the postseason after having a great regular season. Surely, they won't be the last. Harbaugh was rewarded for being the league's best head coach in the regular season. He earned it.

Actor Paul Rudd, he of Marvel Studios' Ant-Man fame, introduced the night's final award: the Associated Press Most Valuable Player. On a large video screen behind Rudd, the candidates for awards throughout the show were introduced in highlights mash-ups of the season. Until the end. For the MVP award, Jackson was the only player featured.

"Now, you might be asking yourself, 'Well, where are the other contenders?'" Rudd said to the audience. "Here's the thing: For only the second time in history, there was just one person that this year everyone voted for. . . . It's pretty incredible. In fact, it's Lamar-velous. Congratulations to this year's most valuable player, Lamar Jackson."

Passed over by 31 teams and his ability to even play QB in the NFL questioned, Jackson that night joined Tom Brady, the most successful quarterback in the game's history, as the only unanimous winners of the AP MVP award. Jackson, who also won the Pro Bowl MVP award, became the youngest passer to ever be selected the league's best player at 22 years, 358 days. Jackson embraced his mother and Lewis before making his way up the steps to the stage to claim his hardware–and to finally let it all out.

"There has been a lot of doubt going on, me being a running back, a receiver, stuff like that. That came when I got to the league," Jackson said in his acceptance speech. "I didn't want to talk about that, the doubters. I wanted to talk about the ones who believed in me."

Even Polian, the Hall of Fame executive who once said Jackson should switch to wideout, finally came around to seeing Jackson as a quarterback.

"I was wrong, because I used the old, traditional quarterback standard with him, which is clearly why John Harbaugh and Ozzie Newsome were more prescient than I was," Polian said. "The definition has changed, no question."[106]

About that much, both Polian and Jackson would surely agree.

[16]

PATRICK MAHOMES

KANSAS CITY CHIEFS QUARTERBACK Patrick Mahomes grabbed his television remote and hit the power-off button. He couldn't stomach the images on the screen another second. It was May 26, 2020, and Mahomes was shaken by a news report about a Black man named George Floyd, who a day earlier had been killed in Minneapolis by police while being arrested on suspicion of passing a counterfeit $20 bill. The report included a clip of a smartphone video revealing that Derek Chauvin, a white police officer with the Minneapolis Police Department, knelt on Floyd's neck for over nine minutes while Floyd was handcuffed behind his back and lying facedown in the street. Sitting silently in the living room of the Kansas City, Missouri, home he shares with his fiancée, Brittany Matthews; their daughter, Sterling Skye Mahomes; and their dogs, Silver and Steel–an impressive 4,400-square-foot contemporary ranch he purchased for about $2 million in 2019 that's elegantly appointed but definitely understated for the athlete with the most lucrative contract in the history of team sports in the United States–his thoughts quickly turned to his extended family. The young NFL superstar, who three months earlier punctuated his remarkable ascent to the top of the game in only three seasons by directing a historic Super Bowl victory, has uncles and cousins who could have easily faced the kind of inhumane treatment at the hands of police–anywhere in the United States–that Floyd suffered on that fateful day. There's no shortage of disturbing data to support the claim that police are more likely to use force against and kill Black citizens. Black men are about 2.5 times more likely to be killed by police than are white men. Black women are about 1.4 times more likely to be killed by police than are white women. Among all groups, Black men and boys face the highest lifetime risk of having fatal interactions with police: About one in 1,000 Black men and boys will be killed by police. And between the ages of 25 and 29, Black men are killed by police at a rate between 2.8 and 4.1 per 100,000.[107]

The bleak facts weren't new–far from it. But for Mahomes, what played out in the video stirred something unfamiliar within him. The incident seemed different than other fatal interactions between police and people who look like him, many of which had been captured on smartphones in recent years. As it turned out, Mahomes wasn't alone in his thinking.

With government agencies, places of business, and schools nationwide shuttered during the COVID-19 pandemic, hundreds of millions of people were confined to their homes and glued to screens. A captive audience watched Chauvin arrogantly place his hands into his pants pockets and stare defiantly at horrified onlookers as he slowly extinguished Floyd's life. Chauvin's depravity in torturing and killing Floyd (about 11 months later, Chauvin would be convicted on three counts of murder and sentenced to 22.5 years in prison) both horrified the nation and sparked international outrage. Across the United States, people left their lockdowns and took to the streets to protest police brutality and systemic oppression of Black and brown people. The movement soon spread globally, with protestors denouncing racism and police brutality worldwide and declaring solidarity with like-minded demonstrators in the US.

Mahomes could barely think of anything else. He knew he had to do more than sympathize. This was not the time to remain on the sidelines, the man widely considered the NFL's best player told himself. Mahomes, however, wasn't interested in merely making a gesture. He was determined to make a difference. Of course, for Mahomes, doing anything could be perilous for him personally as well as disastrous for his employer—professional sports' most successful and powerful league. For anyone, but especially for someone—still just 24—whose prominence had come in a blinding flash, the issues he confronted were as expansive as they were thorny. Life was coming at Mahomes hard and fast, like a 300-pound defensive tackle.

—

Patrick Lavon Mahomes II was a lucky kid.

By the time he was a preschooler, the child who would grow to become the face of the NFL was as comfortable in a Major League Baseball dugout as he was in a sandbox, his confidence in the former the result of Mahomes tagging along to his dad's place of business regularly. For 11 seasons beginning in 1992, Patrick Sr. pitched for six teams. The Minnesota Twins selected Pat, as he was known to his MLB teammates, in the sixth round of the 1988 MLB Draft. Four years later, the right-hander reached the majors. On September 17, 1995, Pat's then-wife, Randi, gave birth to Patrick, the couple's first child. Patrick's younger brother, Jackson, arrived in 2000. The product of an interracial union—the elder Mahomes is Black and Randi is white—Patrick as a child was taught to judge people as individuals based on their conduct toward others. The approach would become a guiding principle of his life.

At ease around his dad's teammates of all races and ethnicities, Patrick enjoyed showing the big leaguers that he had skills, too. In the New York Mets–New York Yankees World Series of 2000, five-year-old Patrick put a scare into his pops, then a reliever on the Mets' National League pennant-winning club, and left him bursting with pride as well. During batting practice before Game 3 at Shea Stadium, Pat permitted Patrick to accompany him into the outfield– territory that could be dangerous for a tyke as the best baseball players in the world darted about while shagging fly balls during batting practice. Pat wanted his youngster to experience being on one of the biggest stages in sports.

"The coaches were wary that he was going to get hit," he recalled, "but I told them if he gets hit one time, he will learn–then he won't do it again. As I was saying it, Robin Ventura hit a ball out to left-center."

It was a towering shot, heading right toward the little guy, who was barely bigger than a toddler. Pat had a bad moment. He even imagined Randi's reaction if little Patrick was injured while under his supervision in a setting, and participating in an activity, clearly way beyond his years. But to the delight of the Mets (and undoubtedly to Pat's relief), Patrick tracked down the ball and made a nifty running catch with his little glove. The play provided a glimpse into Patrick's potential in baseball. It would be the first of many.[108]

As the years passed, and Patrick excelled in baseball at every level, Pat thought Patrick would follow him into the family business. In 2010, when Patrick was 14, he appeared on ESPN, playing shortstop for a team from Tyler, Texas, where he was born–the runner-up to Taipei in that year's Junior League World Series. By the time Patrick enrolled at Whitehouse High in Whitehouse, Texas, he was already an area youth-sports standout. He would soon become a three-sport star for Whitehouse in baseball, basketball, and football. On the baseball team, Mahomes played multiple positions, shining whether at the plate, in the field, or on the mound. When he played left-center field, would-be doubles and triples often died a quick death in his glove. But pitching, not surprisingly, was really Patrick's thing.

In a high school playoff game, Mahomes tossed a 16-strikeout no-hitter. He only gave up one run on a wild pitch in the third inning. With a fastball clocked consistently in the low 90 mph range, Patrick, as a senior, emerged as an MLB prospect, and one who was highly regarded by some teams. The Detroit Tigers topped that list. The Tigers selected Pat's boy in the 37th round of the 2014 MLB Draft. By that time, however, Patrick had already committed to play football at Texas Tech. Pat had made it clear to MLB teams: His son was focused on playing college football. Pat, however, probably wouldn't have mounted much of an argument if Patrick had suddenly changed his mind and decided to stick with baseball a little longer, if for nothing else than just to see how high his son could rise in a sport Pat was sure he could succeed in as a professional. In MLB circles, the word was that Patrick would have gone much higher in the draft had he not been so dug in on pursuing a football career. He possessed all the tools needed for a big league run. Of that, Tim Grieve, the Tigers' area scout covering Texas during Patrick's time in high school, was certain. That's why Grieve hoped the young man would give his first true love another shot.

"The thing that stood out about [Patrick] the most, first and foremost, you knew going in that he was a football player. That was his passion. You were kind of hoping against hope a little bit that you could talk this kid into playing baseball," said Grieve, who was instrumental in the Tigers' decision to pick Patrick. "You watch him play football, that's kind of the way he played baseball. . . . He was an unbelievable athlete. He didn't do a lot of the summer stuff [in baseball], a lot of the select [team] stuff, so he maybe wasn't the polished baseball player that some of these other kids were. But he was a superior athlete.

"He was probably one of the best high school basketball players in the state. We drafted him as a pitcher, but you probably could've made a decent argument that this kid was just as good as a position player. I only saw him pitch, but . . . he played center field for his team, he hit in the middle of the order. He swung a wood bat when the other kids were hitting with aluminum bats. It was just an athlete that you could dream on. He was a football guy, but he showed you the arm strength, the athleticism. He could hit, he had strength. Just a really interesting kid. But it was going to take some time because of the lack of polish. But you could really, really dream on him being really good someday."[109]

As a pitcher, Patrick had plenty of room to grow. In addition to having a good fastball for a high school senior, he had unrefined off-speed stuff that, well, could have become well refined by top-notch pitching instructors in the Tigers' farm system, Grieve believed.

"He was a kid that was going to pitch in that eighty-nine to ninety-two [mph] range. I'm sure there were days where he threw harder than that, I think I saw him touching ninety-three, touching ninety-four," Grieve said. "He would shape a breaking ball, he showed you that he had it. It was a little hit and miss, but every third or fourth one, you said, 'Okay, that's going to be plenty good enough.'

"He had a changeup that he really didn't use a whole lot. It wasn't one of the bigger classification high schools [in Texas], so his fastball, curveball, and throwing high school-ish decent strikes was plenty good enough to beat the typical team he was going to play against. The typical game when you went and saw him play, he was so much better than everyone else that he was going to win. He was always the best player on the field."[110]

In Pat, Grieve had an ally. Well, sort of.

Patrick was so good in both baseball and basketball, Pat was convinced that his son's future would be in one of those two sports. And football is just so dangerous. Until Patrick's senior year in high school, Pat continued to lobby hard for baseball.

"We had just visited Texas and he was coming back home and I was trying to talk him out of playing football," the elder Mahomes said. "And he said, 'Dad, I just want to try it one time. I will be the QB this year.' What I was trying to tell him was 'Why take the chance of getting hurt when you know your future is going to be in one of these two other sports?' He had never once concentrated on one thing, and I thought it was going to be either basketball or baseball for him."[111]

In 13 games as a senior at Whitehouse High, Patrick passed for 4,619 yards and an astounding touchdown to interception ratio of 50 to 6. "It didn't take me long to realize he was a pretty good quarterback," Pat said.[112]

By his sophomore year at Texas Tech in Lubbock, Texas, Patrick was in command of the Red Raiders' offense. He delivered a 4,653-yard, 36-touchdown passing performance that year, then did even better as a junior: 41 touchdown passes and more than 5,000 yards passing. Patrick led the Football Bowl Subdivision (FBS) in yards passing, and he joined Marcus Mariota, who played collegiately at the University of Oregon, as the only players from a major conference in FBS history to throw 40 touchdown passes and rush for 10 touchdowns in the same season. And then there was the Red Raiders' 66–59 loss to the Oklahoma Sooners in which Mahomes racked up 734 passing yards with 5 touchdowns and 819 total yards—an FBS record.

Yep. Patrick's decision to attend college and focus on football turned out exceedingly well. Even Grieve, who had called Mahomes to inform him he had been drafted by the Tigers, admitted as much.

"He was actually already at that point on campus in Lubbock. I didn't know that at the time," Grieve said. "But when I called him and talked to him, I said, 'Hey look, this is just us rewarding you for an unbelievable high school career. I don't have the money to pay you what you might've been looking for, but you earned this and I just want to congratulate you on getting drafted.' He was very thankful and honest and said, 'Hey, this is what I'm going to do. I'm going to play football.' But he thanked me for it. I remember hanging up and thinking, 'That's a kid I'm going to root for.' A very down-to-earth, humble, good kid."[113]

—

It was early in the spring of 2017, and something big was happening. All those visits and workouts with teams across the NFL. The buzz around each trip. The signs were all there. And they turned out to be right.

The Kansas City Chiefs selected the former Texas Tech quarterback 10th overall, completing Mahomes's surprising ascent in the NFL draft. The second of only three quarterbacks chosen in the first round in that draft class–North Carolina's Mitchell Trubisky went second overall to the Chicago Bears, and Clemson standout Deshaun Watson went 12th to the Houston Texans–Mahomes wound up with the Chiefs after they paid a steep price to move up the board for a signal-caller considered the rawest high-profile player available at the position. Kansas City swapped positions with the Buffalo Bills, moving from 27th to 10th. To persuade the Bills to make the deal, the Chiefs also gave up their pick in the third round (91st overall) and a 2018 first-rounder. Kansas City head coach Andy Reid loved what he saw in Mahomes and didn't want to risk losing him. Based on the chatter around the league entering the first round, Reid had reason to be concerned.

Before every draft, there are players whose stock rises or falls quickly based on their performances in private workouts and how they come across in interviews with team decision-makers. In the run-up to the 2017 draft, Mahomes's stock was jumping. More and more clubs were trying to get on his schedule. Mahomes bounced around the country like a rock star on tour, improving his standing with each stop.

Even so, many so-called experts expressed doubts that Mahomes would be a successful NFL starter, let alone a star. A potential all-time great? Forget about it.

Sure, Mahomes amassed oh-wow numbers during three seasons at Texas Tech. But skeptics could point to the many Texas Tech passers before him who had produced stats that prompted football fans to do double takes—but fell flat in the NFL. Arizona Cardinals head coach Kliff Kingsbury, University of Southern California offensive coordinator Graham Harrell, and B. J. Symons, who set 11 NCAA records with the Red Raiders, are on that list, to name a few. But of the Red Raiders' notable alumni, only Mahomes was a first-round pick. Still, few outside of the Chiefs' organization were convinced that Mahomes would be the exception.

In the school's "Air Raid" offense, a system in which the quarterback works from the shotgun formation and spreads out the defense by utilizing three-, four-, and five-receiver sets, Red Raiders passers lit it up. It's not the ideal college offense, however, for preparing quarterbacks to play in pro-style NFL systems, in which signal-callers regularly operate under center and the running game usually has a significant role in an overall offensive strategy.

Before being drafted, Mahomes acknowledged he had a whole lot to learn about playing under center, how to protect the football, and the complexities of running a traditional NFL offense. But the Chiefs chose to overlook the potential downsides. In compensation for the risk, they got an athletic passer who possessed outstanding arm strength as well as someone who, from an early age while watching his big-league-pitcher dad, learned what it took to succeed in professional sports. From his days as a standout prep passer through his record-setting college run, Mahomes displayed the requisite smarts and work ethic to make it big in the sport's highest level. As an understudy to Chiefs starter Alex Smith during the 2017–18 season, Mahomes kept his focus on the field. But his eyes remained open off of it. Mahomes carefully observed fan reaction to the player protests. He understood exactly what happened to Kaepernick for daring to take a stand, or more accurately, a knee. Mahomes, as a rookie, had to feel his way around in a new work environment. Even as he was trying to find his footing as a pro quarterback, he was also trying to find his voice as a young man. Mahomes had a lot coming at him as the Chiefs' presumptive franchise-quarterback-in-waiting and a Black QB at the dawn of a new era for Black QBs in the NFL.

When Mahomes's opportunity finally came at the beginning of his second season, he showed that the Chiefs had chosen wisely.

—

Before trailblazer Marlin Briscoe would answer any questions, he had a few of his own. And Briscoe–the first African American to start at quarterback in pro football's modern era in the United States–got right to the point.

"You do understand how incredible this kid is and why what he's doing is so special, right?" Briscoe said of Mahomes. "He has everything–the arm, the smarts, the athleticism. You see what he has done already, and he has everything he needs to stay on top for a long time. And after everything that so many of us who came before him went through, after everything we had to deal with, man, wouldn't that really be something?"

In the evolution of the Black quarterback, Mahomes represents a new level.

Black passers have led teams to the Super Bowl. They've won the Associated Press NFL Most Valuable Player award. One is even enshrined in the Pro Football Hall of Fame. Never, however, in league history has an African American passer been the consensus No. 1 player at his position. Mahomes is that guy. He's the embodiment of a belief that all the Black pioneers at the position have held: that if the field eventually became level, or at least something close to it, Black quarterbacks would thrive–and one would emerge as the best regardless of race. Mahomes fulfilled their belief.

With his no-look throws, passes launched from contortionist arm angles, and video game–like stats in the 2018–19 season, Mahomes, in only his first season as a starter and second in the NFL, made us reimagine what's possible from the position while becoming only the third Black signal-caller to win the AP MVP Award. The NFL had not seen the likes of Dan Marino since the former Miami Dolphins great retired after the 1999–2000 season. In the previous generation, Marino also wowed the football world while emerging as the league's best player in only his second pro season. En route to earning the game's top individual distinction, Mahomes had a Marino-like impact, leading the league with 50 touchdown passes and throwing for almost 5,100 yards. But unlike Marino, or any other player who lined up under center and barked orders in the NFL before him, Mahomes improvised in a manner one might expect to see from a youngster during recess on a middle-school playground–not a multimillion-dollar professional athlete performing in front of 70,000 rabid fans with a playoff berth at stake. On so many occasions during his breakthrough season, Mahomes left his coaches, teammates, and Chiefs fans scratching their heads and asking, "Did he really just do that?" The no-look passes got everyone talking the most.

Mahomes's first no-look pass in an NFL game occurred during his only start as a rookie. In Week 17 of the 2017–18 season, with the Chiefs locked into their seeding for the postseason and Smith getting the day off, Mahomes showed his sleight-of-hand work against the Denver Broncos after revealing the trick to teammates in practice throughout the season.

On a first-and-10 play, Mahomes saw a defender closing in and spotted a Chiefs receiver crossing the field out of the corner of his eye. He knew that if he kept looking straight downfield, a linebacker in zone coverage would come off enough for him to make a throw to

Albert Wilson on the boundary. And that's exactly what happened. Think about the fact that Mahomes made this gutsy play in his first NFL start. "It's not like I mean to throw no-look passes," Mahomes said. "I think it kind of happens out of instinct. As I do it, I'm like, *Dang, I didn't even mean to do that.*"[114]

Briscoe gets it. He used to get into a similar groove, too, "And when it happens, you just start doing things in the flow of that game that you probably wouldn't do if you thought about it [beforehand]. When you watch him out there, when you see the things he does, you see he's playing with a confidence, with freedom, to play the way he needs to play to be the best he can be on every play.

"That's not the way we [the Black QB pioneers] were really able to play. We would do some things on instinct—but we also would try to [consciously] pull back sometimes. We knew we didn't have that freedom to totally be who we wanted to be, who we knew we could be out there, if we wanted to [stay in the game]. So the fact that he had that freedom, that confidence, and it all helped him get off to such a great start . . . it was just great to see."

In 2018, his first season atop the Chiefs' depth chart, Mahomes started hot and remained that way. He had four touchdown passes in a 38–28 Week 1 victory over the Los Angeles Chargers. That was great. But in Week 2, Mahomes was even better: He had six touchdown passes as the Chiefs outlasted the Pittsburgh Steelers, 42–37. After only two games, Mahomes had 10 TD passes and zero interceptions. For many quarterbacks, that's a great two months. The next season, during the Chiefs' Super Bowl championship run, Mahomes displayed a flair for the dramatic during the most important time of the year—the postseason. While guiding the Chiefs to their second Super Bowl title (it had been exactly half a century since Kansas City defeated Minnesota in the fourth Super Bowl), Mahomes became the only QB in NFL history to lead a team to three victories in one postseason in which it trailed by at least 10 points in each game.

When Mahomes received the MVP honor, Briscoe beamed. After Mahomes rallied Kansas City to its Super Bowl victory over the San Francisco 49ers, Briscoe took pride in the fact that his battles decades earlier helped clear a path for Mahomes to rise higher than any Black man at the position in the sport's history.

Whenever the Chiefs play, the Long Beach, California, resident makes sure he's in front of his television. According to Briscoe, there's no better show in football.

"I have to be honest about it: It does make me proud to watch him play," Briscoe said. "The things I had to deal with and others had to deal with, when you see a young kid like this come along, it makes you feel good about . . . the doors that you helped open. There have been a lot of talented [Black quarterbacks]. That's for sure. But this kid . . . there's just really something about him."

Mahomes knows the old-timers are watching and "definitely can understand" why they're rooting so hard for him. "For me, it's all about going out there and playing the game I love. But at the same time, you see the things, you see everybody supporting you," Mahomes said. "I'm going to go out there and try to make everybody proud. All of those guys, guys like [Briscoe], Warren Moon, Doug Williams, and so many others, are the reason I'm playing the quarterback position today.

"They were the first to do it. They were the first ones to show that the Black quarterback could be great. They were the first ones to show that the Black quarterback could be a pocket quarterback, could run teams, and could make plays. They gave me the opportunity to play the position, and then end up in the NFL and in Super Bowls and winning a Super Bowl. Those guys came before me and set the standard. I was able to come behind them and just be who I am."

—

During Super Bowl XXII in 1988, Williams ended the racist myth that Black passers lacked the smarts and leadership ability to win championships. By the time Russell Wilson helped the Seattle Seahawks crush the Broncos during Super Bowl XLVIII in 2014, his race wasn't the biggest story of the day. Likewise, when Cam Newton led the Carolina Panthers to Super Bowl 50 in 2016, he didn't face a volley of questions about whether he measured up.

In addition to Mahomes, Steve McNair, Newton, and Lamar Jackson of the Baltimore Ravens have won the league's MVP Award. Football fans can find Warren Moon's bronze bust at the Pro Football Hall of Fame in Canton, Ohio. Randall Cunningham was known as "the Ultimate Weapon."

Here's the thing, though: Cunningham and Moon played during an era in which Joe Montana, Dan Marino, and John Elway took turns standing atop the mountain. By the time Newton and Wilson entered the league, the long-running debate was whether Peyton Manning or Aaron Rodgers were better than Tom Brady, who, as the winner of the most Super Bowls, is the most successful quarterback of all time.

But now Mahomes is the player all other quarterbacks are chasing. And it's not only about winning Super Bowls or MVP awards. Mahomes's performance is the yardstick for how other quarterbacks are measured. Michael Jordan didn't win the NBA championship or MVP award every year of his career. But the combination of his smarts, athletic excellence, and competitive drive set the standard by which all basketball players were rated during Jordan's era. The same thing can be said for LeBron James in today's NBA. Mahomes has become the measuring stick in the NFL.

Another common trait among the three: pettiness. Mahomes, Jordan, James, and the rest of their spectacularly accomplished ilk–Brady is near the front of that short line, too–view the world through the same skewed lens, which makes watching them work so much fun for the rest of us. After word emerged that James had finished second to Giannis Antetokounmpo of the Milwaukee Bucks in voting for the 2019–20 NBA MVP award, James did anything but hide his anger. He made it clear: He took finishing second personally. James acknowledged that the perceived snub helped fuel him in guiding the Los Angeles Lakers to that season's NBA championship. The fact that Antetokounmpo deserved the award was beside the point. James uses all manners of slight, real and imagined, and disappointment to help propel him higher.

As skilled as James is at it, he has nothing on Jordan. In ESPN Films' *The Last Dance*, Jordan explained, repeatedly, he "took it personal." The aggrieved Jordan reached so many peaks with the help of so many (and mostly imagined, apparently) attacks, it was hard to keep track of them all. Early in his career, Mahomes embarked on a revenge tour of sorts. It began during the 2019–20 season. In a victory over the Chicago Bears, Mahomes was shown counting to 10 on his fingers while celebrating a touchdown pass. For casual NFL fans, a brief history lesson: The Bears made a horrific decision in bypassing Mahomes in the 2017 draft and selecting Trubisky, who turned out to be a major disappointment.

During a Chiefs win in the 2020–21 season over Baltimore, Mahomes again was shown counting, that time to four. Before this season, Mahomes was ranked fourth on the NFL's annual NFL Top 100 list. Jackson, the Ravens' star quarterback, was selected No. 1. Then, in the playoffs that season, Mahomes added another notch on his belt by dispatching Buffalo Bills quarterback Josh Allen, metaphorically speaking.

Mahomes "took it personal" that All-Pro voters that season selected both him and Allen as co–second-team QBs. It's not that Mahomes lacks respect for Jackson, Allen, or even Trubisky, for that matter. It's just that Mahomes, like many superstars, is perpetually in search of an edge. Just enough of a boost to help him be better than the other guy.

"I have so much passion for this game, and stuff just kind of happens when I'm on the field and competing," Mahomes said. "It's funny to me how everyone makes a big deal out of it [the counting], but it really all comes from my love for this game, wanting to compete and wanting to win."

Mahomes's competitiveness is among the traits that Mike Shanahan admires most.

Considered among the greatest offensive play callers in NFL history, Shanahan, while serving as the 49ers' offensive coordinator in the early 1990s, helped Steve Young develop into a Super Bowl winner and a future Hall of Famer. Then, as the Denver Broncos head coach in the late 1990s, Shanahan partnered with another future Hall of Famer, John Elway, to help the Broncos win back-to-back Super Bowl titles. When it comes to recognizing talented quarterbacks, Shanahan's bona fides are beyond reproach.

Which makes his assessment of Mahomes all the more impressive.

"What separates him is his ability to extend plays. He extends plays better than any quarterback I've ever seen," said Shanahan, who began coaching in the NFL in 1984. "And to have the accuracy that he has [on the move] is just . . . I've never seen anything like it. He's also just got a great feel for the game. Not many people I've ever seen, especially this early in his career, can do the things he's done. No way."

In his first three seasons as a starter, including the playoffs, Mahomes ranked first among NFL quarterbacks in victories, passing touchdowns, passing yards, 300-yard passing games, yards per attempt, and Total QBR, the metric that accounts for all of a quarterback's contributions on every play. Mahomes's historic start prompted many NFL legends to reevaluate how to measure even the best quarterbacks. Former Washington head coach Joe Gibbs, who led the franchise to four Super Bowls, winning three with three different quarterbacks, marvels at Mahomes's repertoire.

"Everyone has got a thought about Patrick Mahomes," the Hall of Famer said. "This guy is so gifted, and he can make so many plays for you in so many different ways. With Mahomes, what's so unusual is that he . . . he can just do everything. He's shown he can throw on the run and make things happen. He also does it from the pocket. He's just a gifted guy."

—

Andy Reid knows exactly what he has in Mahomes: the total package.

With Mahomes, Reid has made all the right moves, beginning with having Mahomes sit and learn as a rookie. Reid is among the best in the business at putting quarterbacks in position to perform at their best. In Mahomes, Reid, who once mentored a young Brett Favre and had a long, fruitful run with Donovan McNabb, has the most gifted protégé of his career.

"Certain guys have great vision and can see the field. [But] it's one thing knowing it and seeing it on the field and being able to execute it," Reid said. "These top quarterbacks . . . they have that. They can see things that the average guy can't, right? That's why they're the best in the business. With Patrick, he's been blessed with the vision and he's very intelligent.

"Great quarterbacks, they have that ability [to lead]. He's young, but he has that ability to influence and make people around him better. He does it with his teammates. He brings a certain energy with him. This is him. . . . That is who he is and what he is."

According to Donovan McNabb, Mahomes couldn't be in business with a better partner. McNabb has monitored Mahomes's fast rise under Reid, who picked McNabb second overall in the groundbreaking 1999 NFL draft–the only draft in which three Black quarterbacks were selected in the first round–and sacrificed heavily to trade up in the 2017 draft to get Mahomes, partly because Mahomes reminded Reid of McNabb.

"Listen, and I know this may sound strange based on what

Mahomes has done so far, all of his success, but he's just getting started," said McNabb, who teamed with Reid to lead the Philadelphia Eagles to five NFC championship games and Super Bowl XXXIX in 2005. "The thing about Andy is, he's going to always protect him. He's always going to have those big guys up front that will give him the time he needs to work. That's what Andy always starts with, because he understands what it takes.

"A lot of guys [coaches] say they get that, but they don't show it. They don't really put guys in the position to succeed. But believe me, Andy really gets it. He's always thinking about it. And Andy is always going to have weapons for him. He's just going to keep building, building and building around him. Mahomes is comfortable with what they're doing now, and he really is, but it's going to go to even a better place, because that's what Andy does. With Andy, he's in a really good place to do all the things he wants to do."

What Mahomes wants to do is a long list, and one of those to-do items is no less than surpassing Tom Brady's gaudiest achievement: leading more teams to Super Bowl victories than any other passer. Brady's jewelry haul is intimidating, but for Mahomes it's motivation, just as Boston Celtics great Bill Russell's record of 11 NBA championships was to Michael Jordan, inspiring him to be the first in the gym and the last to leave. Mahomes and Jordan, geniuses at their craft, compete with themselves even more than they do others; perfection is their daily opponent. And although they realize that foe can't be vanquished, the battle is for them nonetheless worthwhile.

———

During an otherwise-uneventful Super Bowl LIV news conference in Miami in late January 2020, Mahomes paused to ponder a question about the importance of being a Black quarterback playing for the NFL championship. Mahomes hadn't been especially vocal on matters of race in his first three seasons, but as only the seventh

Black starting quarterback in the 54-year history of the Super Bowl to that point, he understood the significance of the moment.

"The best thing about it is you're showing kids that no matter where you grow up, what race you are, that you can achieve your dream," Mahomes said then. "For me, being a Black quarterback–having a Black dad and a white mom–it just shows that it doesn't matter where you come from."

Just in case anyone was wondering, Mahomes made sure he identified himself as being a Black quarterback. With skin in the game–literally–Mahomes in late May 2020 was ready, despite the risks, to leave no doubt about his position on what happened to Floyd. A phone call from a fellow NFL headliner would lead to providing Mahomes with the vehicle to drive home his point.

Four days after Chauvin finally removed his knee from the neck of Floyd's corpse, NFL commissioner Roger Goodell issued a statement on the incident and two other recent killings of Black people that received widespread media coverage. The statement read:

The NFL family is greatly saddened by the tragic events across our country. The protesters' reactions to these incidents reflect the pain, anger and frustration that so many of us feel. Our deepest condolences go out to the family of Mr. George Floyd and to those who have lost loved ones, including the families of Ms. Breonna Taylor in Louisville, and Mr. Ahmaud Arbery, the cousin of Tracy Walker of the Detroit Lions.

As current events dramatically underscore, there remains much more to do as a country and as a league. These tragedies inform the NFL's commitment and our ongoing efforts. There remains an urgent need for action. We recognize the power of our platform in communities and as part of the fabric of American society. We embrace that responsibility and are committed to continuing the important work to address these systemic issues together with our players, clubs and partners.

Considering the tightrope the league walked back then around the issues of systemic racism and police brutality, the statement was in keeping with the times. But what Goodell and NFL team owners didn't realize was that times were changing rapidly.

From the moment former San Francisco 49ers quarterback Colin Kaepernick started the NFL player-protest movement—which evolved into a new civil rights movement in sports—during the 2016–17 season, Goodell and club owners were a step slow while being squeezed on two fronts. They tried to mollify supporters of President Donald Trump, a group that also comprises a huge part of the league's immense fan base, by never offering a full-throated endorsement of the players' demonstrations during the playing of "The Star-Spangled Banner." The players were the other side of the vise. With such a large part of the league's workforce being Black (among players, African American representation in the NFL reached about 70 percent during the 2016–2017 season), Goodell and team owners couldn't outright dismiss the players' concerns. The league's leaders struggled to find a sweet spot between the two sides because, well, one didn't exist.

The NFL reached perhaps the best decision it could with the bottom line always paramount for franchise owners: The league provided considerable funding for the players' social justice efforts. With resources in hand, players redirected their energy from demonstrating during the national anthem to supporting grassroots organizations that aspired to increase equity in society, especially those pushing for criminal justice reform. Although it took longer than team owners would have preferred, the NFL succeeded in defusing the situation.

But for many NFL players, and even some employees within the league office, three words immediately came to mind after Goodell's statement about the killing of Floyd was released: not good enough.

—

Chauvin's actions represented stark examples of police brutality and systemic oppression (arguably the most egregious ever caught on video), the conduct that inspired the large-scale NFL player protests during the 2016 and 2017 seasons. As the commissioner of an overwhelmingly Black league, Goodell should have delivered a forceful and explicit condemnation of police brutality and systemic racism, which was conspicuously absent from his statement. The statement fell woefully short of addressing the moment, some league employees believed. An NFL social media staffer named Bryndon Minter was among them.

Embarrassed by the league's insufficient response, Minter went rogue. He contacted Michael Thomas, an All-Pro wide receiver with the New Orleans Saints who's active on social media, about creating content–a video unauthorized by the league office or any NFL club– that would put league owners on notice. Thomas loved the idea and took the lead in recruiting other league stars. For the production to be a hit, Thomas knew he needed the biggest in the NFL's constellation: Mahomes. Having Mahomes attached to the players' project would make NFL club owners and decision-makers take notice. Fortunately for Thomas, Minter, and the other star players, he caught Mahomes at just the right moment, the moment when the league's best player was looking for a way to engage. By participating in the players' video, Mahomes realized he would leave no doubt about his position on other matters of race. Of course, there were risks involved. Mahomes weighed them–and the correct choice still jumped off the page.

"Before you do anything, you have to think about it," Mahomes said. "You have to examine what positives can come from anything you do, and what negatives can come from anything you do. For me,

I knew that I had to take a stand. I had to be a part of this video. I had to be a part of the change . . . a part of the movement.

"And me having my platform, I knew that it would mean a lot. Not only for me, but also for everybody who came before me and everyone who comes after me. I knew that I had to be a part of it because . . . it was just time to take that step. I mean, again, yeah, I thought about it. But enough was enough. We needed to take a stand–I needed to."

On June 4, 2020, under #StrongerTogether, Thomas and the other players involved in the project posted the finished product to their Twitter accounts. Mahomes was among a group of more than a dozen Black NFL stars who pushed owners to acknowledge past wrongs and truly stand with them, asking the league to admit it erred in its response to peaceful NFL player protests of police brutality and systemic oppression, condemn racism, and affirm that Black lives matter.

Thomas, who led the NFL in receptions during the 2018–19 and 2019–20 seasons, opens the one-minute, 11-second video. "It's been ten days since George Floyd was brutally murdered," Thomas says. He's followed by a cadre of A-listers, including Mahomes, Houston Texans QB Deshaun Watson, New York Giants running back Saquon Barkley, Cleveland Browns wide receiver Odell Beckham Jr., Dallas Cowboys running back Ezekiel Elliott, and Chiefs safety Tyrann Mathieu, who alternate between appearing on-screen individually as well as collectively in the video mash-up as they continue to recite the statement Thomas started. "How many times do we need to ask you to listen to your players? What will it take? For one of us to be murdered by police brutality?" Then they all ask, "What if I was George Floyd?" From there, the players pivot. One after another, they recite the names of Black people killed during interactions with law enforcement officers or armed vigilantes.

"I am George Floyd. I am Breonna Taylor. I am Ahmaud Arbery. I am Eric Garner. I am Laquan McDonald. I am Tamir Rice. I am Trayvon Martin. I am Walter Scott. I am Michael Brown Jr. I am Samuel Dubose. I am Frank Smart. I am Phillip White. I am Jordan Baker." The video closes with the players making their specific requests of team owners and league leaders. "We will not be silenced. We assert our right to peacefully protest. It shouldn't take this long to admit. So, on behalf of the National Football League, this is what we, the players, would like to hear you state: 'We, the National Football League, condemn racism and the systematic oppression of Black people. We, the National Football League, admit wrong in silencing our players from peacefully protesting. We, the National Football League, believe Black lives matter.'"

The NFL responded quickly to the video, issuing a statement the same night the players released it. In the statement, which the league office posted to social media, the NFL said it stands with the Black community. The statement read:

This is a time of self-reflection for all–the NFL is no exception. We stand with the Black community because black lives matter.

Through Inspire Change [the league's social justice arm], the NFL, Players and our partners have supported programs and initiatives throughout the country to address systemic racism. We will continue using our platform to challenge the injustice around us.

To date we have donated $44 million to support hundreds of worthy organizations. This year, we are committing an additional $20 million to these causes and we will accelerate efforts to highlight their critical work.

We know that we can and need to do more.

As league executives, coaches, and players burned up the phone lines and wore out their thumbs texting one another about the video and the NFL's rapid response, one name dominated the discussions and text threads: Mahomes.

It wasn't just that Mahomes joined in. He played a key role, looking into the camera and declaring for the first time in the video, "Black lives matter."

To that point, the NFL had not acknowledged the Black Lives Matter movement, which was formed to protest incidents of police brutality and racially motivated violence against Black people. In stoking culture wars to his political advantage, former president Trump has regularly railed against BLM for, among other things, as he spun it, being "a symbol of hate." Mahomes's decision to go all in on the video–especially regarding a topic that NFL power brokers had strenuously avoided–put the NFL in a difficult position.

When the quarterback who's standing atop the mountain looks into the camera and declares, "Black lives matter," well, it suddenly becomes time for Goodell to explain the realities of navigating the new world to his billionaire bosses. Once the players' video dropped, with Mahomes essentially having top billing in it, Goodell was on the clock. Ignoring the players' bold move was simply not on the table. No longer could the NFL offer its considerable social justice funding alone as proof it fully supports the majority of its on-field workforce. Backed into a corner and having only one viable option, Goodell chose it.

In a remarkable video response to what even some pushing for change within the game considered to be an ambitious, to say the least, series of requests made by the NFL stars in their video, Goodell the next day admitted the league erred in how it handled peaceful NFL player protests of police brutality and systemic oppression, condemned racism, and affirmed that black lives matter, pledging his allegiance to the players in the battle for equal justice under the law.

Doug Williams, the first Black quarterback to start in a Super

"Arrowhead is a place where we have a lot of fun and show unity, so it was the perfect place to come together, vote, and use our voice," Mahomes said. "Doing that, helping to make it happen, was very important to me."

He wasn't finished.

Before the Chiefs played host to the Houston Texans in Week 1 of the 2020–21 season, with the United States still on lockdown because of the COVID-19 pandemic and tensions high as the long overdue reckoning on the United States' history of racism continued unabated, Mahomes and Houston quarterback Deshaun Watson organized a pregame "moment of unity." As kickoff approached, players from both teams stood on the 50-yard line at Arrowhead Stadium and locked arms in unison. After the public-address announcer asked for a moment of silence, boos from the crowd were audible. And predictable.

"There are always people who are going to be like that. I think we all know that," Mahomes said. "But to just boo unity . . . was definitely disappointing. But at the same time, there were a lot of people who showed support [at the stadium] before and after that. I really have a lot of respect for *those* people, because they stood behind us when not all people did."

Kaepernick dragged the NFL, figuratively kicking and screaming, into the national discussion about police brutality and systemic oppression. Mahomes picked up that standard and prodded the league to capitulate on opposing protesting and to openly support its players. Two Black quarterbacks took stands that moved the NFL to new places, much to the chagrin of franchise owners. It was the fulfillment of the worst nightmares of the racist owners of decades past: that Black men would become quarterbacks and lead on–and off–the field. Leading from a Black perspective will always be different.

Because Mahomes is a Black quarterback, a Black man, issues of race, as he explained in his own words, affect him and his family

Bowl and be selected the game's MVP, lauded Mahomes for stepping out front. *Far* out front.

"You look at what was going on at the time in the country, with all those young people out marching in the streets every day and demanding change, and you just understood something was happening. Things were different," Williams said. "You saw so many young people leading in those marches. So many young people standing up and saying, 'This has to stop.' Then you look at a guy like Mahomes, who's a young guy himself, and he's leading in his way in the league. We're talking about a young man who wasn't even twenty-five yet.

"But he decided he had to take a stand just like so many other people his age and even younger. Now, when you're talking about a quarterback, it has to start on the field. If you want people to follow you, you have to prove you can lead them, which he definitely did. MVP of the league, Super Bowl winner, Super Bowl MVP, All-Pro, Pro Bowler–you can't lead better than that in the league. You can't make a greater impact than that. So when you look at it all, with what he has done in such a short time on the field, nothing he does as a leader surprises me. It doesn't surprise me at all."

—

For Mahomes, the video was just a start. He quickly shifted his focus to expanding voting during the 2020 presidential election. Mahomes and his 15 and the Mahomies Foundation, along with the Chiefs' organization and the Hunt family (which owns the franchise), purchased new voting machines–for a "six-figure" sum the parties split equally, according to Chiefs president Mark Donovan–and received government approval to open up Kansas City's Arrowhead Stadium as a polling place. After finding his voice and putting it to use, Mahomes dipped into his pocket to help many others express themselves at the ballot box.

differently than they would, say, Peyton Manning, Tom Brady, or Drew Brees. At one point during the players' video, Mahomes says, "I am Tamir Rice," referring to the 12-year-old Black boy who was shot and killed by a Cleveland police officer in 2014. Fact is, John Elway or Joe Montana couldn't have gone there.

"Having a Black dad and having a white mom, and just growing up in the locker room my whole life because of my dad and my own [sports involvement], with people from all different races and communities, is what really formed how I am today," Mahomes said. "Being around so many different people from different backgrounds . . . I got a good perspective on where everyone is coming from.

"You don't have to agree with everything everyone says, but what you try to do is understand how they grew up and you listen. You really listen to what they're saying. Then, after that, you make the right choices for yourself. And you try to bring people together. And you try to do the right thing as much as you can, every single day, to set an example."

His name is Patrick Lavon Mahomes II. He's the best Black quarterback in the history of the NFL. And by the time he's done, the qualifier may no longer be needed.

EPILOGUE

The symbolism that marked the end of the NFL's first 100 years and the beginning of its next was as obvious as it was powerful.

When the then-defending Super Bowl champion Kansas City Chiefs played host to the Houston Texans in the league's 2020–21 curtain-raiser, quarterbacks Patrick Mahomes and Deshaun Watson shared the spotlight. As the late, iconic musical artist and civil rights activist Nina Simone would have said, oh, to be young, gifted, and Black.

Nothing in the NFL's regular season scheduling occurs because of happenstance. By pairing Kansas City and Houston in that season's kickoff matchup (Mahomes led the Chiefs to a 34–20 victory), the white men who controlled the marionette strings of professional sports' most successful and powerful league acknowledged the obvious: The drawing power and influence of superstar Black QBs have changed the NFL forever.

In bygone seasons, eyebrows would have been raised if two Black men–who play the defining position in professional sports– were featured in the league's first game of a new season. But on and off the field, this new generation of spectacularly talented and unapologetically Black passers has changed the game.

Emboldened by the influence they wield because of their once-unfathomable success, they speak their mind publicly on myriad issues and in a manner off-limits to the Black men on whose shoulders they stand. They use not only their voices but also their expansive social media platforms to challenge the status quo and push for progress in the areas most resistant to it. They're change agents in helmets and shoulder pads, influencing important discussions way beyond the arenas in which they work.

As the NFL reached its centennial on Aug. 20, 2020, Black quarterbacks, historically the league's most marginalized group, had come to occupy a position among its most powerful. In the face of innumerable ignominious slights, they persevered and completed an arduous journey 100 years in the making, mirroring the Black experience in America overall.

While speaking out, these sports heroes have redefined who's permitted to participate in the best of the American experience. They're assured of at least being heard because of the standing they've achieved, and they're determined to keep spreading their message.

They've drawn lines in the sand that even the ubiquitous NFL does not dare cross. The reality is, team owners can't risk alienating their most important employees. That's just not good business. And above all else, NFL club owners know what sells.

Understanding a significant shift has occurred, team owners have tried to signify "We finally get it." In addition to publicly committing to increase their social justice footprint heading into the 2020–21 season, pledging to donate $250 million over a 10-year period, the league arranged to have "Lift Every Voice and Sing," traditionally known as the Black national anthem, played during Week 1.

The messages "It Takes All of Us" and "End Racism" were stenciled on all end zone borders. The end zone messages were intended to demonstrate "how football and the NFL brings people together to work as one and use our example and our actions to help conquer racism," according to an internal league memo. What's more, players were given the option to wear helmet decals honoring victims of systemic racism. Before Colin Kaepernick took a stand and Mahomes and other Black QBs made their feelings clear, it was unimaginable to think that the NFL would ever go to such places.

Of course, progress is not perfection.

Anyone who has read to this point knows that the soul-crushing racism woven into the fabric of America and the NFL cannot be removed quickly. There are still many frontiers to conquer in pursuit of finally achieving a level playing field, or something as close to it as possible. In the NFL, the battle has shifted from excluding Black men from playing behind center to keeping them locked out of the head coach's office.

Team owners are about as eager to hire Black men to lead their coaching staffs and run their franchises as they are to pay federal estate taxes.

Over the previous five hiring cycles completed before the start of the 2022–23 NFL season, there were 36 openings for head coaches. Four Black men were hired to fill positions. Four.

In the last cycle, white coaches were chosen for seven of the nine openings. Mike Tomlin of the Steelers and Lovie Smith of the Houston Texans are the only Black coaches still leading teams. Mike McDaniel of the Dolphins, whose father is Black, is biracial. Ron Rivera of the Washington Commanders and Robert Saleh of the New York Jets are the league's other minority head coaches. Remember: The league has 32 teams.

Entering this season, the league has seven Black general managers. The NFL has never had more than that number. It took the league 100 years to hire its first team president—and it still has only two.

Things have been so abysmal for so long regarding inclusive hiring, former Miami Dolphins head coach Brian Flores in February 2022 filed a racial-discrimination lawsuit—which seeks class-action status—against the NFL. In the court of public opinion, the NFL hasn't come up with good answers to explain its hiring problems. In the court of law, it will have to do better.

In responding publicly to Flores's lawsuit, the NFL said the coach's action was without merit. Then only four days later, commissioner Roger Goodell revealed in a memo sent to owners that the league understood the concerns expressed by Flores and others, and it planned to initiate a comprehensive review of its entire approach to diversity, equity, and inclusion.

On one hand, the NFL argued that everyone should just move

along because it told us there's supposedly nothing to see regarding Flores's claims. And on the other, the league acknowledged its hiring process is broken and that its policies must be reviewed.

Talk about speaking out of both sides of your mouth.

Of course, doublespeak and misdirection from the NFL regarding matters of race are nothing new. All because of their racism, league officials for decades convinced themselves that Black men were incapable of thriving at quarterback. Even after Doug Williams's myth-busting performance in Super Bowl XXII, it was still a long, slow climb for Black quarterbacks to occupy the perch they do today. Similarly, despite the achievements of men such as Tony Dungy and Jerry Reese–the first Black head coach and general manager, respectively, to win Super Bowl championships–the slog continues for Black coaches and executives to receive opportunities for career advancement like that of their white counterparts.

Clearly, the job is not finished.

That's the thing, however, about movements: They're ongoing.

Whether the discussion is centered narrowly on the NFL or expanded to include America in a societal context, we know that the scourge of racism will not be eradicated quickly regardless of how many Black people acquire power. But the rise of the Black quarterback ensures that America can no longer ignore these issues as easily as it once did. They're now always front and center because of some of the most prominent faces in the game and America.

ACKNOWLEDGMENTS

I never expected to write my first book while navigating the breakup of my marriage, my mom's declining health, and juggling my kids' sports schedules as a single dad. But such is life. You take the good with the bad, and every second I spent reporting and writing *Rise of the Black Quarterback: What It Means for America* was definitely time well spent. I owe so much to a core group of friends who encouraged me and supported me throughout the process: Judge Rossie Alston; Darrell Fry; Jeff Granger Jr.; Cindy Greenya; Todd Harmonson; Tom and Melissa McGinn; Cynthia Wesley, MD (aka "Dr. Cyn"); and Tony Wyllie. Then there's my girlfriend, Shanon Lee, who came into my life unexpectedly and provided me with the love and support I needed to get the book across the finish line. Thank you for bringing balance to my life, baby. Many years ago, legendary editor and author Tom Shroder pushed me to expand my thinking about writing. Tom also challenged me to produce the best manuscript possible. I'll forever be indebted to him for that, too.

I've had wise mentors through the years, starting with Emelina Reid. During difficult times, my mom set an incredibly positive example for me and my brothers, Jonathan and Justin. We owe her everything. Jolene Combs, my first journalism professor, inspired my love of the craft. I broke into the business at the *Daily Breeze* in Torrance, California, when Mike Waldner took a chance on a teenager. Longtime *Los Angeles Times* sports editor Bill Dwyre gave me my big break in the business, assigning a wet-behind-the-ears reporter to cover the Los Angeles Dodgers. When I was 19, Kevin Merida told me, "Never stop reporting." Those words have provided the foundation for my career. I wouldn't have reached this point without Kevin's belief in me—and his support of this book. Emilio Garcia-Ruiz is one of those editors who inspires reporters to climb higher. Emi brought me to the *Washington Post* and helped me realize my potential, though I'll never admit that to him. Matt Vita gave me a column and the runway to figure out how to write it. I'm at ESPN because Rob King and Patrick Stiegman thought I could contribute. I hope I've proved them right. Every writer should be lucky enough to have an editor and advocate who cares as much as Raina Kelley. Lisa Wilson and Matt Wong were fabulous supervisors whom I've come to count among my confidants.

So many of my colleagues and friends have contributed to shaping my thinking about the quarterback position: Matthew Berry, Ryan Clark, Domonique Foxworth, Dan Graziano, Paul Gutierrez, John Keim, John Pluym, Jim Trotter, and Seth Wickersham. Many scholars and civil rights leaders were generous with their time, permitting me to pick their brains about the ongoing struggle for social justice. Dr. Jody D. Armour, Dr. Todd Boyd (aka "Notorious Ph.D."), Dr. N. Jeremi Duru, Dr. Harry Edwards, Dr. Eddie S. Glaude Jr., Dr. Richard E. Lapchick, and Dr. T. M. Robinson-Mosley couldn't have been more accommodating. Journalist and author William C. Rhoden and Dr. Charles K. Ross provided a launching pad for my book.

Many public relations officials helped immeasurably in arranging interviews with players and coaches. Ted Crews of the Kansas City Chiefs, Mark Dalton of the Arizona Cardinals, and Michael Houck of the Oklahoma Sooners were clutch. The book wouldn't have happened without the Black QB trailblazers who entrusted me with their stories: Marlin Briscoe, James "Shack" Harris, Warren Moon, and Doug Williams. The stars who came behind them were similarly helpful: Randall Cunningham, Donovan McNabb, and Michael Vick. Patrick Mahomes and Kyler Murray, two of the current generation's brightest lights, were absolutely great. And there were so many others–Tony Dungy, Joe Gibbs, and Paul Tagliabue, to name a few–who aided me in the process. And, of course, I must give a shout-out to my Andscape family and to my Line Brothers–Charvin Anderson, Steve Burke, William Hicks, and Deon Scott–who have had my back for all these years. To everyone who assisted in the making of *Rise of the Black Quarterback: What It Means for America*, I thank you so much.

ENDNOTES

1 *Breaking the Color Barrier: The Story of the First African American NFL Head Coach, Frederick "Fritz" Pollard,* p 9.

2 *Breaking the Color Barrier: The Story of the First African American NFL Head Coach, Frederick "Fritz" Pollard,* p 10.

3 *Outside the Lines: African Americans and the Integration of the National Football League,* p 24.

4 *Fritz Pollard: Pioneer in Racial Advancement,* p 41.

5 *Breaking the Color Barrier: The Story of the First African American NFL Head Coach, Frederick "Fritz" Pollard,* p 18.

6 *Breaking the Color Barrier: The Story of the First African American NFL Head Coach, Frederick "Fritz" Pollard,* p 20.

7 *Breaking the Color Barrier: The Story of the First African American NFL Head Coach, Frederick "Fritz" Pollard,* p 20–21.

8 *Breaking the Color Barrier: The Story of the First African American NFL Head Coach, Frederick "Fritz" Pollard,* p 30.

9 *Breaking the Color Barrier: The Story of the First African American NFL Head Coach, Frederick "Fritz" Pollard,* p 30.

10 *Breaking the Color Barrier: The Story of the First African-American NFL Head Coach, Frederick "Fritz" Pollard,* p 30–31.

11 *A Hard Road to Glory: A History of the African-American Athlete, 1619–1918,* p 99.

12 *Breaking the Color Barrier: The Story of the First African American NFL Head Coach, Frederick "Fritz" Pollard,* p 32.

13 *Breaking the Color Barrier: The Story of the First African American NFL Head Coach, Frederick "Fritz" Pollard,* p 32–33.

14 *About Fritz Pollard* (brown.edu).

15 *Outside the Lines,* p 24.

16 *A Hard Road to Glory: A History of the African-American Athlete, 1619–1918,* p 102.

17 *Breaking the Color Barrier: The Story of the First African American NFL Head Coach, Frederick "Fritz" Pollard,* p 35

18 *Outside the Lines,* p 25.

19 *Pasadena Star-News,* December 24, 2018, https://www.pasadenastarnews.com/2018/12/24/

rose-bowl-game-trailblazer-fritz-pollard-made-history-in-pasadena/.

20 *About Fritz Pollard* (brown.edu)

21 *Outside the Lines,* p 26.

22 *Outside the Lines,* p 26–27.

23 *Outside the Lines,* p 28.

24 *Outside the Lines,* p 29.

25 *A Hard Road to Glory: A History of the African-American Athlete, 1619–1918,* p 98

26 *A Hard Road to Glory: A History of the African-American Athlete, 1619–1918,* p 100.

27 *Outside the Lines,* p 19.

28 *Hard Road to Glory: A History of the African-American Athlete, 1619–1918,* p 100.

29 *A Hard Road to Glory: A History of the African-American Athlete, 1619–1918,* p 100–101.

30 Paul Robeson Excluded From Football Game—African American Registry (aaregistry.org)

31 *A Hard Road to Glory: A History of the African-American Athlete, 1619–1918,* p 100–101.

32 *Outside the Lines,* p 33.

33 *A Hard Road to Glory: A History of the African-American Athlete, 1619–1918,* p 107.

34 *Columbus Dispatch,* November 21, 2019

35 *Outside the Lines,* p 34.

36 *Outside the Lines,* p 34.

37 *Outside the Lines,* p 32.

38 *Outside the Lines,* p 35.

39 *Outside the Lines,* p 36.

40 *Outside the Lines,* p 22.

41 *Outside the Lines,* p 22.

42 *Outside the Lines,* p 52.

43 *Outside the Lines,* p 37.

44 *Outside the Lines,* p 44.

45 *Outside the Lines,* p 52.

46 *Outside the Lines,* p 52.

47 *Outside the Lines,* p 53.

48 *Outside the Lines,* p 53–54.

49 *Outside the Lines,* p 53.

50 *Outside the Lines: African Americans and the Integration of the National Football League,* p 77.

51 *Outside the Lines: African Americans and the Integration of the National Football League,* p 78.

52 *Outside the Lines: African Americans and the Integration of the National Football League, p 83–84.*

53 *Outside the Lines: African Americans and the Integration of the National Football League, p 84–85.*

54 *Third and a Mile: The Trials and Triumphs of the Black Quarterback,* p 65.

55 *Third and a Mile: The Trials and Triumphs of the Black Quarterback,* p 66.

56 *Third and a Mile: The Trials and Triumphs of the Black Quarterback,* p 65.

57 *Third and a Mile: The Trials and Triumphs of the Black Quarterback,* p 68.

58 Jerry Bembry. "George Taliaferro Played Quarterback and a Whole Lot More: At 90 Years Old, the First African-American Drafted into the NFL Recalls a Career in which He Took on Seven Positions." ESPN's *Andscape* (formerly *The Undefeated*). September 28, 2017.

59 Jerry Bembry. "George Taliaferro Played Quarterback and a Whole Lot More: At 90 Years Old, the First African-American Drafted into the NFL Recalls a Career in which He Took on Seven Positions." ESPN's *Andscape* (formerly *The Undefeated*). September 28, 2017.

60 Jerry Bembry. "George Taliaferro Played Quarterback and a Whole Lot More: At 90 Years Old, the First African-American Drafted into the NFL Recalls a Career in which He Took on Seven Positions." ESPN's *Andscape* (formerly *The Undefeated*). September 28, 2017.

61 Jerry Bembry. "George Taliaferro Played Quarterback and a Whole Lot More: At 90 Years Old, the First African-American Drafted into the NFL Recalls a Career in which He Took on Seven Positions." ESPN's *Andscape* (formerly *The Undefeated*). September 28, 2017.

62 Jerry Bembry. "George Taliaferro Played Quarterback and a Whole Lot More: At 90 Years Old, the First African-American Drafted into the NFL Recalls a Career in which He Took on Seven Positions." ESPN's *Andscape* (formerly *The Undefeated*). September 28, 2017.

63 Jerry Bembry. "George Taliaferro Played Quarterback and a Whole Lot More: At 90 Years Old, the First African-American Drafted into the NFL Recalls a Career in which He Took on Seven Positions." ESPN's *Andscape* (formerly *The Undefeated*). September 28, 2017.

64 *Third and a Mile: The Trials and Triumphs of the Black Quarterback,* p 70.

65 *Third and a Mile: The Trials and Triumphs of the Black Quarterback,* p 71-72.

66 *Third and a Mile: The Trials and Triumphs of the Black Quarterback,* p 71.

67 *Saturday Night Live* Transcripts: Fran Tarkenton: 01/29/77: *Black Perspective*—SNL Transcripts Tonight (jt.org)

68 Michael Lee. "We All Thought that He Would Be the One." *The Washington Post.* November, 12, 2021.

69 *Third and a Mile: The Trials and Triumphs of the Black Quarterback,* p 83.

70 *Third and a Mile: The Trials and Triumphs of the Black Quarterback,* p 82.

71 *Third and a Mile: The Trials and Triumphs of the Black Quarterback,* p 85.
72 *Third and a Mile: The Trials and Triumphs of the Black Quarterback,* p 99.
73 *Third and a Mile: The Trials and Triumphs of the Black Quarterback,* p 88.
74 *Third and a Mile: The Trials and Triumphs of the Black Quarterback,* p 89.
75 *Third and a Mile: The Trials and Triumphs of the Black Quarterback,* p 93.
76 *Third and a Mile: The Trials and Triumphs of the Black Quarterback,* p 92.
77 *Third and a Mile: The Trials and Triumphs of the Black Quarterback,* p 92.
78 *Third and a Mile: The Trials and Triumphs of the Black Quarterback,* p 97.
79 *Third and a Mile: The Trials and Triumphs of the Black Quarterback,* p 29.
80 *Third and a Mile: The Trials and Triumphs of the Black Quarterback,* p 33.
81 *Third and a Mile: The Trials and Triumphs of the Black Quarterback,* p 35.
82 *Third and a Mile: The Trials and Triumphs of the Black Quarterback,* p 35.
83 *Third and a Mile: The Trials and Triumphs of the Black Quarterback,* p 38.
84 Leigh Montville, "Father Moon: At Every Stage of His Carefully Plotted Life, Oiler Quarterback Warren Moon Has Shown Wisdom Beyond His Years," *Sports Illustrated,* September 27, 1993.

85 Leigh Montville, "Father Moon: At Every Stage of His Carefully Plotted Life, Oiler Quarterback Warren Moon Has Shown Wisdom Beyond His Years," *Sports Illustrated,* September 27, 1993.
86 Leigh Montville, "Father Moon: At Every Stage of His Carefully Plotted Life, Oiler Quarterback Warren Moon Has Shown Wisdom Beyond His Years," *Sports Illustrated,* September 27, 1993.
87 Justin Tinsley. "Steve McNair Went Third in the NFL Draft 25 Years Ago. We May Never See Another HBCU Player Go as High: A Look at the Numbers and What They Tell Us." ESPN's *Andscape* (formerly *The Undefeated*). April 22, 2020.
88 Justin Tinsley. "Steve McNair Went Third in the NFL Draft 25 Years Ago. We May Never See Another HBCU Player Go as High: A Look at the Numbers and What They Tell Us." ESPN's *Andscape* (formerly *The Undefeated*). April 22, 2020.
89 Kelley D. Evans. "Michael Vick's Next Chapter Includes Forgiving Himself and Guiding Young Athletes. The Retired QB Has Started Sports Academies and Is Pushing His

Brand V7." ESPN's *Andscape* (formerly *The Undefeated*). May 2, 2017.
90 *Colin in Black & White.* Netflix, 2021.
91 Steve Wyche. "Colin Kaepernick Explains Why He Sat During the National Anthem." NFL Media, August 27, 2016.
92 Steve Wyche. "Colin Kaepernick Explains Why He Sat During the National Anthem." NFL Media, August 27, 2016.
93 Jesse Washington. "Still No Anthem, Still No Regrets for Mahmoud Abdul-Rauf. NBA Star Lost Millions After Sitting in 1996—And He'd Do It Again." ESPN's *Andscape* (formerly *The Undefeated*). September, 1 2016.
94 Jesse Washington. "Still No Anthem, Still No Regrets for Mahmoud Abdul-Rauf. NBA Star Lost Millions After Sitting in 1996—And He'd Do It Again." ESPN's *Andscape* (formerly *The Undefeated*). September, 1 2016.
95 Jesse Washington. "Still No Anthem, Still No Regrets for Mahmoud Abdul-Rauf. NBA Star Lost Millions After Sitting in 1996—And He'd Do It Again." ESPN's *Andscape* (formerly *The Undefeated*). September, 1 2016.
96 Clinton Yates. "Football or Baseball for Kyler

Murray? It's Time to Play Ball." ESPN's *Andscape* (formerly *The Undefeated*). December 28, 2018.

97 Clinton Yates. "Football or Baseball for Kyler Murray? It's Time to Play Ball." ESPN's *Andscape* (formerly *The Undefeated*). December 28, 2018.

98 Clinton Yates. "Football or Baseball for Kyler Murray? It's Time to Play Ball." ESPN's *Andscape* (formerly *The Undefeated*). December 28, 2018.

99 Sports Day Staff. "Kyler Murray Opens Up on Leaving Texas A&M, His Difficult Conversation with the Oakland A's and More." *Dallas Morning News.*

100 Andy Vasquez. "NY Jets Players Lined Up for Signed Jerseys from Lamar Jackson After He Destroyed Them." NorthJersey.com. December 13, 2019.

101 Steve Jones. "Quiet and Private, Jackson's Play Speaks Volumes." *Louisville Courier Journal,* November 25, 2016.

102 Scott DeCamp. "West Michigan Coach Who Mentored NFL MVP Lamar Jackson Saw Immense Ability 2012-14." Michigan Live, February 2, 2020.

103 Steve Jones. "Quiet and Private, Jackson's Play Speaks Volumes." *Louis-*

ville Courier Journal, November 25, 2016.

104 Matthew Stevens. "Greg Roman Remaking Ravens Offense: We're Literally Redefining Everything." *Ravens Wire,* February 15, 2019.

105 Lonnae O'Neal. "For Black Fans in Baltimore, Lamar Jackson's Success 'Resonates Way Beyond Football.'" *Andscape* (formerly *The Undefeated*), December 11, 2019.

106 Jarrett Bell. "Bill Polian: 'I Was Wrong' for Saying Lamar Jackson Should Be a Wide Receiver in the NFL." *USA Today,* November 6, 2019.

107 Frank Edwards, Hedwig Lee, and Michael Esposito, "Risk of Being Killed by Police Use of Force in the United States by Age, Race–Ethnicity, and Sex," PNAS (Proceedings of the National Academy of Sciences of the United States of America), August 5, 2019.

108 Nicholas Talbot. "In the Spotlight: Mahomes' Childhood Prepared Him for Big Stage at Texas Tech," *Lubbock Avalanche-Journal.* September 11, 2015.

109 Matt Schoch. "Meet the Man Who Tried to Bring Patrick Mahomes to the Detroit Tigers," *Detroit News.* September 26, 2019.

110 Matt Schoch. "Meet the Man Who Tried to Bring Patrick Mahomes to the Detroit Tigers," *Detroit News.* September 26, 2019.

111 Nicholas Talbot. "In the Spotlight: Mahomes' Childhood Prepared Him for Big Stage at Tech," *Lubbock Avalanche-Journal.* September 11, 2015.

112 Nicholas Talbot. "In the Spotlight: Mahomes' Childhood Prepared Him for Big Stage at Tech," *Lubbock Avalanche-Journal.* September 11, 2015.

113 Matt Schoch. "Meet the Man Who Tried to Bring Patrick Mahomes to the Detroit Tigers," *Detroit News.* September 26, 2019.

114 Jenny Vrentas. "The Mahomes No-Look Pass: A Brief History." *Sports Illustrated,* December, 11 2018.

INDEX

2014 (XLVIII), 5, 252
2016 (50), 5, 252
2020 (LIV), 236, 250, 251, 256
Most Valuable Player (MVP), 4, 88, 107, 228, 263
Swain, Rick, 214
switching positions, 64, 66, 71, 72–73, 74, 75, 82, 84, 85–86, 92, 95, 97, 101, 103, 109, 138, 204, 209, 210, 211–12, 215, 224
Symons, B. J., 247
Syracuse University, 161

T

Tagliabue, Paul, 44–45, 46–47, 48, 49
Taliaferro, George, 66–72
Tampa Bay Buccaneers, 83, 126–31, 132, 135, 138
Tarkenton, Fran, 79–80, 81, 98, 100, 144, 149–50
Tennessee State University (Tigers), 92, 93, 117, 118, 119, 157
Tennessee Titans, 157, 158, 159, 236, 237
Texans (Houston), 4, 7, 246, 260, 264, 267, 269
Texas A&M University (Aggies), 191, 195, 196, 198, 219, 220
Texas Tech (Red Raiders), 196, 243, 245, 246, 247
"thinking positions," opposition to Blacks in, 60–62, 80, 91
Thomas, Michael, 259–60
Thorpe, Jim, 13, 27, 35, 36, 37, 45
Thrower, Willie, 62, 63–64, 65–66, 71, 72, 118, 145
Titans (Tennessee), 157, 158, 159, 236, 237
Tomlin, Mike, 83, 269
Towns, Stephen, 24
Trask, Amy, 93
Trubisky, Mitchell, 246, 253

U

United States Football League, 130, 131
University of Alabama, 72
University of Central Florida, 87, 161, 179
University of Delaware, 228
University of Kentucky, 72, 161, 219
University of Louisville (Cardinals), 211, 212, 215, 216, 217, 218, 219, 220, 221, 223, 224, 226
University of Minnesota (Golden Gophers), 68, 73, 75, 79, 82
University of Mississippi, 72
University of Nevada, Las Vegas/UNLV (Rebels), 150, 151, 173
University of North Carolina, 246
University of Oklahoma (Sooners), 196, 199, 200, 227, 231, 245
University of Oregon, 161, 245
University of Southern California/USC (Trojans), 109, 129, 130, 137, 138, 150, 151, 227, 247
University of Tennessee, 72, 226
University of Washington (Huskies), 84, 136–37, 140–41, 224
University of Wisconsin, 73
University of Wyoming, 223, 227
Upshaw, Gene, 94, 97, 98

V

Vick, Michael, 100, 148, 150, 155, 163–67, 172, 213, 214, 221, 235, 236
Vikings (Minnesota), 81, 98, 143, 149, 155, 157, 158, 161, 162, 250
Vincent, Troy, 77
Virginia Tech University (Hokies), 221

W

Warfield, Paul, 104
Washington Commanders, 166, 269. *See also* Washington Football Team
Washington Football Team, 52, 88, 107, 131, 132–33, 134, 135, 153, 154, 163, 164, 165, 185, 254
Washington, Kenny, 55, 56, 65
Washington State University, 21
Waterfield, Bob, 56
Watson, Deshaun, 4, 6, 8, 78, 106, 246, 260, 264, 267
White, Danny, 85
White, Dwight, 121
Williams, Doug, 1–4, 5, 8, 66, 86, 87, 88, 89, 105, 107–8, 114, 117–18, 122, 125–35, 137, 143, 144, 145, 149, 153, 156–57, 158, 163, 210, 236, 251, 252, 263, 270
Williams, Jay "Ink", 31
Williams, Sidney, Jr., 73
Willis, Bill, 56, 57
Wilson, Albert, 250
Wilson, Russell, 4, 5, 7, 8, 76, 78, 106, 148, 201, 252
Winston, Jameis, 211
Wood, Willie, 150–51
Wooten, John, 51–53, 55, 57–59, 60, 61, 74, 83, 84–85, 87
Wright, Jason, 166–67
Wyche, Steve, 168, 170, 171–72, 173, 174, 175, 176–78, 183, 189

Y

Yale University, 20, 21, 23, 63
Yewcic, Tom, 64
Young, Buddy, 111
Young, Steve, 50, 150, 184, 254